DELIVERING
PUBLIC SERVICES
EFFECTIVELY

DELIVERING
PUBLIC SERVICES
EFFECTIVELY

Tamil Nadu and Beyond

VIVEK S.

FOREWORD BY
JEAN DRÈZE

OXFORD
UNIVERSITY PRESS

OXFORD
UNIVERSITY PRESS

Oxford University Press is a department of the University of Oxford.
It furthers the University's objective of excellence in research, scholarship,
and education by publishing worldwide. Oxford is a registered trademark of
Oxford University Press in the UK and in certain other countries

Published in India by
Oxford University Press
YMCA Library Building, 1 Jai Singh Road, New Delhi 110 001, India

© Oxford University Press 2015

The moral rights of the authors have been asserted

First Edition published in 2015

ISBN-13: 978-0-19-945132-6
ISBN-10: 0-19-945132-X

Typeset in Trump Mediaeval LT Std 9.5/13
by MAP Systems, Bengaluru 560 082, India
Printed in India by Sapra Brothers, New Delhi 110 092

Dedicated to the people of Villupuram district who were generous with their time and knowledge without which this book would never have materialized

Contents

Foreword

In February 2003, Vivek Srinivasan and I spent a few days cycling around the villages of Dharmapuri District in Tamil Nadu visiting primary schools, health centres, fair price shops, and other public facilities. It was a memorable experience, not only because travelling with Vivek was great fun but also because we learnt more from this short journey than from weeks of academic study.

For someone used to the dilapidated and dysfunctional public facilities of rural Uttar Pradesh, it was a revelation to see the opposite in Tamil Nadu. For instance, each of the nine schools we visited enjoyed facilities that would have been quite unusual in north India at that time: a tidy building, basic furniture, teaching aids, drinking water, free textbooks, a nutritious mid-day meal, and regular health check-ups. More importantly, the teachers were teaching, and most of them were even using the blackboard, a rare event in north Indian schools. There was, of course, much scope for improvement, but at least children were learning in a fairly decent and stimulating environment.

We were even more impressed with the health centres. They were clean, lively, and well-staffed. Plenty of medicines were available for free, and there were regular inspections. The walls were plastered with charts and posters giving details of the daily routine, available facilities, progress of various programmes, and related information. Patients streamed in and out, evidently at ease with the system.

The public distribution system (PDS) was no less effective. Fair price shops were open at the stipulated times and people had no difficulty in collecting their rations (not just foodgrains but also other essential commodities—the correct quantity at the correct price. Determined to find some evidence of abuse, we trekked to a remote Dalit hamlet and asked the women there whether the dealer ever cheated them. They laughed. 'What do you mean?' they asked. 'The dealer lives here, if he cheats us we will break his legs.' In rural Uttar Pradesh, Dalit women tend to be sitting ducks for corrupt dealers: most of them know very little about their PDS entitlements, let alone how to defend them.

All this, of course, is relative. The people of Tamil Nadu have endless complaints about public services. But that is partly because they have high standards. If they were not so demanding, things would not be the way they are in Tamil Nadu. Exacting standards create a healthy pressure for further improvements, in turn leading to higher standards.

We were not the first or the last to observe this striking contrast between Tamil Nadu and Uttar Pradesh (or, for that matter, other large north Indian states) in the reach and quality of public services. Leela Visaria had made insightful comparisons, a few years earlier, between health services in Rajasthan and Tamil Nadu (Visaria 2005). More recent studies suggest that Tamil Nadu's ability to deliver effective public services has continued to improve, and extended to new domains. For instance, the standards of implementation of the National Rural Employment Guarantee Act (NREGA), which came into force in February 2006, are better in Tamil Nadu than in most other states. As Vivek's work shows, Tamil Nadu's achievements in this field are evident not just from first-hand observation, but also from a wealth of secondary data.

People often ask 'why' Tamil Nadu has relatively effective and equitable public services, in sharp contrast with many other Indian states. It is hard to give a complete answer to this question. Truth be told, we don't understand these matters very well. But we can give a partial answer—identify some important connections. For instance, it seems plausible that Tamil Nadu has greatly benefited from a rich history of social reforms in the pre-independence period. At a time when Gandhi was entangled in a woolly headed defence of the caste system (more precisely, of *varnashramdharma*), Periyar in Tamil Nadu expounded a devastating critique of it, and also of patriarchy. As Vivek's study shows, his ideas and influence are still alive today. In fact, the two leading parties in Tamil Nadu (DMK and AIADMK) are both direct descendants of the Dravidian movement led by Periyar. Even more importantly perhaps, early social reforms laid the ground for what Vivek aptly calls 'decentralized collective action' later on.

Of course, this observation raises the further question of why these social reforms happened in Tamil Nadu and not, say, in Uttar Pradesh. And there is no simple answer. Yet, the focus on early social reform as one of the drivers of social progress in Tamil Nadu is informative.

Vivek Srinivasan's study fits in this attempt to connect the dots without necessarily uncovering the full picture. He focuses particularly on the emergence of a broad-based commitment to public services. It is often said that 'political will' is the most important factor of success in this field. This is a valid observation as far as it goes, but political will is not born of thin air. In a democratic country, it is the outcome of democratic processes in the broad sense of the term—not just the electoral process but also other forms of democratic practice, from public debate to street action. Vivek's study is an illuminating attempt to understand how effective public services became one of the defining characteristics of Tamil Nadu's approach to development.

For me, one of the most important lessons from this study is how the history of public services in Tamil Nadu is closely connected with struggles of the unprivileged for social justice. Securing access to education, of course, was a paramount concern of these struggles. But the unprivileged, particularly Dalits, also had to fight for other forms of social support at every step. As Vivek notes in his case study of one Dalit hamlet: 'A series of petitions, demonstrations, protests and bargaining marked how each hand pump, street light, road and other services were secured.' This was a bitter, even violent struggle at times—part of India's historic transition from a society geared to the interests of a privileged minority to a democracy of sorts.

There are many other valuable insights in this outstanding study of public services in Tamil Nadu. The canvas is not confined to that particular state: the book also sheds light on a range of larger issues such as the critical importance of public services for the quality of life, the reasons why they tend to be devalued in contemporary political discourse, the value of universalism in social policy, and the social conditions that facilitate decentralized collective action. But let me refrain from giving away the story—over to the author.

Jean Drèze
Ranchi University, 14 April 2014

Preface

This book is being published shortly after India's general elections 2014, which generated fierce debates on whether or not governments should provide basic services for all. On one side of the debate was a set of powerful advocates who demanded the dismantling of even the little welfare that is provided in India—and many of them have the ear of the newly elected National Democratic Alliance (NDA) government. These advocates have argued that public services do not reach people due to corruption and inefficiency and in any case, money spent on them raises fiscal deficit, reduces 'investments', and affects growth.

The arguments are problematic in many ways. Contrary to their arguments, basic services including food programmes reach a large proportion of the beneficiaries and current evidence points to substantial improvements in the delivery of basic public services in the recent years. In other words, the fears of corruption are grossly exaggerated. But there are more fundamental problems with the arguments.

The demand to dismantle services is justified today in the name of economic theories. What it has amounted to is an unprincipled application of ideas from economics in order to eliminate services for the poor while demanding benefits for large corporations and for non-poor. For example, the derisive term 'freebies' is applied to welfare programmes but not to free allocation of coal blocks, land, gas, and other public resources to large corporations. Those who demand the closure of National Rural Employment Guarantee Act (NREGA) based on the assertion that it produces poor quality assets do not extend this argument to urban roads, even though we see so many roads being washed away by rains in every part of India. Economic logic is rarely invoked when large contracts are revised well after the bidding is done even though it is anti-competitive, produces perverse incentives, and also has consequences for fiscal deficit through higher payments. There are many who demand an end to public services based on the argument that there is corruption in it. But the same people rarely argue for an end to privatization of public resources even though the biggest scandals of the recent past were related to it. The examples can go on.

Selectively highlighting problems in government programmes meant for the poor and ignoring equivalent problems in programmes used by the non-poor has been a key characteristic of national public discourse this season. Such partisan demands in the name of economic logic started gaining ground in the 1990s and they attained a particularly high pitch recently. There are those who wonder how far the assault against services will be successful in destroying India's bare minimum welfare programmes. This book addresses that concern by looking at the politics around public services in India's past.

While the application of economic logic has a recent origin, partisan demands themselves have a much longer history. Instead of economic arguments, the framework of caste, gender, and class were used to prevent the common person from gaining access to services a few decades ago, and this was possible given India's deeply unequal past in which a narrow set of elite were able to corner all the resources.

Social movements of the marginalized groups challenged the elite control of politics in independent India and made it difficult to sustain entirely partisan policies. As the common person became more assertive, the demands for the government to address their aspirations grew with it. Basic services like roads, water, health, education, and social security make a huge difference to people's lives and not surprisingly, it has become one of the principal demands of the common person from governments.

In states like Kerala and Tamil Nadu that saw massive social transformation and the decline of elite dominance earlier, governments were forced to address the aspirations of the common person early on, and these states have a much longer history of delivering services effectively. The same kind of social transformation happened in other parts of India, including the Hindi belt, subsequently. This is reflected in the evolving priority to food programmes, education, health, roads, and other services in states like Bihar, Chhattisgarh, Madhya Pradesh, and Orissa in the recent past.

The opportunistic use of economic logic evolved in the context in which the elite have lost the ability to deny public services to the common person in the name of caste, class, and gender (more on this point in the following chapters). One may ask how far the renewed effort in the name of economic logic will be successful. If I may make the bold claim, this will fail much like similar attempts have failed over the last twenty years. Unlike the early independence era where the elite could take others for granted, we have an increasingly assertive common person who demands that the government performs for everyone's benefit, especially by delivering services effectively. In fact, the crux of this book is about how increasing assertion and deepening democracy lie at the heart of the social commitment to public services in Tamil Nadu and elsewhere in India.

There is no doubt that there is an unprecedented assault on services today in the name of economic logic, and it may have a few minor successes in reducing the scope of services here and there. But in the long run these arguments will have to contend with India's deepening democracy and the popular demand for public services. If one were to look at the history of democratic India, one could safely say that governments that ignore the popular demand for services will risk electoral defeat. If democracy continues to deepen over the years, we have every reason to believe that the opportunistic use of economic logic to sustain privilege will fail. If I can twist a commonly used phrase in the media, we have a good reason to believe that good politics will prevail over bad economics. Let me now turn to a brief history of politics around basic public services with the hope that it will shed light on the future.

Acknowledgements

This book is a product of seventeen years of learning which started when I joined the Delhi School of Economics as a graduate student. The ideas in this book have been shaped by my conversations with hundreds of people who generously shared their knowledge with me. Let me start with those who shaped my work without the expectation of gaining anything: my discussants during the field-work. I had formal interviews with fifty people who spent one to twelve hours each sharing their knowledge, time, books, and other resources. As if that were not enough, most of them also fed me sumptuous food, which went a long way toward keeping me happy during the long days of fieldwork.

Kaliyan and his family were my neighbours for many months and they played a major role in shaping my understanding of how things worked in the region. They also served as friends and gracious hosts without whose support my stay at Villupuram would have been much less enriching. Parimalan deserves special thanks for his long discussions and also for fundamentally changing the questions I asked as I went to the field. Manohar, Marti, and Ravi became the fulcrum of my friends circle and my evenings would have been boring without them.

Writers Prathiba Jeyachandran and Ravikumar (also an ex-MLA) helped me clarify the relationship between Dalit activism and social change. Gautham Sannah and Kudiarasan took this a step further.

Many members of CPI (M) served as my discussants and I would like to thank K. Balakrishnan, Chandra Athreya, Geeta, Mani, N. R. Ramasamy, Venkatesh Athreya, and T. R. Vishwanathan. My work would have been impossible without the help of many officials, Panchayat presidents, and Panchayat level workers. The support of the District Collector, Director of District Rural Development Authority, Superintendent of Police, and other officials at the Block offices and Collector's office of Villupuram is gratefully acknowledged.

A large number of Panchayat assistants and Makkal Nala Panialars shared their experiences with me, and provided the most valuable insights on how the government functions at the grassroots. These insights are critical to my work. Their hard work on the ground also makes possible the admirable delivery of public services in Tamil Nadu. I would have liked to enlist the names of all my discussants, but for their safety and owing to the constraints I agreed to with the Institutional Review Board of Syracuse University, I am unable to provide a more extensive list here.

I owe much intellectual debts to my committee, my teachers, and fellow students at Syracuse University. My Chair, John Burdick was a great teacher and an incredibly supportive advisor. I was also lucky to have the guidance of Chandra Mohanty, Jackie Orr, Shubo Basu, John Harriss, and Sue Wadley. During my first trip to the US, my immigration officer asked me if I really wanted to go to Syracuse: 'It is very cold up there', he warned me. Little did he know that I would bask in the warmth of friends! Special thanks to Bandita, Chris, Dana, Diane, Lindsey, Marie-Lou, Saheli, and Umut for sustained companionship and support.

My friends from the Right to Food Campaign (RFC) laid the foundation for this work. Among them, I owe huge debts to Jean Drèze, Kavita Srivatsava, Harsh Mander, Aruna Roy, S. R. Sankaran, and N. C. Saxena. I have admired them for their social commitment and for their understanding of Indian society. My work would have been deeply compromised if they had not shared their knowledge with me. Jean, in particular, was a constant inspiration. His knowledge, ethics, hard work and his constant encouragement have mattered much to me as a person in more ways than I can describe. Other friends, notably Reetika, read my draft and offered detailed comments, to which I am grateful.

No work is complete without the support of friends and family. I have had the fortune of having the most supportive parents. A very special friend entered my life five years ago but has managed to take a rather dominant role in my life. Kristin has by now served as my editor, discussant, friend, host, and my most enthusiastic cheerleader. Kristin, her family, and her friends have offered valuable support over the last few years. Many family members have offered support through the years, and I would like to especially thank Bhuvana Athai, Chinni Perima, Mala Athai Ravi Anna and Mangala Chitti for their extended support to me and my family.

My friends from St. Joseph's College and from St. John's Vestry have provided me the social support without which it would have been difficult to make the unusual career choices that I did. Ram, Balki, and Vijay went on to provide financial assistance to help me get to Syracuse, and they were always there for me in my moments of doubt.

I joined Stanford two years ago to the company of the most supportive colleagues. I owe a lot to Larry Diamond for his inspiration and for ensuring that I have had the time and space to do this work. I also benefited from a friend in a 'rival university'—Rajesh Veeraraghavan—who read, argued, and shaped this work in significant ways. I would also like to thank the team at Oxford University Press for their encouragement and support.

The list can go on, but the book has to start. No acknowledgement can serve as a true and complete list of all the intellectual and social debts that one owes —but I do hope that I have conveyed adequately that this work was not done in a vacuum. Every page to follow owes a debt to someone, and I am mindful that this is a social product that has merely been compiled by me—Thank you.

Abbreviations

All India Anna Dravida Munnetra Kazhagam	AIADMK
All India Women's Democratic Association	AIDWA
All India Trade Union Congress	AITUC
Ante-natal Care	ANC
Backward Castes	BC
Chief Minister	CM
Communist Party of India	CPI
Dravidar Kazhagam	DK
Dravida Munnetra Kazhagam	DMK
Dalit Panthers of India	DPI
Education Guarantee Scheme	EGS
Government of India	GoI
Government of Tamil Nadu	GoTN
India Human Development Survey	IHDS
Integrated Child Development Services	ICDS
M.G. Ramachandran	MGR
Maharashtra Employment Guarantee Scheme	*MEGS*
Member of Legislative Assembly	MLA
Mutually Assured Destruction	MAD
Most Backward Caste	MBC
National Conference	NC
National Federation of Indian Women	NFIW

National Rural Employment Guarantee Act	NREGA
National Family Health Survey-III	NFHS-III
Overhead Water Tank	OHT
Public Affairs Centre	PAC
Public Distribution System	PDS
Primary Health Centre	PHC
Public Works Department	PWD
Right to Food Campaign	RFC
Republican Party of India	RPI
Self-help Group	SHG
Special Economic Zones	SEZ
Tamil Nadu Integrated Nutrition Project	TINP
Targeted Public Distribution System	TPDS
Union Public Service Commission	UPSC

Introduction

The narrow-gauge train line built by the Prince of Gwalior from Gwalior to Sheopur was so much smaller than the standard trains in India that it looked almost like a toy train to me. I took this train in June 2003 during my first trip to the Chambal valley, and with some encouragement I joined a group of colourfully clad men and women on the roof of the train to begin a journey that profoundly changed my worldview. My toy train passed through beautiful sandy ravines interspersed with deep gorges, and a sprinkle of monsoon rain had revived the greenery, making the place serenely beautiful. My view belied the fact that the region was suffering the third consecutive year of drought that had led to widespread hunger and misery across Madhya Pradesh, Rajasthan, and other states. Every now and then I saw stray cattle roaming far away from villages; people who once owned them had let them wander away, unable to feed them and unable to watch them starve to death. There were a few in flesh and blood, but mostly I saw dry skeletons littered everywhere as a marker of the desperation lurking behind the beautiful landscape.

I was there as a part of a team to examine reports of starvation and deaths in Hirapur village. Our hosts led from house to house and gave us a long wooden stick to check if there was any grain in their storage bins, only to feel the empty floor again and again. At least six children had died in the drought of diseases that that they would have survived had they been better nourished. Most children looked visibly malnourished and seemed incapable of surviving even a mild bout of illness. We talked to people about what kind of government programmes were being implemented in their village and found that a few relief works had started to provide employment, but they were closed even while the inhabitants hardly had any store of grain. The state government had decided not to spend any money on school feeding, leaving it to the Panchayats.[1] Since most Panchayats spent less than half-a-rupee on a child a day, children often got just boiled wheat with some salt, and as one of my former teachers put it, *the impoverished children enjoyed even that.*[2]

The cruellest impact of drought was on the elderly people. Destitution was widespread and many old people had to live on the charity of hungry people. At least three elderly people had died the previous year accompanied by severe hunger in that hamlet. We met Gyan Bai, wife of the late Hira, as she was preparing her breakfast. The food consisted of a paste of leaves she collected from the forest; a clear sign that she had no food to eat. She ground the leaves and mixed them with water for food. She used to receive state pensions, which had stopped abruptly the year before, without any reason.

Our hosts insisted that we go to the bank of the canal to meet the old man who was sick. We were led to a row of ramshackle huts that could at most provide some shade from the sun for a part of the day. A frail skeleton of an old man named Duria was sitting inside on a cot. He was too sick even to move from his bed. Like many of the elderly destitutes, he too lived on occasional charity. We did not ask Duria what he does for food. A terribly dusty plate that had not been used for a long time spoke its own eloquent tale.

Like Gyan Bai, Duria used to get a pension that had stopped a while ago. He was too weak to recount how far back this had happened. His son Pappu explained there was no way for him to help his father since he and his children themselves were going hungry. Amidst all this, Duria was not an angry man. He calmly told us that the people of the village were starving and they should be provided employment in the next few months. For himself, he just asked for an injection to cure his illness. He did not ever murmur a complaint about his starvation and complete destitution. He calmly awaited his fate.

Hirapur was just one case among thousands of villages that were homes to such hunger, disease, and avoidable deaths, and I was convinced that a lot could be done to alleviate such widespread misery. Improving school feeding, providing reliable pensions, and ensuring employment were well within the state government's financial capacity; unfortunately they were not political priorities. Most families in Hirapur had received just 20 days of work in wage employment programmes that year, which was hardly adequate to sustain a family in those months. Low budgets to prevent hunger were further eroded by endemic corruption. We verified official accounts of three employment projects, and all three were fudged extensively. The dealer of the ration shop that was supposed to distribute subsidized grains and a few other necessities was mercilessly swindling even the poorest of the poor. We met many pensioners who were regularly cheated of up to two-thirds of their measly pensions, and even those who knew that they were being cheated could not complain for the fear of losing what little they got.

On my way back from Hirapur I started thinking about Tamil Nadu and my perception about my home state underwent a sea change. Until then, I had thought of Tamil politicians as populists who pander people with 'freebies' in order to get votes. I considered Tamil Nadu's extensive nutrition programmes a waste. I guess I acted like a middle-class boy who took basic necessities of life for granted, and so could not appreciate the importance of school feeding, child care, or subsidized food grains, and my thoughts were confirmed by others in similar positions whose ideas made their way to the English language media that I read. The same class background made me devalue these services, since they did not meet my standards. As a result, I was an enthusiastic supporter for winding up these services that were a useless *fiscal strain*. But watching a landscape littered with dead cattle from the top of the toy train forced me to re-evaluate my worldview.

I had started working at that time with the Right to Food Campaign (RFC) in India that was campaigning for greater involvement of the state in addressing hunger.[3] As a part of this work, I travelled to many parts of India and was struck by the regional disparities in how governments functioned—and for whom it worked. RFC's first major campaign was on school feeding and I was surprised by how resistant most state governments were to spend on an issue like that. The Supreme Court of India made school feeding a legal right of children in public schools and had directed all state governments to initiate it by June 2002 (Drèze, Prasad, and Bhatia 2005; Right to Food Campaign 2001). Despite the directive from the court, there was continuous resistance from most state governments and school feeding finally materialized in all states only by June 2006. The resistance for child care for children under six was even higher. In contrast to most states, Tamil Nadu provided these services extensively, and had started doing so decades before the intervention of the Supreme Court.

The villages I visited in Tamil Nadu typically had a range of basic public services including water, schools, child care centres, primary health care, all-weather roads, street lights, electricity, fair price shops, and school feeding. In addition to these services, there were an assortment of entitlements including old age pensions, maternity benefits, and programmes for farmers, and they were routinely accessed by beneficiaries. As people in Tamil Nadu vociferously pointed out throughout my fieldwork, there are major problems in how these programmes work. There was corruption in substantial scale and the quality of services had much room for improvement. The problems in the system are not trivial, but at the same time, Tamil Nadu has also managed to deliver a significant set of services, and these made a huge difference to people's lives.

There are three features of public service delivery that were notable in comparison to most other states. First of all, there is a wide array of services covering education, health, basic civic amenities (water, street lights, roads, etc.), transport, child care, nutrition support, and social protection. Second, these programmes can be found in most villages, and most people have access to them based on massive budgetary and administrative commitments. While a lot of the financial support came from the centre, the administrative effort has been entirely local. Finally, much thought and effort had gone into these programmes, and so the quality of implementation is often far superior to other states, especially those in the Hindi belt with which I was best acquainted.

Let me first discuss the extent of services. Almost every child in the state (i.e. 99.53 per cent) had access to a school in Tamil Nadu within one kilometre (Goyal 2006). Almost all children attended school in the 6–10 age group and there was no gender disparity in Tamil Nadu for this group (International Institute for Population Studies and Macro International 2008) (henceforth, NFHS-III), despite weak laws for compulsory schooling. Every child in a government school got school feeding, uniforms, textbooks and stationery, without the distinction of class, caste, or gender. There were some special incentives available only for a certain group, such as bicycles for girl children who enroll in higher secondary school.

Similarly in the field of health, 98 per cent of all women surveyed in the most recent round of National Family Health Survey (NFHS-III) got ante-natal care (ANC) from a health professional, including 84 per cent from a doctor. ANC was thus almost universal among women, though educated, richer, and urban women tended to get care from doctors rather than trained nurses with some disparity. In terms of ANC, Tamil Nadu ranked the highest among all states in NFHS-III, and the all-India average was 52 per cent. During ANC, 9 out of 10 women received all the mandated services needed to monitor their pregnancy, in which too Tamil Nadu ranked among the best in India. Eighty-eight per cent of all births took place in a health facility, and in this Tamil Nadu ranked only third in the country overall. Ninety-two per cent of women received post natal care, and 87 per cent of them within the first two days as recommended. NFHS-III also reports that Tamil Nadu had the highest proportion of children who were fully immunized against critical diseases such as polio, diphtheria, tetanus, pertussis, and measles. Ninety-seven percent of children lived in an area covered by a child care centre, 94 per cent of households had an improved water source, and 89 per cent of houses had electricity connections.

One of the largest surveys on India's public services done by Public Affairs Centre (PAC survey) (S. Paul, Balakrishnan, and Public Affairs Centre 2006) found that more than 90 per cent of all rural households had a 'ration card' that is essential to access the Public Distribution System (PDS). The PAC survey also found that 90 per cent of the people used the ration shop in the last month or two, and in terms of reliability Tamil Nadu scored much higher than all other states with 73 per cent of the respondents finding the services reliable compared to 51 per cent for the nearest rival, Andhra Pradesh. The national average was 23 per cent.

Tamil Nadu did not distinguish between populations that live below or above poverty line in providing access to the PDS. Following the recommendations of the World Bank, the Government of India (GoI) decided in 1997 to make the PDS 'targeted' and available only to those families identified as living below the poverty line. Given the widely acknowledged unreliability of identifying poor families, and determining what poverty is, this move has remained controversial. Following the GoI directive, the Government of Tamil Nadu (GoTN) decided to introduce targeting but removed it within one week following a spate of protests (Raj Ratnam 2003). GoTN spent a considerable amount of money to cover families that were deemed to be above poverty line by the GoI. By doing so, Tamil Nadu became the only state in India that retained a universal PDS when even states like Kerala switched to targeted PDS in 1997.[4]

One of the most striking elements of Tamil Nadu's commitment to provide public services is its commitment to do so almost universally. This can be seen from the fact that over 90 per cent of the population is able to access education, health, child care, PDS, and other public services as illustrated above. Such a commitment is not easy, since it is costly as well as administratively more and more challenging as governments try to reach underserved populations in remote areas (Table I.1).

The quality of public services is another notable feature in Tamil Nadu. Let me illustrate it by comparing health and child care services in Tamil Nadu and elsewhere. Across India, child care for children under six is provided under the rubric of one programme—the Integrated Child Development Services (ICDS). ICDS was started in 1975 as a national programme to address young children's health, pre-school education, and nutritional needs under one roof, called the Anganwadi. The programme is mainly sponsored by the GoI and it is implemented by the states. Since this is a national programme governed by common programme guidelines, it has a common and comparable framework across the country.

Table I.1 Top Performers in Public Services

State	WTR	HLT	TPT	PDS	EDU	Overall
Andhra Pradesh	7	16	4	2	4	5
Karnataka	2	6	3	3	3	3
Kerala	13	7	7	5	8	6
Tamil Nadu	1	4	2	1	1	1
Maharashtra	5	2	5	4	4	4

Notes: WTR = Water; HLT = Health; TPT = Transport; EDU = Education.
Source: S. Paul, Balakrishnan, and Public Affairs Centre (2006: 93)

The first impressive feature of Tamil Nadu's commitment to child welfare is the rapid expansion of the programme beyond the provisions of the GoI. Using funding from the World Bank, the ICDS system was supplemented by a parallel programme called the Tamil Nadu Integrated Nutrition Project (TINP). TINP supported more centres than the ICDS itself in the 1990s. After the World Bank funding ended in two phases, the centres were integrated with the ICDS programme, thus providing a substantially larger coverage of child care network in the state than was originally envisaged by the GoI.

Qualitative differences between Tamil Nadu and other states could be found in a number of aspects including infrastructure, regularity, range of services, training of workers, regularity of wage payments, and the quality of health, education, and nutrition delivered in the Anganwadi. Many of these are captured in the table below in a large comparative study of ICDS across six Indian states (see Table I.2).

Tamil Nadu ICDS had also initiated a system of training workers to identify disabilities in children at early stages to give them appropriate stimulations to use the plasticity of children's brains in early stages so that some of the disabilities could be overcome. The programme was in the nascent stages during my fieldwork, but the difference between Tamil Nadu and other states even at that stage was remarkable.

Table I.2: Facilities in ICDS Centres of Tamil Nadu and Other States

Facilities	Tamil Nadu	North(a)
Own building	88	18
Kitchen	85	30
Storage facilities	88	58
Medicine kit	81	22
Toilet	44	17
Average hours open per day	6.5	3.5
% children who attend regularly (b)		
Age 0–3	59	20
Age 3–6	87	56
% mothers who report that:		
Pre-school education takes place	89	47
Motivation of the worker is 'high'	67	39
Worker ever visited them at home	58	22
% women who had PNC (d)	100	55
% children who are 'fully immunized' (c)	71	41
Avg. months since training	6	30
% workers who have not been paid (e)	0	22

Notes

(a) Chhattisgarh, Himachal Pradesh, Rajasthan, Uttar Pradesh

(b) Among those enrolled at the local Anganwadi; responses from mothers

(c) Based on assessment of investigators

(d) Among those who delivered a baby during the preceding 12 months

(e) Workers who have not been paid in the last three months before the survey

Source: (Citizens' Initiative for the Rights of Children Under Six 2006)

In the case of health care, apart from ensuring that there is a Public Health Care (PHC) or a sub-centre available at a short distance, a variety of basic measures and creative ideas have gone into making the health system effective (for an overview see M. Das Gupta et al. 2009; Goyal 2006; International Institute for Population Studies and Macro International 2008; Seeta Prabhu 2001; Visaria 2000). Tamil Nadu has a strong cadre of nurses who are well trained and take the health system where it is needed; in fact, Tamil Nadu has one of the highest ratios of nurses per doctor in India. Almost half the doctors in the public health system are women, without which women's access to health care would be seriously compromised. Further, a large proportion of doctors are from lower castes,[5] which makes the health system socially accessible to most people. Apart from this, specialized training in many universities is available only to doctors serving in the public health system, so that their expertise is available widely.

In order to ensure the timely supply of medicines in the health care centres (which is so fundamental yet sorely missing in many states), Tamil Nadu started a pharmaceutical corporation that procures drugs and distributes them centrally. This experiment was successful and even doctors in rural areas rarely complained of running out of medicines. These and other innovations have made the health system dynamic and responsive to health issues and emergencies like the Tsunami of 2004.

While the primary health care system had grown gradually since independence, the system rapidly expanded after M.G. Ramachandran (MGR) became the Chief Minister in 1977. The 1980s saw a dramatic expansion of the primary health care system with support from the GoI. In most states the nationally mandated goal of providing a sub-centre for every 5000 people and a PHC for every 30,000 persons was gradually achieved, but the progress stopped at that. Apart from expanding the number of centres, Tamil Nadu also worked on ensuring at least one woman doctor in each centre, recruiting more support staff, improving the infrastructure, and ensuring regular supply of medicines.

A remarkable fact about Tamil Nadu is that between 1971 and now, life expectancy increased by nearly 20 years from 49.6 to 67 for men and 69.8 for women. Similar achievements have also been made in fields of maternal mortality and various debilitating diseases, among other things, infant mortality rate reduced from 113 to 30 in this period. Tamil Nadu has also managed to reverse the rapid expansion of HIV infection, and its health system played a critical role in ensuring that the state did not suffer from major epidemics like the plague, chikangunia, swine flu, and other epidemics that affected even well-managed states of India, including Gujarat.

All these have been achieved despite the fact that the state spends less than the national average in health expenditure (M. Das Gupta et al. 2009). For most of my readers, systems to ensure regular availability of drugs, presence of doctors, or availability of women doctors may not look like spectacular achievements. Indeed, these are not spectacular. But, the unfortunate fact in India is that even such basic facilities are not available for an unacceptably large number of people. In this context, Tamil Nadu's achievements, and those of other states like Kerala, are remarkable.

Delivering health, education, child care, and other basic services is a complex task that has to take into account social, physical, technological, economic, geographic, and other considerations. For a system to function well it has to be dynamic, with vision from the top that evolves in response to needs on the ground. It is not unusual to find thoughtful engagement by senior officials with the support of experts in relevant fields. A strong cadre of local bureaucrats who have risen up from the grassroots form a critical part of the administration, and they provide a detailed understanding of the system in formulating policies and plans. There is also a constant feedback from the ground via NGOs, political parties, media, and the public, which I will discuss in detail from the next chapter.

I was first exposed to the dynamism and adaptability of the system when I met a senior official dealing with the PDS in Tamil Nadu (Raj Ratnam 2003). He explained how the GoTN focussed on different problems over the years including physical access, problems in measurement, corruption through ghost cardholders, illegal switching of better quality goods for worse during transport, corruption by private ration shop dealers, etc. Each issue was taken up systematically and creative ideas were tried to address them.

For example, Tamil Nadu tried a major experiment with the PDS in the late 1990s by issuing coupons to ration-card holders to get their food and other entitlements. Normally, a card holder is supposed to take her card to the shop to get her entitlements. The shopkeeper is expected to verify the card, and issue the goods after making entries in her records and in the ration card. Since it is difficult to cross-verify each ration card, it was easy for the shopkeeper to write false entries in the registers with people who did not collect their rations. Cardholders also complained that ration dealers denied them their supplies, which could potentially be pilfered. Further, a large volume of bogus cards were issued that were used for corruption. In order to address these problems, GoTN decided to issue coupons each year to cardholders. Shopkeepers were expected to collect a signed copy of the coupon when anyone was offered her entitlement, and this was the basis for reimbursement to the shopkeeper.

The introduction of coupon system made it unprofitable to deny card holders their entitlement, thus making it more likely that dealers would deliver the entitlement. Coupons were distributed not through the PDS, but through a network of school teachers and other public servants making it difficult to create bogus coupons within a well-established network. The government had announced that those who did not get the coupons in the previous year will not be eligible to get it in the following year, but following protests this was quickly withdrawn. Finally, responding to complaints that poorer people are unable to buy their entitlements for a month in one installment, the entitlements were issued in multiple small coupons.

Such ideas are based on a simple understanding of the situation and none of this is out of the ordinary. Unfortunately, simple and ordinary ideas that could easily be introduced are often not done in the government, and this makes government-run facilities dysfunctional and poorly organized. As with this example, case studies of well-run public services in India typically attribute the successes to simple common sense measures that could have been conceived locally without the need for costly expertise. The experience of Tamil Nadu and other successful Indian states indicate that financial, administrative, and knowledge resources are well within the capacity of a state that is committed to provide a basic public service to its people. What truly matters is the commitment to provide basic public services effectively to **common people**[6].

Considering that basic public services are well within the capacity of most governments in India, I was puzzled as to why only a few states like Tamil Nadu, Kerala, and Himachal Pradesh developed the commitment to providing them extensively, while others lagged behind with devastating impact on the lives of so many.

I took this as the central puzzle for my doctoral dissertation but focussed exclusively on why Tamil Nadu developed its social commitment. The first section of this book looks at the evolution of that priority in Tamil Nadu. In the second section I argue that the insights from Tamil Nadu could be helpful in understanding the prevalence or the lack of commitment to services in other states.

Related questions and answers

Before I get into that story of how Tamil Nadu developed a commitment to services, I would like to discuss how this and some closely related questions have been dealt with by other authors in three literatures: human development, political economy, and comparative politics. My intellectual starting point into this question was the *human development* literature that provides a broad view of 'development' by taking into account different aspects of human well-being. Scholars of this tradition have argued that we cannot reliably understand what is happening to people's well-being by looking at narrow indicators such as economic growth or the level of poverty. If we look at basic indicators of well-being such as longevity, literacy, nutrition, health, etc. there are many cases where poorer regions (in which governments provide basic services extensively) do significantly better than their richer counterparts (where services are often not a priority). To get a better understanding of people's well-being, this literature measures health, education, and other factors that are broadly agreed in the society as critical for a decent life.

Apart from measuring indicators of well-being, this literature has also looked at what contributes to it. As Sen and Drèze have articulated (Drèze and Sen 1995; 2002), well-being can be improved by a variety of strategies including land reforms, pro-market measures, social reforms, etc.[7] In the process these scholars have argued that public services can have far-reaching consequences to people's well-being. Such an assessment of public services is rare in social science scholarship on India, which I will elaborate below. Human development scholars have also argued that most states do not provide these services with disastrous consequences.

But in this milieu, some states have shown a remarkable political commitment, the impact of which can be seen in much better levels of health, education, longevity, and other basic indicators of well-being. The literature also identifies Tamil Nadu, Kerala, and Himachal Pradesh as exceptional performers (Citizens' Initiative for the Rights of Children Under Six 2006; Drèze and Khera 2002, 2011, 2012; Goyal 2006; Khera 2011b; Planning Commission 2001; The Probe Team, Drèze, and De 1999). The focus of the human development literature has been on understanding how public services contribute to human development and most works in this tradition do not deal with the question of why some governments develop the socio-political commitment to provide services to all. The puzzle became the starting point of my study. Given the longer history of Kerala's success in such policies, there is some literature examining the 'Kerala model', but there was very little on other good performers including Tamil Nadu and Himachal Pradesh. That gap motivated this study.

The closest work on Tamil Nadu's political commitment to services is *Ethnicity and Populist Mobilisation* (Subramanian 1999). In this work, Narendra Subramaniam starts with the question of why Tamil Nadu's successful ethnic mobilzation did not lead to conflicts as we have seen in most other parts of the world, including neighbouring Sri Lanka. In the process he argues that Dravidian parties were able to maintain peace by being inclusive of all social groups, and sustaining the support of the newly assertive groups through populist policies. He also indicates that there was a strong electoral competition and the party cadres had relative autonomy that enabled them to offer support to alternate parties or visions, which forced these parties to be responsive.

Dravidian parties responded with populist policies that were crucial in keeping them in power, and the promises of distributing tangible benefits to key support groups enabled mobilization. He calls this a form of clientelism, and argues that, 'parties and regimes show an affinity towards clientelism if the promise of ready benefits appears likely to attract significant clientele' (Subramanian 1999: 65–66). This is a persuasive argument but it raises the question of why the same did not happen in other states of India. After all, services have proven to be immensely popular wherever they have been introduced and politicians such as N.T. Rama Rao and Y.S. Rajashekara Reddy of Andhra Pradesh, Digvijay Singh of Madhya Pradesh, and Raman Singh of Chhattisgarh among others have proven that creating services leads to tremendous electoral support. There is every reason to believe that services lead to immense popularity but very few regimes have resorted to this to sustain power even in the face of serious competition. A part of that answer lies in the fact that dominant communities have consistently opposed the provision of services to marginalized groups in the name of caste, class, or gender. This history of extending roads, water, school feeding, jobs, monetary support, and every other service to marginalized groups was fraught with conflict. It is true that politicians who extend services to these groups would be popular among them—but it could cost support of the dominant communities who decided the political fate of the candidates.

Narendra Subramaniam's insights, that electoral pressures in the context of autonomous cadres who could shift their support, is without doubt an important part of the story. This has to be complemented by understanding how the ground was created for the leaders to be populist, how the cadre autonomy was achieved and how communities that were violently prevented from using existing services were able to access them. Answers to these questions lie at the grassroots and not party politics with which Subramaniam was concerned. I will focus heavily on that side of the story in this book.

While works on the political commitment to services in Tamil Nadu are rare, there is now an impressive corpus of works that try to understand the differences in the commitment to services across India's states in a comparative perspective. One of the earliest works in this tradition was by Myron Weiner (Weiner 1991, 1996) who asked why there is little commitment to making basic education compulsory in India despite the financial ability to do so.[8] He argued that the overarching casteist ideology in India prioritized education only for the caste elite and the value attached to the labour of children from lower castes, rather than their education, underlie the lack of social commitment to universalizing education. Weiner's insight that the social structure, especially the caste system, was at the heart of India's lack of commitment to education will underlie some of my arguments as well. But his work did not account for the rapid changes that were happening to caste equations and its implications for governance. His book was originally published in the 1960s and since then there have been remarkable changes in the caste-relations in India and this alone requires a revision of his argument.

Weiner's work (1991, 1996) is one of the few that focuses on structural conditions and ideology in the construction of policy outcomes. Most other works on this subject attribute good performance to mobilization by the common people in order to secure some benefits of power from the state that is normally controlled by the elite. One could say that there is broad agreement among scholars across disciplines that public action by common people matters for performance. Having agreed that public action matters, there are two questions that have been asked in the literature: Why is there a greater level of public action in some regions, and are there some types of action including certain kinds of movement organization that are likely to be successful in instituting progressive policies?

Both these questions started crystallizing around Kerala, which was the first state in India to get international attention for rapid improvements in human well-being through the delivery of basic public services. The 'Kerala model' was considered to be unique within India and so analysts were focussed on what was unique about Kerala in trying to understand it. These works have attributed Kerala's success to factors such as enlightened princes of the past who expanded services, influence of matrilineal communities in the state that encouraged women to engage in basic public services and, social movements in the state led by the communists.[9] As some scholars have pointed out, the matrilineal society argument cannot take us too far since only a few communities were matrilineal in the state. Similarly, the enlightened princes may have started progressive policies but they were available to a very small section of the population—even though this was considerably higher than other parts of India at independence. Given the fact that Kerala had some of the worst forms of casteism in India at that time, services were traditionally restricted to few communities and this was expanded only with struggle by social movements.

Overall, the weight of argument on Kerala's performance has been on intense mobilization in the state.

Kerala has a history of mobilization along the lines of caste, religion, class, and other identities. Despite this rich history, analysts have tended to attribute Kerala's success to class mobilization led by the Communist Party. A good example of this can be found in the works of Patrick Heller who has argued that the communist movement starting in the 1930s has been instrumental in creating an agenda for public services such as health, education, and nutrition (Heller 1999). He argues that the success of the movement in mobilizing at the grassroots and in forming governments periodically in Kerala enabled the movement to make services a policy priority. Heller acknowledges that there were other powerful social movements in Kerala that did not mobilize along the lines of class, but these for him were only stepping stones for a strong communist movement to emerge. He has even argued that identity movements do not have a public content and do not look at economic policies, and so even though many other states have had strong identity movements, public services or other pro-people issues did not become a priority in these states (Heller 2000). In his works, Kerala represents an island of success and that success was enabled by class-based mobilization. This argument is widely accepted in public discourse.[10]

The idea that mobilization is likely to result in progressive policies only if it is along the lines of class is also represented in the works of other scholars such as Atul Kohli. In his iconic work (Kohli 1983) he argues that West Bengal was the most successful state when it came to land reforms and based on this experience he argues that class mobilization through an organized political party that could handle conflicts is most likely to succeed in redistributive reforms. He also argues that such a political party should have limited membership of the elite, a coherent leadership, and a pragmatic attitude towards change in order to be successful in carrying out contentious land reforms.

The focus on class mobilization has continued in Kohli's works for over two decades including in his recent work (Kohli 2012), where he looks at the success of states in reducing poverty. In this, he divides Indian states into three broad types: neo-patrimonial, social democratic, and developmental. He argues that neo-patrimonial states tend to have politics focused on leaders and this kind of politics lacks a public agenda, whereas social democratic states are the most successful in combating poverty. Social democratic states are defined as those that have strong left of centre parties built upon class mobilization. Kerala and West Bengal feature in this list and he points out that they have been among the top states in combating poverty.

Unlike Kerala or West Bengal, Left parties have never come to power in Tamil Nadu and class mobilization has been overshadowed by identity movements in the state. In this context, Kohli (2012) argues that even though there has been tremendous mobilization in Tamil Nadu, it has not been able to succeed due to the fact that mobilization was not carried out through strong and well-organized parties (a debatable claim), giving rise to populist leaders. His reading of politics in Tamil Nadu is best summarized in his statement, *'While such leaders are just as capable as neo-patrimonial leaders in a state like Uttar Pradesh of breaking the state economies... several factors limit their destructive tendencies: mass pressure from a mobilised electorate, better quality state bureaucracy, and the political weakness of feudal-like Zamindars'* (Kohli 2012: 158). Kohli looks at the political process in Tamil Nadu as a case of flawed democratization since the dominant form of mobilization in the state was not along the lines of class. Interestingly, he cites Tamil Nadu as the second most successful state in reducing poverty following Kerala (see Figure 3.5 in Kohli 2012: 152) but he does not discuss this success in his work.

Kohli's argument that Tamil Nadu had a case of failed mobilization is reflected in Heller's work and also other authors such as M.S.S. Pandian (Pandian 1989, 1990, 1992). Pandian asked how such an impressive history of mobilization failed to influence the political leaders and he answers that by looking at M. G. Ramachandran (MGR), one of the most popular chief ministers in Tamil Nadu's history. Under MGR there was a substantial expansion of schooling, health care, school feeding, child care, and other services in Tamil Nadu. Pandian dismisses these programmes by arguing that they do not address structural issues[11] and based on this he asked how common people could support a chief minister who acted against their own interests. He attributes this to the successful appropriation of popular symbols of resistance by MGR through his movies. These endeared him to the masses, but MGR appropriated these symbols in a 'perverse way' (Pandian 1992: 140) by removing the revolutionary spirit of these symbols (see also Pandian 1989). MGR's regime led to a dramatic expansion of school enrollment and reduced gender and caste gaps in basic education. It also led to dramatic improvements in longevity, infant mortality, maternal mortality, and other outcomes. If services and these outcomes were valued, Pandian's notion that MGR functioned against the interest of the people would not have been tenable—and that would have removed the basis of his analysis of what was wrong with the system that enabled this to happen.

What we see in the works cited above is a kind of double devaluation of the the political processes and their outcomes in Tamil Nadu. There is first a devaluation of mobilization around identity over class. In addition there is an unstated devaluation of public services in favour of the classic 'class agenda' involving land reforms, unionization of workers, and redistribution of property (more on this in later chapters). While all these authors argue that there was impressive mobilization in Tamil Nadu, it was seen as a failed process that did not lead to deep democratization in the state. Thus, it is not just enough to have mobilization, but mobilization should have certain kinds of ideological orientation and organization to be successful.

Any analytical work that tries to understand the reasons behind 'success' or 'failure' of states has to have underlying yardsticks through which success is assessed. There is a long tradition of scholarship in India that values what I call as the class agenda. The fact that West Bengal and Kerala had some measure of land reforms has made them famous examples of 'successful' states. Without any doubt, class-mobilization was at the heart of this success and it is well-known that most identity movements did not espouse land reforms. In this tradition, movements that did not lead to land reforms have been strongly criticized, and other achievements that they may have produced have been undermined given the preference of the left-oriented scholars for the class agenda. Since class mobilization was not dominant in Tamil Nadu and because it did not produce land reforms, the political process in the state has been analysed through the lens of double devaluation. Thanks to this, Tamil Nadu's politics has been characterized as a failure despite its success in combating poverty and its substantial improvements to human development.

The works of Kohli, Pandian, and Heller have what one could call a *leftist orientation*. In parallel, there is now a growing tradition of research with a *rightist-orientation* where 'good politics' is that which leads to neoliberal reforms. Like the leftist scholars, neoliberal scholars also view public services as a negative policy choice that is the result of poor political processes–or as the media puts it, a case of *bad politics winning over good economics*. This perspective is widely shared in the academia in India and is of course not restricted to the country. For example, Jaywardena (Jaywardena 2004) describes the expansion of services in Sri Lanka with words such as *dirigiste, political opportunism, paralyzing growth, market failures, populist* and even *villain of the piece*. His article looks at 'problems' like populism and electoral pressures, and how they prevent economic technocrats from devising 'good policies' that would promote economic growth. The author even advises technocrats to implement unpopular policies as soon as a new government is elected, so that such reforms at the forefront during the next elections.

Jaywardena evaluates human well-being mainly in terms of overall economic growth, and in his perspective public services are a hindrance to investment and growth. It is well known that Sri Lanka has achieved high levels of human development compared to its South Asian neighbours or countries with similar levels of income as a result of its commitment to services. If he had valued these services, electoral pressures would have been analysed as a positive force that pressured politicians to institute 'good policies' and there would have been no need to strategize on how to enable politicians to take an unpopular decision.

As illustrated above, the values of authors have analytic consequences. Since public services have been traditionally devalued both by the Left and the Right in favour of different types of structural reforms, both sides have criticized socio-political conditions that have led to the radical expansion of services with the result that they present a lopsided perspective of politics. I should clarify that I do not see the value basis as an analytical problem in all cases. Instead, I believe in the importance of trying to understand the success and failures of states based on different vantage points. Each perspective tends to highlight different aspects of the society, and read together they will help us to understand complex realities with greater sophistication.

I have chosen public services as my vantage point based on the idea that services contribute tremendously to human well-being. With this valuation, I do not look at Tamil Nadu as a case of failed mobilization, and this alone requires a fresh perspective on Tamil politics. By placing Tamil Nadu as a successful case, I hope to bring an epistemic variety to our understanding of what kinds of mobilization could lead to a commitment to human well-being through progressive policies. In other words, I felt that building this case study could challenge notions around the importance of class-based mobilization for progressive policies.

Tamil Nadu's success indicates that rather than ask what kind of mobilization would lead to progressive policies, a more productive question is the more basic question of why there are different levels of mobilization across regions in the first place. There is a body of works on India that identify social conditions that lead to greater public action, and not surprisingly, they differ based on the disciplinary location of the scholarship. Using the political economy approach, some economists have argued that the creation of public goods requires collective effort, but there is a cost to such collaboration. People choose to act collectively if the cost of action exceeds the expected individual benefits.[12] One such cost is finding common priorities to act upon. Some social conditions make collective agreement difficult, which increases the transaction cost and demotivates collective action. Such social conditions can occur when there are strong asymmetries of information (Banerjee, Banerji, and Duflo 2007) or diversity in the population (Banerjee, Iyer, and Somanathan 2005; Banerjee and Iyer 2005). In the latter case it is argued that preferences and priorities tend to be different in a diverse society and learning about common priorities involves a lot of effort that can demotivate collective action.

There is no denying that information and common identities can help in fostering a culture of cooperation. While this is a reasonable premise, there are serious limitations in the understanding of what constitutes identity and how identities shape action. For example, these authors look at identity exclusively as 'ethnic' identity comprised of caste, religion, and language, and this is assumed to be static. The history of every major social movement in India— communist, Dravidian, Dalit, backward caste, etc—involved the creation of new identities and new forms of solidarity that cut across narrowly defined 'ethnic' identities. In taking a static view of what an identity is, and a narrow one at that, this literature ignores some of the key dynamics of politics in India.

In addition I believe that there are more fundamental reasons than 'transaction costs' as to why people engage or refrain from collective action. Among other things these works do not look at the demand for services as a contentious affair that happens in a context of unequal power relations. Perhaps because of the fact that these works are bound by the confines of economics, they ignore power relations even when discussing why Zamindari areas underperform other parts of India. Even in this case with well-documented culture of domination and violence by the elite, the authors argue that these areas have low collective action due to a strong class-based differentiation in these regions that has been created by the Zamindari system. These differences between the elite and the common person lead to different *aspirations* that make collective action difficult. While I would agree with these authors in saying that collective action matters in determining collective priorities, there is very little overlap between my work and theirs in understanding what enables collective action in some places compared to others. In this respect, I am more sympathetic to the works of Heller (1999), Kohli (2012), and others who take into account the dynamics of power and provide a rich context to mobilization in their analysis.

A different strand of thought within economics on why there could be greater public action in some regions can be found in the human development tradition. These scholars see people's agency as the fundamental vehicle of change, and their ability to use their agency to secure change effectively depends on their capabilities (e.g. income, education, social networks, etc.) and also on social conditions that enable or curtail their freedoms. One prominent argument in this literature is that women engage with basic public services more directly than men, and so they are more likely to demand better provision of services (Drèze and Sen 2013; Sinha 2014). But this demand may not be effective if women do not have basic freedoms to travel to various public agencies, speak their opinion freely, and be heard with respect.[13] Women are better able to use their agency in societies that provide them greater freedoms, such as greater decision-making in the family, physical mobility, and an atmosphere where they can speak in public without censure. The success of Kerala is attributed in this literature to the greater freedoms enjoyed by women in the state, and it is also the case that women enjoy greater freedoms in other good performers including Tamil Nadu and Himachal Pradesh. Beyond these states, there is also evidence that the provision of services improves where women have a greater control of political decision-making (Brulè 2013; Chattopadhyay and Duflo 2004).

The human development literature was my intellectual starting point into this research and it gave me two main insights into why there could be higher levels of public action by the common people in some regions. One, people in these regions had the income, education, health, and other capabilities that enabled them to use their agency effectively. Second, social conditions permitted greater freedoms in these regions in social, cultural, political, and economic domains–all of which are important in the exercise of human agency in collective decision-making. While the literature provided me with a conceptual basis for understanding public action, the specific context of what these conditions were and how they changed in Tamil Nadu still required examination. Some of that help came from sociologists and political scientists working on power relations in India (Béteille 1996; Frankel and Rao 1990; Jaffrelot 2003; Kapur et al. 2010; Mendelsohn 1993; Srinivas 1987; Yadav 1999).

Since one of my fundamental puzzles became why Tamil Nadu had such a strong culture of public action, and how it came to demand public services, I also took inspiration from scholarship on collective action that had dealt with similar questions in other contexts. As McAdam et al. summarized conveniently (McAdam, McCarthy, and Zald 1996), there are two broad approaches to the question of why movements arise. The first looks at factors internal to the organization such as availability of resources, social networks, etc. that enable action (also see Diani and McAdam 2003; Giugni, McAdam, and Tilly 1999). The second looks at external conditions that either favour or repress mobilization (Goodwin and Jasper 1999; Kreisi and Weisler 1999; McAdam, Tarrow, and Tilly 2001; Tarrow 1996). The possibilities, concerns, and analogies raised by these literatures formed the core of my informal questionnaire that I used with my discussants during the fieldwork.

I started my fieldwork based on the notion that existing literature on my question gave me useful insights, but I rarely found them adequate for the reasons I offered above. I sought to bridge that gap by learning from officials, politicians, activists, beneficiaries, media persons and others engaged in different levels of public service delivery in Tamil Nadu. After all, they understood the system best. I spent one year doing participant observation in government offices[14] and at Panchayat offices to look at what drives their performance. In the initial stages I worked at the grassroots level in the Villupuram district of Tamil Nadu and in the later stages I conducted interviews with people who have state level experience to confirm which of the insights from Villupuram were more broadly applicable in Tamil Nadu.

During my conversations I asked my discussants what they thought might explain Tamil Nadu's performance, and I also offered different possible explanations I took seriously based on the literature and my previous experiences. This enabled my discussants to point out new facts that I have not accounted for previously, confirm some of my suspicions, or challenge them. Sometimes they brought me books and insisted that I read them or got me phone numbers of people to whom I should. More than once I was asked what kind of a researcher I was if I did not interview someone who was diametrically opposed to their own views! When new ideas came up, I took them back to my key discussants to get their views on it, and I also read literature dealing with the topic. In this recursive process, some themes stood out and they were broadly agreed upon by my discussants. These themes form the backbone of my argument in this book.

These discussions confirmed that public action played a very critical role in Tamil Nadu, as has been suggested in the literature. But there were some surprises. To begin with, discussants argued that the kind of public action that one sees today in Tamil Nadu is very recent and dates back to the 1970s at most. This was a surprising claim considering the fact that Tamil Nadu has a rich history of social movements that date back to the mid-nineteenth century. They helped me understand the difference between the great social movements of the past and the widespread decentralized collective action we see today. In the process they also reflected on changes in movement organization and socio-political conditions that led to the kind of public action we see today, which in turn lies behind Tamil Nadu's commitment to public services. I will discuss these ideas starting with a presentation on the contemporary nature of public action in the region.

Notes

1. Panchayats are village level governments comprised of elected members. It can also refer to the informal judicial body of the village or of a caste, but in this work the word is used to refer to elected governments, unless mentioned otherwise.

2. In a conversation with Jean Drèze during summer 2003. I should add here that Jean has also written about this experience in news articles that were published during the drought.

3. For an overview of the campaign, see http://righttofoodindia.org and the following references (Drèze 2004; Drèze and Jaishankar 2005; Khera 2011c; Vivek and Guha-Khasnobis 2007; Vivek and Narayanan 2007).

4. The situation has changed since then, which I discuss later in the book.

5. I use this term to denote Dalits, tribal people, and the BC people.

6. **Important note on vocabulary:** I use the term 'common people' in this book to indicate the poor, women, Dalits, and others who have traditionally suffered from oppressive social conditions. They constitute the majority of the population, and so the label, 'common people' is appropriate. In using this, I recognize that there are other sections of the population such as Tribal people in Tamil Nadu who are severely marginalized and tend to be left out of the system even today. While 'common people' are not the most marginalized, they suffered from oppressive conditions traditionally, and they are the main subject of this work.

7. Drèze and his associates have also worked on the performance of selected public services including education (The Probe Team, Drèze, and De 1999), early childhood care (Citizens' Initiative for the Rights of Children Under Six 2006), employment (Khera 2011c; Khera 2006), school feeding (Drèze and Goyal 2003) and the public distribution system (Khera 2011b; Drèze and Khera 2011). To this rich set, one could add the works of scholars like Mahendra Dev (Mahendra Dev 2001; Mooij and Dev 2004), Seeta Prabhu (Seeta Prabhu 2001; Seeta Prabhu and Sudarshan 2002) and others (Goyal 2006) who have looked at what aspects of the social sector get priority in different states. Finally, there are important large scale surveys on public services in India that have also contributed to our understanding of how states perform when it comes to basic public services. The most important of these include the National Family Health Survey series, Public Affairs Centre survey of five basic public services and the India human development survey of 2005. Others such as the National Sample Survey series, the census, etc. also ask questions that are valuable to understanding the provision of public services and human well-being.

8. In these works Weiner (1991;1996) focussed narrowly on the legislation of compulsory schooling and did not give credit to rapidly expanding school enrollments without a law.

9. A sample of works discussing these ideas include (Casinader 1995; Franke and Chasin 1989; Heller 1999; Lieten 2002; Mathew 1999; R. Jeffrey 1994; R. Jeffrey 1976; Ramusack 2003; R. Jeffrey 2001).

10. Another work that advocates this line powerfully is (Franke and Chasin 1989).

11. For example, in one of his articles he dismisses MGR's record by saying, 'The eleven-year rule of MGR did not cause any particular structural changes in the economy to benefit the subaltern classes in Tamil Nadu' (Pandian 1989).

12. This goes back to the work of Mancur Olson who brought in the question of why individuals participate in collective action in his famous 1965 article reprinted in (Olson 2012).

13. The relationship between Sen's conception of development as freedoms and its application to women's agency is discussed at length in (Agarwal, Humphries, and Robeyns 2005).

14. These were primarily the Collector's office in my district and various Block Development Offices. I interviewed state level officials but did not spend time observing at this level.

Section I

1

Uncontrollable People

Since I wanted to understand what drives the commitment to public services, I decided to spend a considerable amount of time in government offices during my fieldwork with the expectation that the factors driving a government's performance will be most visible there. Most of this time was spent at the district level and below[1] where programmes are actually implemented, while I also did interviews with state level officials where high-level policies are created. In a context where there was virtually no material incentive for good or bad performance, the decisions that government workers made were mostly based on different pulls and pressures that they faced. Accounting for these provided me with the fundamental insights into how the government functions in Tamil Nadu.

Senior officials and politicians were an important source pressure on grassroots officials, as it would be expected. Large landed farmers, political party office bearers and contractors were also influential. These are common sources of pressure across the world, but none of this helps us understand what makes the government deliver to the common person. In Tamil Nadu, common people were also able to exert pressure on officials, which made them devote a part of their attention to delivering broad-based public services. Unlike contractors, traders or large famers, most common people did not have the money, position or status to exert influence; instead, they had to rely on public action to put pressure and to get some attention to their aspirations.

While officials and others I discussed with agreed that public action was intense in Tamil Nadu and it forced the government to perform, most people also argued that public action of this sort was relatively new and it dated back at most to the 1970s. This was a surprising claim since Tamil Nadu was home to many large social movements including the Dravidian and communist movements. During the course of my fieldwork it became clear that these large social movements typically had a presence only in a few villages in any given district and most people participated only in large scale protests organized outside their villages. What changed since the 1960s was a culture of constant challenge by individuals and along with it collective action that was initiated at the village level. I will deal with this form of decentralized collective action in the next chapter and will give an account of public action by individuals here.

During the course of my fieldwork, it became clear that the distinction between the great social movements of the past and decentralized public action was analytically important and it held the clue to understanding Tamil Nadu's commitment to ensuring that services functioned well and were provided nearly universally. This made it important for me to understand what led to the kind of decentralized public action one sees today. I got the answer to that question during my discussions with the implementing agents who helped me to understand the contemporary nature of public action and how this was enabled. Interestingly, these conversations helped me to see public action through the eyes of people who are the targets of action rather than those who engage in the protests, which is the normal vantage point taken in the collective action literature. I have constructed a conversation below based on quotes from my discussants in order to convey the emotional quality of the discussion that will help us appreciate the social context of their work. I have masked the identity of the speakers by presenting only their official capacity in order to protect them.

Not surprisingly, those at the receiving end of action were rarely appreciative of it, and thus their portrayal of it was seldom positive.

Other discussants including activists, journalists, and common citizens had different perspectives of action that I will elaborate in the next few chapters. In this chapter, I have presented only the widely held views of those engaged in implementing government programmes. Apart from the intrinsic merit in the perspective of an important set of people, this will help us to understand what shapes their performance. Through this, I hope to illustrate the different forms of day-to-day public action that these agents were confronted with and also provide a clue as to what changed from the seventies that resulted in widespread public action.

During my fieldwork in 2007–08, the largest and the best funded programme implemented in rural areas was the National Rural Employment Guarantee Act (NREGA). NREGA was a wage employment programme meant to provide fall-back employment to labourers, based on a law that guarantees work for anyone who applies for work and is willing to do hard physical labour until their family gets up to 100 days of work in a year.[2] The law requires that work be provided to anyone who sought it, but the implementing agents had an incentive to reduce the numbers in order to reduce their workload (which is considerable), enable better supervision and to make the programme manageable. This required them to dissuade people from accessing NREGA work.

> **Panchayat President (President)**: We are sometimes forced to turn a few people away because there are too many already, [but] they will refuse to leave and just sit where I can see them. What can we do about them? After a while we are forced to take them.
>
> **Village Level Worker (VLW)**: We try telling people at times that we can take only one person per family for work, but they don't agree. [An extra-legal rule they tried in order to limit the number of people without being unfair to some families]. They say, we are in trouble [poverty] ourselves and the government gives us 100 days of work, when are you going to give it to me? When people trouble us like this [*torture kodukkara pothu*] we are unable to do any work. That's why things are difficult for us.
>
> **President's husband**: There is nothing that people do not know about NREGA. People know that they won't get their wage if they do not sign on the muster roll and so they come and demand why their signature has not been taken. Workers of communist parties are

always hovering around me when I write the muster roll (attendance register for beneficiaries of NREGA) to see what names I am writing. And they even talk law to us! One man told me that during rainy season when we don't offer any work, I have to pay people an unemployment allowance, is that the case?

There was a debate among the group around that question, and at least at the village level, I found that the implementing agents were now and then confronted by activists who were well read about government programmes and laws. In most villages some activist or an educated young person armed herself with handbooks that provide basic information on entitlements in NREGA and other programs. While the implementing agents were normally better versed with the rules governing various programmes, they also had to regularly encounter people who knew these laws, and thus could use them to their advantage.

Knowledge about government programmes and entitlements was not restricted to activists. Most people I met knew what the entitlements were supposed to be in most major services. One of my favourite memories from my fieldwork was meeting the servant maid of a friend in New Delhi who had left Tamil Nadu three decades ago. When I told her that I was doing my PhD she immediately asked me to check a new scholarship introduced by the Chief Minister for higher education! This knowledge enabled people to identify problems in getting their entitlements in the first place, and it also gave them a strategic advantage when bargaining with officials.

President: People can be very aggressive and my assistant was beaten up one day.

President's Husband: One man in my village has two wives, and he wanted two different job cards with his name that could be given to each of his wives. Rules say that you can give just one card to each family. Tell me, what do I do about a case like this?

VLW: They don't care about any rules, they just order us and ask us to do what they say...We are now so used to bending (he said, indicating how they have to accommodate all kinds of demands, reasonable and unreasonable). They are uncontrollable. They work where they feel like, don't accept measurements, come late and go early. If we try to control them, we get abused—it is humiliating even to narrate it...

VLW 2: ...that is, people use uncivilized words. We feel bad about doing this work and we keep wondering why we came to this line of work. For example, we are supposed to send the number of people working in the project that day to our superiors in the district office at 10.30 am. [This cleaver rule was introduced by the Tamil Nadu government to make field level officials commit to the number of workers before the day ends. After 10.30 am, a senior official may visit the project on any day and by just doing a headcount of labourers, she will be able to assess if there is corruption in the form of ghost workers in the attendance register. Once the field official commits to the number of workers in the morning, they are not allowed to add further names in the register]. We send the SMS at 10.30 am, but people on the other hand claim that we add fake names. They say, he has the register with him and can add names anytime.

President's husband: After we send the SMS to the district office, ten people will report to work; other times when a superior comes to inspect, ten people will go out for urine; some others go out for urgent housework and do things like taking care of animals. Ten to fifteen people go out like this after giving us their names. The officer counts the number of people and will strike their names off since they were not present. But people abuse us when their payment does not come [since their names were removed from the attendance].

VLW: Officers on the other hand tell us how can someone go out without your knowledge [permission], but people don't understand this. People don't understand that it is we who get caught in case of trouble. When we explain this to people they joke by saying, this fellow acts as if he gives us the money from his grandmother's coffers.

VLW 2: On one occasion, ten people's wages were deducted since they were absent when the official came for inspection. These people had come and had worked but they went back home for some errands. When they learned that they will not be paid, they came to fight. They argued that they had come on that day and they had worked. Four other people supported them and said they were present that day. When I asked them why they were not there during the inspection, they said they had gone out for some reason. They give their reasons and four other people support them. Then I had to give them the money even without any account [illegally]. If I don't pay, I get abused; they say, don't think that you are a big shot who can get away with it.

Presidents and field-level workers consistently argued that they had a combative relationship with people in their villages. Without restriction of class, caste, or gender people took up their issues assertively. They would make their case, call others for support, and if need be they did not hesitate to have heated arguments with some hard words said by either parties. This kind of a relationship cannot be found when people are confronted with more senior officials, when the majority of common people tend to get more deferential. But at the grassroots where programmes were implemented, such deference was rare to find, and this relationship enabled people to put a lot more pressure on the grassroots officials. As a result, grassroots level workers found it difficult to work if policies they implemented did not conform to the aspirations or the realities of the people in that region. In order to make their work possible, they bended the rules created by the state and central governments and also made strong representations to their seniors for a change in rules.

Arguments and abuses were of course not the only form of public action. As I indicated above, the mere act of sitting in a visible place and refusing to move can put moral pressure on the agents. Such forms of pressure were combined with strategic voting that was a constant source of pressure for people competing in Panchayat level elections.

> **President**: There are people who shirk, and they don't even bother to stand in the line to collect their payments. Those who actually work, stand in the line... but not the shirkers. They would say, where is that man—the president; is this why we voted for you [that we have to spend our time in lines]?

Many labourers that I had met during the stay concurred with the views of the president. One of them put the issue somewhat colourfully: 'If the president asks us to do what we do not wish to do, we would fight with him and it would lead to problems for the president. What can he do about it? He can try and insist, and even shout at people to work – but he can't bring the spade and do all the work himself, can he?' He also asked, 'Who will get into trouble if we do not do the work? It's the president and other senior people. We will not get into trouble. So the president has to make adjustments with the bureaucrats for whatever work was done.' Such brazen comments were likely to come only among those to whom the president or other officials were obliged through familial or other relations, though some resistance was not uncommon among others.

> **President's husband**: Between the vice president, ward members, and me [who comprise of the elected Panchayat officials], there is a large web of relatives and others that are close to us. We don't have a way out but to give them some concessions [*Salugai*] now and then. It may be some relative of mine. It may be someone close to the vice president or a Ward member. We cannot say no. They will create problems. They take the issue elsewhere [e.g. they can create trouble during his children's marriage or when he needs a loan]. But others quickly demand that they be treated as these people. In this condition, people within the village cannot enforce work norms.

While patronage through a web of relationships is never an acceptable form of governance, there was an implicit democratization of patronage due to the fact that the social background of the elected and administrative officials had changed in the region. Only a few decades ago, most of the elected officials were from elite castes and families, and so were the administrators. The broadening of the social base of those in government has also resulted in the broadening of patronage networks. I will discuss its implications for governance below.

> **President**: so we often enroll people in NREGA even if they don't work. It's not wrong. [Invoking an old poet] It is like what Valluvar said in his *Kural*: *Nellukku iraitha neer vaikkal vazhi oodi; pullukkum ange pusiumam* [water that is meant for the paddy, will also irrigate the grass along the canals]. The water may be for the paddy field, but it is useful for a lot of others. Grass uses it, crows drink it, and people use it and what not. Of course, paddy grows but in the process the president, clerks, disabled people and others also get the benefit of NREGA. At least 10 per cent of people in the muster roll will be those who are not working.

> **VLW**: Some infants come to the worksite and we asked an old

woman who was not feeling well to take care of the children. [This job is physically less demanding] and another woman who is equally old immediately complained and said that she wants to do that work. She then bargained for the work to be rotated between them every alternate week, and then a younger woman of 20 asked me, won't these children sleep if I take care of them? I want that job.

President: Due to people's technology like television and other things, people have a lot of awareness. These things have not made people wise, but cunning. In that, people have improved. A young man in the worksite was not working. When I asked him why, he said that another person who was actually 60 years old was not working much. I asked him why you should compare yourself with a 60-year-old man. Don't you understand that he is old and he cannot work as much as a 30-year-old man that you are? And do you know what he told me for this? He said, whether you're 60 years old or 30 years old it is Rs. 80 per day and you should let me work the same amount as that man does. Why should I work more?

Presidents faced intense competition, and it was not easy to extend some benefits to one set of people while ignoring others. This created intense pressure for creating benefits that were nearly universal, or for creating a system that could be considered fair and legitimate, such as rotating an easier job among potential workers. For example, a block official once asked a president to select 100 people among poor Dalits for Indira Awas Yojana, a programme for providing free housing for the poor. Once he did that, the official asked him to select 50 people who were most deserving from that list. Finally the official sanctioned just 25 houses prompting the president to say, 'Look at my bald head...it is like stabbing me right there. Now a lot of people are going to complain about me'.

VLW: Now all the other 75 will put petitions against him now, she said with a chuckle.

President's husband: Everybody else will now start complaining that the president has done them in [*theethu kattitaru*]. What can you tell all those who did not get the house?

President: There is also an issue of community in this. I belong to the Vanniyar caste and my brother here an *Adi-dravidar* [Tamil term for Dalit]. Whenever a work needs to be done, I try and do it first in the colony [Dalit neighbourhood]. This is because there is already a feeling of separation, and if we do something first for my own area, it will be immediately seen in communal lines. I don't want them to feel that a Vanniyar president has left Dalit people behind, I am concerned about it.

President's husband: It is fear, we are afraid of it.

President: At the same time people of my caste get upset to see me doing things elsewhere. They say that I am your relative, but you go and do things for someone else. This is what my people think. I try and tell them that you are all related to me as uncles and cousins, and you will be willing to wait a little. I cannot expect them to do that. See how fundamental our problems are? They then tell me that you got more votes from us, how can you go to another place and do the work? I try and tell people that even if I got ten votes here and five votes there, both should be treated the same. *Unlike presidents of the past, we have to face all this* [emphasis mine].

These social tensions were aggravated by political competition, which was intense. Every Panchayat president had his or her share of 'enemies'[3] within the village who would incite people at every opportunity, making it difficult for the president to take actions that seem narrowly partisan; that would make them lose their support base. In an intensely competitive atmosphere, Panchayat elections were often held on the basis of narrow calculations, such that an aspirant needed to win only a certain number of votes to win the election, and thus could target the benefits only to some families. But, this calculation did not work equally well when mobilizing votes for the state or the national elections, for which local contestants acted as mobilizing agents. There was thus constant pressure to not lose support, if it can be avoided at all. The enemies were typically young aspirants for office who sought to create a base for themselves by helping people with applications for government benefits, and in other ways. Unlike the presidents of the past, current day presidents did not have dominance either through disproportionate wealth or other means to quash dissent. Apart from inciting people in the village, the enemies also registered petitions of wrongdoing against the president with higher officials and monitoring bodies.

President's husband: We on our part, get very scared even if we hear that the Collector is coming. Our legs start shaking, and we start feeling like someone who is making illegal alcohol. [People around him laughed and enjoyed this analogy, and some of them asserted 'oh yes that's true']. We run away at times when we see the squad [of inspectors] as if we were smugglers of sandalwood or gold. That's how we have to escape at times.

President: Some people also freely dial the number [of the collector's mobile phone]. It is available to everyone today. You just need to have one rupee, you can put it on the [public] phone and dial the collector. On three occasions in my Panchayat, the vice president himself incited people to call the collector and file complaints. On all three occasions a squad came. The first time, when they came, they took a detailed attendance and everybody was present. What happens next? A week or two later they put a one rupee coin again and call the collector. Often people step out to take a leak or for a small break. If officials come when we are not there, we do not get a chance to explain this, and we get into trouble. If the vice president is there, since he does not like me, he twists it to his own methods.

President's husband: Do you know what their satisfaction is? Look at how I made you dance with fear [*aatam kattiten*] with just one rupee! They're proud of it.

President's husband: A 15-year-old boy [from a poor family] wanted to come to work to save money for school. I told him not to come to the worksite, since it will spoil his studies. He told me that he wanted to come and work on vacation days. He has a reason, but if I give him work I will get caught for employing child labour. There are many complexities involved. People have written the law, often sitting in an A/C room.

Presidents constantly pointed out that in order to serve their democratic function, they often have to twist rules that were created in the state and national capitals. While one may have disagreements with this particular case, there were many cases where presidents had to circumvent laws in order to ensure that the very spirit of the law was maintained. But this made them vulnerable to the bureaucracy, which was in charge of ensuring that rules are followed. It also made them dependent on the support of senior politicians who had leverage over bureaucrats. As a result of this vulnerability, even the few Panchayat presidents who were elected as candidates with no affiliation to a political party had to secure the support of some party for their sustenance after getting elected.

Not all circumventions of the law were empowering in the sense that presidents also had to accommodate the demands of local notables that went against the aspirations of other constituents in their Panchayat. For example, a few presidents told me [often in a hushed voice] that farmers were under tremendous pressure since labourers preferred NREGA work to agricultural work. At critical times they were faced with labour shortages, and they put pressure on the Panchayat presidents to ensure that adequate labourers are available for work. Since NREGA was a demand driven programme, presidents did not have the legal room to offer work at a time of their choice, and so they adopt various extra-legal measures to accomplish that. The dominant theme was that they are democratically elected and so have to respond to various constituencies.

This need to accommodate conflicting demands created a lot of pressure in their day-to-day work. An important feature of this tension is that it came from many different social locations. Senior politicians, bureaucrats, farmers, landless labourers, women from different classes, Dalits, agricultural labourers —all had some ability to put pressure on the president. The consequence of this is that the actions of the president had to take into account the aspirations of most social groups in the village, even if she gave priority to some sets of people.

> **President**: *I wish I were a president 30 years back. They did not have to face any of these issues.*

The life of the presidents and grassroots workers resembled a battlefield. It was fraught with tension, competing demands, uncertainty, and challenges in every possible form. There were the subtle challenges such as people refusing to go away when they were refused work. Other challenges were more overt, and even aggressive. Presidents were constantly reminded that they had to return to the people for votes. Presidents were attacked at times of their weakness, such as occasions when they required social support or times when they got into trouble with officials.

Presidents and officials complained bitterly that insubordination, questioning, challenging, and organized collective action were day-to-day affairs in their lives. They also argued that it was uncommon among the Panchayat presidents of the yesteryears. Most people agreed that this form of challenge by the common person was a phenomenon that went back at most to the 1970s. Before that, presidents and other people in influential positions were treated with respect and deference and were not challenged on a regular basis. It was even uncommon for common people to enter a police station or the block office in order to put forward their representation. These places were the preserve of the narrow elite.

Panchayat presidents of the previous generations came from the elite families, typically large landlords belonging to the upper caste. The domination that they had over the village life was extensive. They owned a significant proportion of the land and they were the most important source of employment for most people. Even government employees including postmasters, teachers and others depended on these families for a variety of services from providing cheap housing to subsidizing their consumption. Such patronage, ownership of land, and other factors gave them a dominance in village life that made it difficult or impossible for common people to question and challenge them. This is not to say that there were no challenges from the common person earlier. But the intensity of the challenges and its relentlessness have changed unmistakably in the Tamil context. The breakdown of this dominance has led to numerous day-to-day struggles in all aspects of governmental work—with profound implications on governance.

The critical aspect of the social change in the eyes of the implementing agents was that people were not easy to control anymore. The inability to control led to incessant challenges, complaints, and electoral threats etc. that forced the agents to pay attention to the aspirations of the common person. They now have to balance these competing demands with those of the more powerful groups. A programme like NREGA that gave the agricultural labourers bargaining power over farmers would have been quashed easily at a time when the farmers were totally dominant. Today, even land-owning presidents had to create an extensive amount of employment in NREGA but they undermined the legal guarantee, thus balancing the demands both of the agricultural labourer and farmers.

This feature goes well beyond NREGA. Public services such as water, schools, health facilities, street lights, etc. were typically installed only in the elite areas before the seventies. The Dalits

and also other Backward Caste (BC) communities were often prohibited from using these facilities even if they were physically
accessible to them. Such restrictions also applied to women for
a range of services including schools. In order to access services,
marginalized groups had to challenge the local elite, which was
not possible when the elite were dominant. That dominance has
crumbled in recent decades, unleashing a culture of challenge that
the elite in the government cannot ignore. When the elite were
able to dominate the marginalized social groups, these groups were
unable to challenge the system to create access to services. That
dominance has now crumbled, which has unleashed a culture of
challenge that those in governments cannot ignore.

The day-to-day challenges also had another profound impact.
Implementing agencies had regular meetings at the block level and
they were vociferous in their opposition to infeasible rules that
reflected badly on them. Thus, many of the centrally created rules
and regulations that did not suit local conditions came under tremendous criticism. For example, wage in NREGA is paid on task
rate (i.e. based on the amount of work done), and it is supposed to
be set in such a way that a labourer working diligently for seven
hours in a day will be able to earn the legal minimum wage. When
NREGA was initially implemented, the Government of Tamil
Nadu (GoTN) prepared a schedule of rates based on the experience
of Public Works Department (PWD), where labourers work along
with machines. The use of machinery enables greater output per
person in such works, and the same cannot be expected in NREGA
where the use of labour-displacing machines is prohibited by law.
As a result of using PWD rates, workers were paid unduly low wages, resulting in protests in different parts of Tamil Nadu. The GoTN
responded by increasing the rates by 60 per cent, and once again by
60 per cent (Rural Development and Panchayati Raj Department,
Government of Tamil Nadu 2006; Rural Development and
Panchayati Raj Department, Government of Tamil Nadu 2007).[4]

Such challenges forced the implementing agencies to address
these grievances in order to minimize conflict. The impact of these
changes were profound and it contributed to a better functioning
government overall. There is no denying that pressure of this sort
can also undermine some programmes. To take NREGA as an

example, labourers, officials and others engaged in the programme all had an incentive not to work hard, and thus there were many cases where hundreds of labourers spent a considerable amount of time without any noticeable outcome. While empowerment of this sort comes with notable problems, the overall impact of pressure was to make the government work more efficiently.

The effectiveness of government programmes depended not just on broad institutional parameters; seemingly small details also had major consequences for how well a programme functions on the ground and who is able to benefit from it. The details are often localized and are highly contextual, making it difficult for them to be logically deduced from above. Thus, unless there is serious iteration of such rules based on feedback from the ground, it is unlikely that centralized government programmes will ever be efficient or functional. Programmes that affect the powerful get that feedback and thus tend to be more effective. In Tamil Nadu, public action provided that feedback and it enabled constant iteration of the programme design, which helped the programmes to become more functional and effective. The mix of pressures from all social groups has resulted in a system where the government tends to deliver some benefits widely, while at the same time indulge in large scale corruption and nepotism. While nepotism has been a constant factor in Tamil politics, no government today can hope to retain power without delivering some benefit to the broadest section of the population. The uncontrollable people have ensured that.

Notes

1. This included Panchayat offices, the Block Development Office (that implements most programmes) and the Collector's office at the district level (that oversees the implementation of most public services).

2. For an introduction to the programme see (Drèze, Dey, and Khera 2006).

3. A word commonly used by the presidents themselves.

4. Mihir Shah among others have written on the challenge of fixing an appropriate schedule of rates and its importance to the programme overall (Vijay Shankar et al. 2006; Shah 2009).

2

Thirty Years of Collective Action*

One of the exercises I undertook during my fieldwork was to list the services that were available in a village and ask knowledge-able individuals if they knew of any collective effort to secure or maintain these services. In most cases, there was a long history of action dating back to the 1970s and 80s. As an activist put it, they would struggle one year and get 100 metres of road, street lights required another protest, and many basic amenities had to be gained through a continuous process of collective action lasting decades. Such struggles were carried out by collectives that were

* This chapter is mainly based on several rounds of interviews with a Dalit activist, who I shall call Parthasarathy here. Interviews with him were complemented by discussions with a few others in the Dalit habita-tion, with his family members outside the village, other activists in the region who know the village well, and with literature available on this region. The presentation here is based on the issues that were acknowl-edged by most of my sources. In certain cases, there were divergent points of view, as is inevitably the case. I have retained the subjective narrative by my main interviewee for the most part, based on my conviction that the subjective position of the interviewee is important, and that it explains important aspects of social change. The chapter should be read and interpreted with that in mind.

formed at the village or the sub-village level. These collectives have become vehicles for sustained collective action over various grievances. An important feature of such action is that it is initiated and sustained with local efforts although it benefits from external resources. This has to be distinguished from top-down efforts that are often taken up by political parties in order to have a coordinated action on issues selected by the state level leadership. I call the former phenomenon *decentralized collective action*.

Decentralized action was very common and some instances of it could be found in a district on a daily basis. Such episodes were rare before the 1970s, much like the acts of individual resistance described in the previous chapter. Apart from the fact that episodes of action started after the 1970s, there were a few other notable similarities between this form of action across villages. In most cases, action was galvanized by youngsters– typically with some level of education. In most cases, mobilization was segregated by caste, class, and other differences. Given the fact that residences are strictly segregated in Tamil Nadu, mobilization also tended to be located in certain habitations within villages, except when it was led by the communists who were able to bring together different caste groups within a village, barring the traditional landed elite.

For strategic and substantive reasons, most of these groups started as 'social service' organizations dealing with education, health, and other immediate demands of the community. Activity at this stage strictly involved petitioning the government for some service, and often a non-controversial one so that it was not opposed by powerful sections of the village society. The demand for some types of public services at a small scale did not directly affect the interests of the dominant sections, compared to a demand for land reforms or other divisive agenda. This is one important reason as to why local organizations started by focusing on public services. Eventually, most of these groups started taking up political and social issues because it became inevitable, and also because it became safer to do so once they were established. Some youngsters who galvanized the community started with a political vision, and were biding their time to contest in elections or to take up contentious issues once they gained organizational strength. Others who sought to work mainly on issues like education and health were forced to act on untouchability, voting rights, and political mobilization without which they were unable to advance their agenda.

Another important feature of such mobilization was that it was typically initiated within the village and organized through local efforts. In the process, the local organizers tended to use external networks for some aspects of strategic support, advice on organizing, contacts with the administration, legal support, etc. Decentralized collective action was extensive and played a crucial role in bringing public services to un-served areas and in ensuring that previously excluded social groups gained access to these services.

In order to illustrate the nature of decentralized collective action, I will present its history in the Dalit habitation of a village I shall call Erani. While Erani's history is unique in all its details, its broad features were representative of the struggles that I encountered in other villages. When it comes to public services, Erani was similar to most villages I have visited in Tamil Nadu. The Dalit habitation (called 'colony') had all weather roads, electricity, street lights, potable water, bridges to access nearby villages, flood protection barriers, and other infrastructure. All inhabitants had easy access to functional schools, a well-equipped primary health care centre, a fair price shop, and a child care centre. Many were beneficiaries of governmental programmes such as maternity cash benefits, subsidized housing, old age pension, subsidized loans, etc. Almost 300 families out of 500 had received titles for homestead land. There were also occupational support systems provided by the government including a milk cooperative, support for buying agricultural implements, common threshing facilities, seed and fertilizer cooperatives, etc. While these were provided at the village level, there were also public services provided at the broader level including an impressive public transport system accessible to all people of this habitation.

The Dalit habitation was divided from the main village (called 'Oor') by the national highway, a common phenomenon in villages that have metal roads. While the Oor was close to the highway, the colony was about 1 km away from it. In rural Tamil Nadu, Dalit habitations are separated as a rule from the main village where Caste Hindus live. Being politically more powerful, Caste Hindus have traditionally managed to corner budgets and thus their areas were typically better furnished. Even where facilities were present and physically accessible, Dalits have historically been prevented from accessing them, making social access as important as physical availability. For example, as early as 1935 there was a public school in Erani but not one Dalit child was enrolled since they were afraid to access it. Dalits were keen on educating their children and had even identified some land in their part of the village for a school to be built, but neither was a school built, nor was the existing school socially accessible. Over the years both social and physical access to these public services have changed considerably, I will review some of that story here.

There were three main caste groups in the village: the *Forward Castes* comprising mainly of Reddiars, the numerically significant *Backward castes (BCs)* consisting mainly of Vanniyars and *Dalits* who have typically been about half the village population. Through the last century one family belonging to the Reddiar caste held most land in the village. The estimate of land owned by this family varied from 300 acres to 1000 acres, but by any account, this family owned more land than any other family in the district. The family has been politically important, especially with the Congress party.

Dalits were by and large landless and worked mostly as labourers with Caste Hindu families. Traditionally, Dalit families were attached to some patron family among Caste Hindus who were referred to as *Aandai*. The Dalit family was referred to as *Padi Aal* where padi refers to a measure of rice; the term literally means a person who works for measures of rice. Many families were also bonded through fairly small debts taken at atrocious rates of interest for marriage, illness, funerals, and other expenses. The *Padi Aal* and his family started work early in the morning at the cowshed that they had to clean and deposit the dung in the field or its storage area. They fed the cows and took care of them. Children under 15 grazed cows and older people worked at the *Andai's* house for just food, without any cash wage. Apart from this and farm work, the *Padi Aal's* family had to do other work for the family such as announcing deaths and making funeral arrangements. As in other parts of India, many of these tasks were essential for social life, but were unpaid and considered socially demeaning.

The older generation got little or no monetary wages for the physically demanding work that they did. When people worked in the farms they were given porridge in the morning and evening. During harvest, labourers got measures of paddy and one new piece of cloth each year. Many families migrated to nearby towns for a small part of the year when there was no agricultural work. Income from all these measures was so low that they had little savings to fall back on. When alternate employment opportunities were low, dependence on Caste Hindus for employment and help during emergencies was acute, and this gave Caste Hindus an overwhelming influence over the Dalit population, and it enabled the domination of Dalits.

Beginnings of change

The struggle for change in Erani was not well-documented before the 1970s. Elders in the area recalled one occasion of protest for higher wages before the 1960s when six families attempted to boycott work. There was also an account of Dalits demanding a school in the 1930s indicating that there was some collective effort at securing education for Dalit children, but it was not clear if the effort was sustained and assertive; whatever the effort was, the demand did not materialize. What was clear though is that there were no major struggles in the collective memory of the community until the 1970s. Parthasarathy[1] and his family played a catalytic role in the struggles since.

Parthasarathy's elder brother was the first person to go to school in the colony. It took some boldness from his mother to enroll him in school since Caste Hindus led by the large landlord (referred to as 'the Reddiar' henceforth) refused to let Dalit children attend school. The school was in the Backward Caste (BC) area and teachers were Caste Hindus. Parthasarathy recalls his brother telling him that teachers did not differentiate much between Dalits and Caste Hindus given their Gandhian orientation, but they were not in a position to challenge the social structure since they were all, as my respondent put it, 'in Reddiar's custody'. Their houses were in Reddiar's land, they got grains from him and he had an influence on their job.

Despite the attitude of the teachers, there were many forms of discrimination at school. His brother was expected to call Caste Hindu children 'sir' even in primary school. He could not drink water unless someone served it to him, and of course, the mere act of going to school took some courage on the part of the child since it was located in a hostile neighbourhood.

His mother's fight with the local power holders to educate his elder brother bore fruit when the Indian Constitution came into force in 1952 and mandated that 25 per cent of all public employment be reserved for Scheduled Castes and Scheduled Tribes. This ensured that his brother with a school education got a job as a police constable in 1959. The stable employment and salary in turn helped all his brothers get higher education. Parthasarathy himself did a technical diploma and his brothers graduated with different degrees and one of them got a job in the army and the other became a pharmacist with the Indian Railways.

The experience of Parthasarathy and his brothers at school was reasonably different from that of their elder brother or other Dalit children in Erani. Their elder brother was posted outside the village and the officially provided housing was typically in the Caste Hindu area. 'We never had a problem ... he was neat and tidy since he was a police officer, and it was never apparent that we were Dalits. They [the Caste Hindus] were less well dressed than us, and so there was no discrimination ... [At school] every now and then we won in sports and were given a prize in the assembly. We have about 50 certificates, even at the district level. We were always referred to as Periyavar PC's [Police Constable] brothers. So, I never felt like a Dalit there', Parthasarathy recalled. He was also elected school pupil leader in higher secondary school.

Like most government servants, his brother was transferred periodically to different places and all the brothers moved with him. Cuddalore, where they lived for the longest time, was a site of intense politics. It was one of the hubs of the Dravidian movement and it also had active communists, Dalit leaders and nationalists. Parthasarathy was introduced to Ambedkar's ideas and to the Republican Party of India (RPI) through his relatives when he was at college at Cuddalore, the district capital at that time.

Outside the village the brothers did not face much caste discrimination but had to encounter it during their periodic visits to the village. He studied in his native village for just one year, and he recalled:

> Teachers used to support me then saying that I was a good student. But the situation was such that SC boys will call the BC students as sir or *ayya* ... hierarchy among students was just like that of adults. That one year, I felt discrimination. I was beaten-up by the students [on occasions] and mother had to intervene. There had been big problems.

Some years later he took a bicycle and went to the Oor to visit the post office, which was at the Reddiar's house. Dalits were not allowed to ride bicycles and seeing someone on a bicycle, Reddiar enquired who it was with his servants. A Dalit servant of his told him that it was Mayandi's son and Reddiar called for him.

> When he shouted ... I knew the situation at that time and I felt afraid. I was 17 or 18 then and [being young] I had the mental frame to resist, but I should not uselessly get caught in his place, is it not? So I came out alertly. His servant came running shouting 'Reddiar is calling'. I told him to go mind his business; if Reddiar calls, go answer him. I said that and returned home hurriedly.

The ban on bicycles was widely practised across South India and was a part of a basket of things Dalits could not do. Rules of caste prevented Dalits in most parts of South India from wearing footwear, riding vehicles, accessing common wells, and other public amenities, eating in common restaurants, attending school, covering the upper part of their bodies in the presence of Caste Hindus, among other things. There have been many cases where Dalits were not permitted to use metal vessels for cooking in their own homes or to carry water in metal pots. While these were reasonably common across most untouchable castes, specific castes had more crushing socially imposed unfreedoms. *Purada Vannas* were considered so polluting that they were not allowed to come out during the day so that the higher castes need not even see them (B. R. Ambedkar and Rodrigues 2002).

Subjugation was inscribed in such detail that even simple acts as wearing a shirt or riding a bicycle required power and high status. Though I was mainly doing a study on provision of public services, these issues invariably cropped up in all my interviews. Initially it was surprising and looked to me like interesting but irrelevant details. But over time it became clear to me that struggles on untouchability were closely related to struggles to get educated or to get clean water. In a society where norms of caste, class, and gender explicitly prohibited certain groups from accessing most basic amenities, the struggle for public services is not just a struggle for big budgets. They are, first and foremost, power struggles waged by those lower in the hierarchy to get an equal status, to boldly violate the boundaries that regulate their lives, and to access services that were not created for them.

Two years after the cycle incident Parthasarathy was waiting at a bus stop wearing pants, shirt, and shoes. He recalls a Vanniyar remarking condescendingly to a bystander of his caste, 'Who is this — is this Mayandi's son? Look at him he's wearing a pant and a shirt! Is he the son of the guy who used to do coolie work for *Padayachi*?' He recalls a local Caste Hindu bystander challenging the other by asking him why Mayandi's son shouldn't wear pants. Norms of caste were being questioned both by those who were affected and also by those who belonged to dominant groups. By 1979 when this incident happened Tamil society was poised for rapid changes preceded by decades of anti-caste movements and major political changes. In my opinion the bystander's retort indicates that these changes had begun.

In the same year Parthasarathy decided to settle in his village and take up political work. He talked to most people in the colony and formed an 'Ambedkar *Mandram*' or Ambedkar Society with 25 young men. Ambedkar Mandram is a common phenomenon among Dalit hamlets in the region, and Erani is by no means distinguished in forming one. To begin with, members of the Mandram were exclusively Dalit men. When I probed on the nature of membership, I found no reason why women were not invited to be members, except that it was the norm and it was adhered to by this young educated activist as well. The Mandram started focussing on 'social issues' by working for basic facilities like water, roads, housing, and street lights. The first three years were spent in writing petitions and waiting for answers of which they got none. In a more assertive vein they organized a major march for the first time in 1982, three years after they had consolidated the organization.

The assertive turn

Over the years a housing crisis had developed in the village due to the rising population. Dalits were typically landless in Erani as they were in most parts of Tamil Nadu. Dalits of that habitation were collectively awarded 1 acre and 14 cents of land in 1885 as a part of Communal Award.[2] This was inadequate to support 500 families and over time people had started building houses illegally in the river forest region adjoining the village. 'This happened automatically. The forest department controlled this land and they were forcing us to move. [But] where can we go? There was no land in the colony and we could not go to Reddiar's land. At that stage we had to struggle', Parthasarathy recalled.

Despite the air of inevitability in his statement, people had lived in such precarious conditions for entire lifetimes. The housing crisis had evolved over decades but the Dalits could not do much to act on this without suitable political opportunities or resources. Social movement literature has stressed that grievances can exist forever without an outlet and organizing can provide the context to translate grievances to action (Giugni, McAdam, and Tilly 1999). While organization is important, I do not think that it explains collective action sufficiently in this hamlet or the other villages I studied during the fieldwork. Habitations in rural Tamil Nadu tend to have very strong social ties that are solidified by common ceremonies, problems, occupations, and the sheer smallness of area. In Erani and other villages, there were clear indications that people had organized previously. To understand the assertive turn, we have to go beyond the strength of social ties, which we will discover as the story evolves.

During 1979–82 they sent several petitions for homestead land and housing without any response from the Collector's office. In 1982 the whole colony decided to go on a march to the district capital, then at Cuddalore, about 50 miles from the village. For the first time they organized under the banner of Republican Party of India (RPI), a political party started by Ambedkar. The march was organized under the leadership of Aravinthan, Parthasarathy's nephew, and was assisted by the party. The two-day march was organized on the 13th and 14th April coinciding with Ambedkar's birthday. The party arranged for their stay and for food along the route at Nellikuppam, the first industrial town in the district and the site of early trade union movement in the state. Incidentally, I found references to Nellikuppam in most of my interviews in that region, indicating the effect that movements have in producing leaders and other resources to support activism elsewhere. At the district capital an eminent lawyer and a district leader of the party joined them to talk to the Collector.

The march was a mixed success. The District Collector spoke to the forest department and directed them to stop harassing those living illegally on forest land until an alternate arrangement could be found. He also spoke to the Welfare Officer to find them suitable lands and to arrange housing facilities. This must have been a huge success at that time for the group, but the battle continued for the next fourteen years until they finally got the lands; and the struggle for housing continued. Following the march, people of the Erani colony took up a succession of struggles for water, street lights, road, etc. A list of struggles I documented is given in Table 2.1 below.

Table 2.1   Episodes of Contention in Erani 1977–2001

Year(s)	Event
1977	Parthasarathy goes to the post office on a bicycle
1979–81	Petitions to Taluk officer for housing plots
1979–81	Petitions demanding basic amenities like water, electricity and roads
1982	March to Cuddalore for land and housing
1982	Campaign to install hand pumps for water in the village

1982–83	Demand for better water supply system than the 'Kumar type' water pump with a shallow reach. The administration drilled a deeper bore and installed a hand pump in it.
1982–84	Campaign to stop Dalit children from being cowherds, and to go to school instead.
1982–90	Campaign encouraging migration of youngsters, instead of working for local landlords known to treat them in demeaning ways
1982–92	Started the Ambedkar tuition centre to assist children with education, and to prepare children for college.
1983	Hunger-fast by all Colony residents demanding land titles
1983	Fast and pot breaking for water
1983	Struggles to locate hand pumps in the palm grove, a public land that some Dalit families had occupied with competing claims by the Reddiar
1984	Aravinthan contested in the MLA election
1984	Mobilizing youngsters and external support to counter the violence unleashed on them for establishing a political party office
1984	'Hut Service Scheme' to provide one free light bulb with electric connection to each house was not implemented in the Colony. Residents declared agitation prompting the officials to respond. The Reddiar protested that connections were made to houses in 'his land'. They went as a village to protest this
1984	Violating restrictions on wearing footwear, riding bicycles and other civic restrictions on Dalits
1985–91	Campaign to obtain a share of the auctions of public resources
1985	Bargained with the BC candidate competing against the Reddiar's nominee in the Panchayat elections. RPI's candidate contested with the DMK candidate and won the Vice-President's position in the election
1985–88	Non-formal education and adult education schemes of the government organised through RPI members
1985–90	Street lights were introduced with Panchayat funds through the support of the vice president

1985–90	Installation of additional street lights
1985–90	Construction of cemetery access road
1985–90	Demanded and got two bridges across the canal connecting neighbouring village
1985–90	Cement road with Panchayat funds
1985–90	Cement road with MLA funds
1985–95	Following-up on the case in high court brought by Reddiar against land titles for homestead lands
1987	Protest in front of Taluk office demanding land titles
1989	Petition and resolution through the Panchayat for overhead tank to enable tap water at home.
Date not clear	Petition to chairman of the Panchayat Board and their MLA for an overhead water tank
1991	Fast and protest announced in front of Block Office for overhead tank, and a series of other issues
1993	Demanding the removal of the two tumbler system, one of the forms of untouchability, in the local tea shop.
1995	All residents of Colony go to meet the District Revenue Officer during his 'mass contact' programme and announce a road block if litigation in high court against land title is not resolved immediately.
1996	March to Collector's office at Villupuram for land title distribution after land was allotted but the titles were not distributed formally
1996	Titles issued. Initially titles were issued for a part of the people. All of them refused to receive their titles until it came for all
1996	Protesting that politicians should not distribute land titles first in the AIADMK regime, then in the DMK regime.
2001	Demanding mini water tanks with the local MLA and received 3 tanks

Source: Author

Though each struggle was interesting I will concentrate on the struggle for water since it illustrates many features of decentralized collective action in Tamil Nadu, and the intricacies of local politics that affected the provision of something as fundamental as water. The struggle started with petitions for water pumps that were sent periodically between 1979 and 1982, and like other petitions this had no response. In 1983 the colony decided to organize a fast and 'pot breaking' protest, a common form of protest for water. Residents demanding water brought old pots with them in a procession symbolizing that their pots are empty when they should be holding water. After holding a public meeting in front of the water board, they planned to smash the pots on the gates of the office, conveying their anger symbolically. Though I have heard of no case turning violent, this is an aggressive form of protest that keeps the local police on tenterhooks. Typically this is preceded by intense mobilization and the production of pamphlets and other materials announcing the protest.

Talking about the responsiveness of officials to more aggressive protests Parthasarathy said:

> When we organize a hunger strike, a Gandhian protest, things are not taken seriously. It is peaceful and does not cause any disruption to the country. Officials don't even hear of these protests, they don't respond. If we go for a road block, all officials come to meet us at once. If we do an office blockade by locking an office that does not function, things are different. This may lead to a lathi-charge, police may have to be involved and it will become a big issue and they [local officials] will have to respond to collector's office and others - just for water. So they come to you at once and negotiate and make arrangements quickly.

Like Parthasarathy, other activist interviewees displayed a keen sense of strategic use of public attention, and protests were often designed to this effect with humour, art, music, visual representations, and even the creative use of social tensions. The pot breaking event is at times preceded by stringing pots along the highway for a week to secure public attention. A group of people with shaved heads in pattai-namam protests or a string of pots in pot breaking are also visually attractive and draw immediate attention to the collective problem.

While some repertoires use humour to attract attention, a few use complex social and political calculations in an effort to create social unrest to gain public attention for their grievance. Let me illustrate using the mock funeral protest, which is one of the best examples of the creative use of social tension for obtaining a service.

One of the rules of caste is that each caste has a strictly assigned location for cremation. No person of one caste can be cremated in the location meant for another. There are also well defined routes by which the dead bodies are to be taken to the funeral ground and any deviation to this is not tolerated. The seriousness of the situation can be gauged by the following incident. Towards the end of my fieldwork there was a mini-riot in a village of Villupuram district where the police had to fire their guns killing two people. The riot was triggered when the mother of a priest of the local Catholic Church died. The priest was a Dalit by origin and presided over a population consisting of Dalit christians as well as higher caste members. When his mother expired, Dalits belonging to the church insisted on taking the funeral procession along the common village road and burying her in the common (read upper caste) cremation ground. This led to a protest by upper caste Christians who vandalized the church and many houses in the Dalit Colony. Local cadres of the Dalit Panthers of India party (DPI) got reinforcements from outside leading to a clash between castes leaving two people dead in the ensuing police firing. The details of the incident are complex and I do not wish to get into them here, but the seriousness of the funeral rule can be understood by the fact that even the priest of a Catholic Church presiding over the village was not immune to it.

Reflecting their lack of power, Dalit funerals face tremendous problems in many villages. Often the sites are a long distance away from their habitations. While places that the procession cannot enter are strictly demarcated, there is often no road to the cremation ground. The land around them is at times owned by others and in such cases Dalits have to step through property owned by others to cremate their dead people. This difficult process is often exacerbated by insults from owners of the land. Further, the lack of a road also means that in order to access the cremation ground, processions often have to go through marshes or jungles of thorn trees. The process can be so acutely frustrating that at times bodies are thrown away to rot in the marshes.

This issue highlights the powerlessness of Dalits and how the powerlessness has translated into the inability to secure basic facilities that are fundamental to their social lives. These frustrations point to the fact that the demand for cremation facilities is not just a matter of resources. Since public services were also used as a way of imposing caste-based discrimination, the demand for services also becomes a struggle against the caste system and caste-based discrimination. In this case, the demand for cremation facilities and funeral processions became occasions for inscribing and contesting the status of castes.

A specific form of protest has developed in the region to demand access roads and proper cremation facilities. These involve taking up a mock funeral procession from the Dalit quarter deliberately violating the path marked for Dalit funeral processions. Naturally, mock funeral processions happen under a tense atmosphere and keep the administration and the police in tenterhooks. Typically a long process of demanding cremation facilities takes place before mock funerals are announced, and mock funeral processions are announced only when these fail. The announcement itself typically creates a situation for bargaining, often bringing a tense administration to the table. A local activist described one of the first mock funerals he attended in the following terms:

> As we took the [fake] body along, people were surprised and they stopped whatever they were doing abruptly to come and watch what was happening. People stopped eating halfway through, and dropped all things. A funeral procession does not go this way and everybody started anticipating big trouble. It was a big surprise to every one. This could turn into a riot since different bodies are buried in different places.

Creating social tension is an essential part of this protest since it drives the administration with its power to the negotiating table. I got to observe this while I spent time in the local police station and the administrative offices. During one such protest, the Police Inspector introduced me to his colleagues by saying, 'He is here to study what kind of problems these protests create for the police!' It is well known that access to public amenities are unequal for people belonging to different communities, and the administration often ignores this inequality knowing that creating common or identical facilities may lead to caste tensions. The demand for amenities by lower castes are taken as a challenge to caste status by those above them leading to resentment and even violent suppression. The administration typically preferred to leave these contests to people within a village and did not interfere unless it feared overt tensions or violence would occur. If a protest created a tense situation, it enabled the administration to step in with its power to settle the issue by either fulfilling the demands (by going against prevailing norms) or by stifling the protest. Where the organization was strong, Dalits have had a better chance at using the power of the administration to settle their grievance.

The use of public attention should be seen in the context of sharply competitive politics in Tamil Nadu. Politics has been competitive since 1952, the very first election after India's independence, and political parties have found it difficult to take their position for granted. Under this context, parties are cautious about negative publicity. The state government also monitors protests closely by compiling detailed dossiers of *negative news files* each day.[3] These are monitored by the ministers and senior bureaucrats in charge of various departments. These are not unusual practices across India but the potential for such news to affect the legitimacy of the government is taken more seriously in a competitive political atmosphere. This, in turn, meant that officials at the district and block levels tried to avoid coming into the gaze of senior officials and suffering humiliation, and thus tended to react quickly to the possibility of protests. Reflecting this, most of my interviewees said that their demands were met before or just after their protests.

Getting back to pot breaking at Erani, just before the procession could reach the government office they were stopped and cordoned off by the police. A senior police officer came personally and persuaded them to press their demands without breaking pots aggressively. In turn he promised to mediate with the officials to expedite the work so that police department does not have to confront *law and order* problems. This yielded immediate results and officials agreed to install hand pumps in the village. But this was just the beginning.

Social arrangements and politics

Provision of public services is never a matter solely of technology, budgets, or administrative will; local politics plays a significant role in the process. Dalits of Erani had long depended on the local landlord for basic amenities including potable water. This gave him clout and the status of a patron. For some years Dalits had depended on the irrigation pump of the Reddiar for potable water. When they started political activities this created problems. Some Dalits activists were harassed by his employees for taking up political activities and were denied water on occasions. Parthasarathy argued that this was one of the reasons for their decision to protest for hand pumps. A simple hand pump thus became a challenge to authority in the village.

Following the pot breaking protest, the administration sent two people to install hand pumps in different locations of the colony. Most families did not own land and some settlements were technically illegal. All the common land in the region was encroached by the local landlord to the point that they were traditionally called 'Reddiar's lands'. While appropriation of common land by private interests was happening on one hand, it is also likely that a lot of land previously owned by the Reddiar family became illegal with the legislation of the land ceiling law. A number of practices were devised by large land owners across India to skirt this law, and this was easily accomplished given their political power. But in the context of contestation, illegality can become a problem despite the wealth and influence of such families.

The installation of hand pumps brought the land question to the fore. Some of the families had been living in lands that 'belonged to the Reddiar' in a traditional sense but to which he did not have legal title. When officials of the water board reached that spot with the equipment, Reddiar sent a word out to them. Parthasarathy argued:

> [Since] he is a senior Congress person ... an official cannot do things independently in the village if it may lead to trouble. Officials are ordinary people from simple families who have taken up the job for their livelihood. They cannot confront these powerful political forces. Even if they had big official titles, when it comes to village issues [they can be asked]: What are you doing? Don't you see

that I am here? [How can] you come and go to the village by your will? Where will you put the bore? Where do you have any land? He started such questions and interfered with the work of installing a bore. To put a bore, just an 8 inch pipe, there was no place and he created trouble.

A lot has been said about landlessness among untouchables and people of lower castes. These debates focus on the lack of ownership of agricultural and homestead lands by Dalits, which make them depend on the other castes for livelihood. What has not been stressed adequately is the utter powerlessness of Dalits in organizing their social space by shaping how public lands are created and used around them. The ability to structure social space can have far reaching consequences to things we wish to pursue, including the demand for public services. The question of space came up often in my interviews. For example, given the small size of landholdings, some fields were totally surrounded by fields of others without any approach road. They have to depend on the goodwill of those around them to even reach the fields on a day-to-day basis. In many villages it was the large landholders who had lands that had road access. In a similar vein, one of the most emotional political issues in Tamil Nadu today relates to having access to funeral grounds for Dalits.

Common lands have effectively been under the control of powerful local people and without these it is impossible to provide most public services. Apart from 'unused lands', public ponds and lakes have also been encroached upon widely over the last few decades in Tamil Nadu, which has been threatening the water infrastructure in the state. Creation of Special Economic Zones (SEZs), large dams, large factories, roads, railways and other facilities too need land. The tussle over land for such projects tend to be publicized widely given their scale. What is not widely publicized is that even the installation of a hand pump or water tank can lead to such challenges, and this routinely happens in densely populated areas.

A bewildered official returned to the colony to report that the Reddiar complained about installing the pump in the palm grove.

Some residents decided to approach a senior official at the district level with this question. They argued with him that it is legally a common land and demanded that the Reddiar produce his title if he claimed the land to be his. The senior official decided to go ahead with the work and thus the pump got installed.

This confrontation reflects a change in the bases of influence with some traditional forms of authority continuing to hold some ground while new forms of influence, such as the modern administration, have become important. My interviewee summed this up neatly:

> Work started again ... and Reddiar did not object to it this time. He did not want a public protest where an impression will spread that Reddiar did not even allow a water pump to be installed in his village. There is a public impression about him: people think that Erani has no problems since Reddiar is there and he will cater to all our needs. That is how people think of him outside the village ... He tried stalling us with the expectation that I will run to him to ask his permission. But he did not expect us to fight and claim our rights. When I met the official directly and talked law, he immediately subsided.

In this context, the Dalits of Erani managed to gain influence with their legal knowledge, organization and strategic use of protests.

Using political means

I mentioned earlier that the march for housing and land was organized under the banner of a political party. In 1984 the Dalits got the endorsement from the RPI for Parthasarathy's nephew to contest in the election for the legislative assembly. He contested unsuccessfully but this electoral participation changed the equations in the village in important ways. To put things in context, Erani is not alone in transforming from some sort of a cooperative association to a political party; it is a common practice amidst a culture of political domination by certain powerful groups. Parthasarathy recalled that if he had attempted to start a political party in the early years of mobilization, he would have been stifled immediately. Though they were politically oriented, it was a conscious decision to start a 'society' rather than a 'party'. This also led them to focus on working for basic amenities for their village rather than taking up other more contentious political goals right away. Many of my other interviewees did the same before they started off politically. In this and other cases, local youngsters were advised by more experienced activists belonging to political parties or social movements on organizing cautiously and strategically. To me this reflected two things: the novelty of their challenge at the village level that required them to be cautious, and at the same time, the maturity of political culture that provided experienced leaders and other resources for youngsters to organize locally.

The decision to contest in the Legislative Assembly election was published in newspapers and the contestant started building a small office by the highway. He also set up a flag post and hoisted the party flag on it.[4] Given the dominance of the Reddiar in the village, no other party had hoisted a flag or taken up overt political action in the village.[5] The fact that Dalits had hoisted a flag and had set up an office close to the highway was too much of a challenge to Caste Hindus. A group came promptly, dismantled the office, threw the furniture into a passing truck and broke the party flag as well.

To ensure that political activities of the Dalits are quashed, Caste Hindus came with sticks and other arms to vandalize the colony. This form of vandalism and the use of systematic violence was widely practised in Tamil Nadu. In fact, the use of mercenaries is one of the dominant political themes of Tamil movies today. This is of course not exclusive to Tamil Nadu. Proper understanding of politics anywhere in India cannot be had without understanding the systematic the and selective use of violence by non-state actors in controlling other social groups. Prior to this incident, Parthasarathy and other Dalit interviewees recalled Dalit huts being burned periodically in their villages over the decades when influential sections of the village had any grievance against Dalits.

When Caste Hindus came to attack the colony, they were challenged this time by Dalit youth, and the invaders returned without causing extensive damage. Before they could regroup and attack again, the Dalits organized support from other villages. They got the support of Dalit residents from a prominent colony in a nearby town. A public meeting was organized at Erani with important leaders from the town to demonstrate their support. They also managed to get support from other sympathizers. One important source of support came from a Naxal organization in a village nearby. That organization followed a brand of communist ideology and was sympathetic to the cause of Dalits, but it was headed by a BC person. This enabled him to talk to BCs of his and other villages to ensure that they did not group with Erani BCs in attacking the Colony there. He persuaded people that it was a village level problem that should be settled within that village and thus reduced the strength of the attackers.

Aravinthan was not successful in contesting the Assembly election but efforts to capture political power continued. In 1985 Panchayat elections were organized in Tamil Nadu without any special reservations for women or for SCs and STs. Consistent mobilization since 1979 ensured that the colony represented a solid block of votes that could be mobilized by the Dalits themselves, who were no longer under the control of the local landlord. Using the power of their numbers, the Dalits negotiated with several aspirants for positions among the BCs. They demanded a share in positions, revenues and the promise to use Panchayat funds to build basic amenities for the colony. Their candidate for Panchayat polls succeeded with Aravinthan contesting for the post of vice president. In the following five years street lights, roads, and a series of other facilities were built in the colony through the Panchayat. The Panchayat also passed a resolution demanding an overhead water tank (OHT) for the colony. That brings us back to demand for water.

The resolution was passed in 1989 towards the end of the Panchayat's term. Due to litigation demanding reservation in Panchayat elections, no election was organized at the Panchayat level between 1990 and 1996 in Tamil Nadu.[6] In the absence of a Panchayat they announced another protest in 1991 for the OHT. The fact that a Panchayat had resolved for it strengthened their demand for the tank, and before the protest could take place, officials agreed to build the overhead tank in the village. Locating the tank led to the same set of issues that were faced in locating the hand pump, but by then Parthasarathy had learned how to handle it. Building the OHT meant that water was available at the doorstep, if not very close to most houses. But being a tall structure it needed a strong motor that required three phases of electricity connections. Thanks to power shortage, electricity was often not available in one of the three, rendering the OHT dry routinely. The practical alternative that the Water Board had devised was to build 'mini-tanks' that can be operated with small motors requiring just one phase of power that is available at most times.

In 1996 the Assembly went to poll again and RPI had an alliance with the All India Anna Dravida Munnetra Kazhagam (AIADMK) that came to power. Parthasarathy, like most other political mediators, was conscious of the votes he commanded and the difference it could make to political aspirants in a competitive atmosphere. Using this clout, he made their Member of Legislative Assembly (MLA) sanction three mini-tanks for the colony, with his funds. Apart from these efforts to secure infrastructure, there have been efforts to ensure that the facilities are well-maintained and kept functional. This included at one point a demand to change the employee who was not cleaning the tank periodically as he was supposed to.

The struggle for potable drinking water had to engage with political, social, legal, and technological challenges and it was waged for nearly twenty years. While the struggle for clean water had quietened by 2008, other struggles continued, especially for housing. Allotment of houses was delayed, among other things, by a litigation that the Reddiar initiated against issuing land titles to the Dalits. Interestingly while he had effective control over the land, the Reddiar did not have a legal claim to it. So he argued in the court that the land housed his water pump that was used for public purposes including providing water for land cultivated by Dalits. With the government's lawyers not turning up for hearings, the case lingered for almost ten years. Finally Dalits went to the officials and announced a protest prompting the government to settle the case and award titles.

The extension of water to the least powerful illustrates the story of Tamil Nadu's commitment to public services. In many villages like Erani, direct water supply to houses was started decades ago but only to limited sections of the village in which the elite lived. Political organization and assertive bargaining were needed to extend these services to other sections of the village. Negotiations with power holders from the Panchayat to those competing at the state level played a crucial role in extending public services, and such negotiations would not have been possible without political organization. But political organization in itself was a major challenge under an environment of domination. Individual acts of resistance, including simple acts like wearing pants or driving bicycles, were precursors to organization in such conditions. Resisting control, organization and political mobilization were all important parts of the story of how Tamil Nadu developed a commitment to public services.

Economic and social struggles

I started my fieldwork in order to understand what drove the commitment to public services and found it impossible to understand this without paying attention to the struggles for dignity, political participation, better wages, mobility, and other issues. Struggles on these issues had direct and indirect connections to the question of public services. As I argued before, there were direct restrictions on people's access to public services based on their caste, gender, and other aspects of identity. In this sense, the struggles over these issues have a direct connection to the struggle for services. At the same time, such struggles were also related to basic civic, social, economic, and political freedoms. The expansion of such basic freedoms had an impact on people's agency that in turn enabled them to stand up, participate, bargain, and collect some of what was their due. I will return to this discussion after a brief overview of some of these struggles in Erani.

Erani saw several struggles for higher wages and other livelihood issues. Parthasarathy remembered that the whole village had boycotted work around India's independence on the issue of wages. Six families alone went to work and they were boycotted by other families for many years subsequently. Since this happened before his birth he did not have a clear account of the incident. Police records in the region indicated that there were several long drawn wage struggles in other villages, especially those with communist activists; it is possible that the Erani struggles were related. In any case, there were no considerable collective wage struggles in Erani between 1950 and 1980 when the Ambedkar Mandram became active.

By the 1980s, there were three scales of wages within the village for similar agricultural work. A government-run seed farm gave agricultural labourers the official minimum wage, which was substantially higher than the wage paid by smaller land-owners and other private employers. The lowest wage was paid by the Reddiar who used his power as the patron to suppress wages. This issue was taken up by residents of the colony when they sent a petition demanding the enforcement of legal minimum wage to the *Thasildhar*, the head of the revenue administration in the district. This opened the space for negotiation. The smaller landholders quickly accepted a minor increase in wages but the Reddiar held out. Most people working with the Reddiar by then were members of the RPI, and so a night meeting was easily convened in which people were convinced to skip work the next day. When Reddiar's *mestri* (a manager who deals with labourers on behalf of the big man) came the next day, he found that no one was willing to work. In the ensuing negotiation, workers demanded that a party member replace the *mestri* who belonged to the same caste as the Reddiar. Apart from facilitating negotiations this was a tactical step that gave labourers control over the hiring process. In the negotiations that followed the Reddiar agreed to increase the wage by Rs. 2, which was less than what was demanded, but it was accepted by the group. Following that, there have been periodic wage negotiations to increase wages, but these have been accomplished with much less struggle in the recent years.

Apart from wage struggles, there have been numerous small struggles involving livelihood issues. Traditionally Dalit children were expected to take care of the goats and cows of Caste Hindus, while there was a ban on their raising goats. In the *MGR period*[7] loans for animal husbandry were offered and the local MLA worked actively to extend it. The scheme involved collective loans to groups that were extended through banks, in which the bank got a subsidy from the government that it passed on to the registered group.

A group was registered in the colony to avail the loan and the formalities were almost complete with the bank when word reached the Reddiar about it. He spoke to the bank's manager and asked him not to extend the loan by arguing that the Dalits do not have any land upon which to graze the goats. In one sense, this is a reasonable objection since goats may damage his crops, but this was done in a discriminatory fashion since the same objection was not extended to Caste Hindus. More importantly, it illustrates how the elite could influence commercial transactions of marginalized groups to their advantage. Consequently the loan was denied and the group was disbanded.

Later Parthasarathy used a provision in the scheme inventively. The scheme specified that loans would be given to any registered group, which could be from a cluster of villages. Using the network of RPI, they formed a group spanning their village and some others, and registered the group in another village. This enabled them to approach a different bank where they had more influence and thus got the loan that was denied to them in their own village. Such a challenge would have been quashed violently not long ago, but their political position had changed considerably, which enabled them to meet such challenges. Goats commanded a good price and some families had made a considerable amount of money by rearing them. This would not have been possible without the social and political clout which had grown over the years.

In a span of twenty years, starting in the 1980s, bonded labour was eliminated in the village and Dalits have stopped performing unpaid labour to Caste Hindus. To put it in Parthasarathy's words again, 'our people are more aware and do not work as slaves in tending to others' cows, processing dung, beating drums, tending the lakes or doing thotti work. All these things are taken away as services from the BCs and they have to do it themselves. Now all work is wage-based'.

Stopping demeaning practices

The opposition to grazing the animals of Caste Hindus was also based on a cultural aspiration. Grazing was seen as a demeaning activity and it was a part of a campaign to stop Dalits from taking up such activities. The low social status of this work was reflected in a common form of scolding that school children in Tamil Nadu face when they do not perform well in school—*you are fit only to be a cowherd*. Such collective opposition to demeaning practices were a part of the strategy to gain greater social status for the whole group. The reference to status made the appeal to stop grazing animals of Caste Hindus more powerful, and within five years of starting, only one family in the colony at Erani was sending their child to graze. Intense pressure was mounted on this family by the whole village which finally forced them to discontinue it. From 1984, no family has continued this practice in the colony.

I mentioned earlier that Dalits had also started violating caste bans on them including wearing footwear, covering upper parts of their body, and riding bicycles. Going further, a decision was made to confront other discriminatory practices. These included refusing to be served food in a demeaning manner, opposing the two-glass system, and other forms of symbolic discrimination. For example, when food was served to Dalits in farms or temple festivals, Caste Hindus had to do it without polluting their vessels. So during lunch in the fields, labourers were made to sit in a row and porridge was poured into their hands from a height so that no vessel will get polluted. In many temples, Dalits were expected to stand at a distance and porridge would be poured from one end of a plantain bark with Dalits receiving it from the other side. Village by village, these practices have disappeared in Tamil Nadu and the range of discrimination against Dalits has narrowed down considerably. While the two-glass system, dress restrictions, and many others are rare today, there are continuing restrictions on using the political space, temple entry, access to funeral facilities, and a set of other issues. Thus, while one cannot say that untouchability has disappeared, the forms of untouchability have become less draconian and Dalits today enjoy freedoms that were unimaginable merely a few decades ago.

Though these practices have disappeared across the region, it happened village by village and practice by practice. I tried to enquire how each of these practices disappeared in each village I studied and found that in most cases some youngsters would engineer a conflict in the village leading to a heated debate that was followed by a nego-tiated change. Let me illustrate this with an example.

In Erani a set of youngsters went to the tea shop and argued with the owner that it was illegal to discriminate between Caste Hindus and Dalits by serving them in two different sets of cups. If the tea shops were to continue the practice, they would register a case against the owner in the police station. This led to a heat-ed argument where some BCs took sides against such practices and some others asked the tea shop owner to serve everyone in a common glass to avoid a legal hassle. The next week, tea was served to customers in disposable glasses but given the cost, it was abandoned in favour of common glasses. The moral challenge against civic unfreedoms raised by the social movements influ-enced both the suppressors and the suppressed. Without this ideo-logical change among the traditional suppressors, local challenges such as the one raised by the youngsters of Erani would not have succeed so easily. I will turn to that in the next chapter.

Parthasarathy and most of my other interviewees were con-scious that social changes cannot come about without deep-rooted personal changes. Campaigns to stop demeaning practices were a reflection of this, since they focussed on the dignity and self-respect of Dalits. In early 1980s, members of the Mandram at Erani started encouraging youngsters to stop working as *Padi Aal* and to migrate instead. Reflecting on his own migration, Parthasarathy argued, 'We had asked youngsters to go out of the village and not be like a bonded labourer here … go out and do anything. You'll at least get knowledge about the surroundings. When they come back after 2–3 years they were tip-top. They earn money and come back bold; it is like they have got some clarity.'[8]

The political education through travel, meetings, newspapers, and vigorous discussions was complemented by the use of political and cultural symbols to the point that politics is reflected in the person strongly. For example, it was common to see people wear-ing *veshtis*[9] and sarees with borders in the colour of their party flag. Houses were filled with political photographs, doors, and windows had party symbols carved in them, and there were other artefacts reflecting the affiliation in many houses. While poorer families did not have many of these artefacts, their houses sported wall paintings of their party's symbol on the outer walls. In the sparsely furnished house of Parthasarathy was a calendar symbolizing Dalit politics. Instead of marking Hindu festivals like *deepavali*, it had Buddhist festivals, birthdays of Dalit leaders, and the anniversary of the massacre of Dalits who were struggling for wages in Venmani village within it.

Marriages too were highly politicized. Practically every marriage of politically involved youngsters during my fieldwork was a variation of 'reform marriage' initiated by Periyar, while there were fewer instances of reform marriages among those who did not hold positions in parties. One of my delightful memories from the field involves overhearing a discussion among people who had just attended a reform marriage of their friend who was involved in the Naxal movement near their village. The bride and the groom read a 'contract', vowing to respect the marriage and each other, based on nine vows. They exchanged garlands and there were speeches, first by the bride and then the groom. The discussants I overheard in the bus gloated over the fact that the marriage was very simple involving little expense — a rare exhibition of pride in a society where marriages are an exhibition of wealth and power.

Reform marriages were initiated by Periyar in the 1920s in opposition to traditional marriages that gave importance to Brahmin priests. Apart from the anti-Brahmin message, these marriages embody a series of other messages such as gender equality and avoiding wasteful spending in wedding ceremonies. Variations of this were used by different parties based on their ideologies. Weddings of Communist Party members were done with a background of the party flag and were presided by party leaders. Similarly, in Parthasarathy's family, following Ambedkar's principles, Buddhist symbols were inserted into the reform marriage.

The profound changes that the Mandram was fighting for required not just a change among their constituents. Activists of the Mandram were careful to frame their message for others as well. When protests against the *Padi Aal* system started they framed the arguments carefully as, 'We only say that we won't be their slaves; we don't want them to be our slaves either. We won't ask you to do our work. This is the basic principle'. This message was repeated in public meetings and they also sought the support of their BC allies, including friends from the Naxal movement in a nearby village, to spread this message.

Given the social distance between Dalits and BCs it was difficult at times to argue directly, and in such circumstances mediation by allies was indispensable. Reflecting on the importance of allies such as the Naxals, Parthasarathy said, 'Since they were an organization that had people from all communities they could talk on our behalf. They would ask what's wrong with our position. Socially and economically we are depressed and want to come out of it and what's wrong with that? What we were speaking in small circles [among Dalits] they were able to say out loud'. Networks of solidarity stretching across castes and classes can play a vital role in mediating especially in times of conflict. Béteille (Béteille 1996, chap. 6) argued that urbanization, education, and electoral politics based on adult franchise among other things have created new networks of solidarity that cut across caste, class, and location. Similarly organizations of the Naxal and communist movements consciously created solidarities that cut across castes, and thus created a platform for change.

Beyond Erani

Such long struggles lasting decades were not uncommon in other villages in the region, and they were instrumental in expanding people's access to services. Activists working on these issues full time often found the progress frustrating, and it was not uncommon to hear them say that the government is unresponsive to their demands. After all, on any given year, there were only a few minor demands, and there were constant frustrations in fulfilling them. While a short-term view of the situation is frustrating, understanding public action over two to three decades conveys a very different picture. Constant action, individually and collectively, have been chipping away various challenges in extending public services, and in ensuring that they are kept functional. Over a period of three decades these small successes have added up and have had a profound impact on the landscape and the lives of people therein.

The progress that Tamil Nadu has made in providing an array of basic public services to most residents cannot be understood without taking into account this kind of lasting decentralized public action.

My discussants identified a set of factors that enabled them to undertake the struggles on socio-economic and cultural issues since the 1970s. Some of them were internal to the community such as growing number of educated youngsters who led the agitations and availability of allies such as lawyers and political leaders who could support their struggles. Thanks to reservation policy of the government and the availability of new economic opportunities many communities had a few people who had gained some wealth and education. This enabled them travel to meet officials or arrange material resources for collective action.

Along with these internal changes that made the collectives stronger there were also a set of external changes that made their struggles more likely to succeed and less likely to be suppressed effectively. These included the introduction of adult franchise, Panchayat elections, job opportunities outside the village, growing power of the administration, undermining traditional forms of power, etc. These added to the strength to the common person in a lopsided struggle.

The internal or external changes I mentioned above did not suddenly happen in the 1970s. Some have been slow and progressive, such as the availability of jobs outside the village; others such as the introduction of adult franchise happened decades before but it took that time for the communities to use the opportunity. Some of these changes had started in the nineteenth century itself and in the 1970s there had matured enough to enable the kind of decentralized collective action seen in Tamil Nadu. These changes allowed people within a habitation of a village to spearhead their own struggle and in my opinion, such long and sustained struggles could not have taken place unless they were led by people in the locality themselves.

One of the most interesting aspects of collective action around services was the sheer variety of ways in which people undertook protests. Marches, meetings, sit-ins, hunger strikes, blocking roads and offices, petitions and postcard campaigns were among some internationally known forms that were widely used. Interestingly there were several other forms that I have not encountered elsewhere, but are used widely in this state. I documented over twenty repertoires of action that were used on grievances relating to public services. There were also specific forms of protests pertaining to social and economic issues are too numerous to mention here. Unlike petitions or marches that are taken up for all kinds of grievances, some of these repertoires are used for specific purposes. For example the ceremony called *Nathu Naduthal* or planting of rice saplings is a protest exclusively for all-weather roads. In this protest, people of the village will gather on a muddy part of the road leading to their village after sufficient advertisement, and they plant rice saplings on the road highlighting its poor state. This is used to shame the administration and sends an unmistakable signal about what their grievance is. Similarly *Panai Udaithal* or breaking of empty pots is taken up as a protest for drinking water, and mock funerals are organzed for cremation facilities. Unlike petitions or marches, these forms of protest send an unmistakable signal about the grievance and they get wide public attention.

The fact that there were over twenty repertoires in itself indicates the extent of collective action in the region — after all, it is difficult to imagine such a variety in a place where collective action is relatively rare. Most people understood what these forms of protest meant, and also the role that they have to play in it. This enabled quick coordination with the result that protests could take place with remarkable coherence at a very short notice, sometimes within moments of learning about a problem. Given below is a brief summary of the repertoires that my interviewees had used to press a grievance. Often, the resolution of a grievance required many episodes of action, and so many of them would have been combined for the resolution of just one grievance.

1. **Blocking roads**: Road blocks are typically carried out after representations and other forms of protest do not work. Often,

highways are chosen for blocking since this creates maximum disruption.

2. **Burning puppets**: When protests on issues of corruption or political wrong-doing happen, puppets symbolizing the perpetrator are burned in a public display of rage. This form of protest is typically personalized and is taken up when a particular politician or official is singled out for protest.

3. **Collective bargaining**: Representations are made to bargain with political parties and with aspirants for various political offices as conditions for offering support during elections. This method accounts for an important part of the services that were extended in villages.

4. **Collective refusal to accept wages**: When a group feels that they have not got adequate wages for the work they did in a public work programme, they would collectively refuse to accept the wage paid to them. This is tactical since it leaves money in the hands of the official, which is not encouraged by the government. Further, an account cannot be closed and so it would create problems during audits. This helps start a negotiation.

5. **Cutting trees**: This was particularly taken up in a large scale by the PMK party where the highway would be blocked for a long duration by cutting trees and throwing them across the road.

6. **Fasting**: Most fasts are organized for the duration of a day, and on rare occasions there are *fast unto death* protests. These are used after the initial stage of demands, but are often used before more disruptive techniques such as road blocks.

7. **Legal action**: In an era where legal entitlements have been created around public services, courts are periodically approached in order to ensure the extension of services to certain habitations or people. In addition, legal action is often required in the process of using some other repertoire of contention since episodes of protests lead to arrests and other kinds of action by the administration. Sometimes, legal action is required not against the administration but against an opposing social group that creates barriers to accessing public services.

8. **Letter writing**: Each person in the village is encouraged to write a letter demanding some amenity to a responsible official.

This happens at an early stage and is intended as a show of strength.

9. **Locking the government office**: In a display of anger, the 'dysfunctional' government office is locked by an angry mob of protesters. This is at times done with a few officials inside the office for a brief period until negotiations start. This is a highly disruptive tactic and is taken up only when there is sufficient number of people in the protests. It is taken up only at later stages when a legitimate demand for some amenity is not met.

10. **Mock funerals**: A mock funeral procession is taken out on a route that deliberately violates the route marked for funeral processions of a caste in order to create tensions and to demand cremation facilities.

11. **Paddy planting**: Paddy is transplanted in the road symbolizing how muddy the road is, and thus difficult to use. Apart from being disruptive, this is also visually appealing and thus invites media attention, and also the attention of passers-by.

12. **Pattai-Namam protest**: Dozens of people shave their heads and wear the highly brahminical symbols of pattai (three horizontal lines of white ash across the forehead) or Namam (a white U shaped line spliced by a vertical red line on the forehead, typically worn by Vaishnavite Brahmins in Tamil Nadu). 'Giving a namam' has the colloquial meaning that stands for being cheated, and pattai-namam protests are typically used when a promise by some official does not materialize. The sight of dozens of men with shaved heads and decorated foreheads is visually appealing, this gets quick media attention.

13. **Petitions**: One of the first stages of collective action in almost all cases, where petitions are sent to responsible government offices at different levels. Sometimes these are sent directly to the chief minister's office with an understanding that they are forwarded to the responsible officials.

14. **Pot breaking**: Protesters take empty earthen pots in a procession and smash the empty pots in front of a government office that is responsible for providing water facilities. The empty pot is symbolic of water shortage, and this action is typically taken at a later stage when representations do not work.

15. **Processions**: A common form of protest to signal the strength of demand.

16. **Publicity**: Wall writing, putting up flags, notices announcing grievances, sticking posters in public spaces, distributing pamphlets, hanging empty pots along the road, and a variety of other measures are taken to invite public attention to a grievance after petitions have gone without any response for a reasonable time period.

17. **Representations**: A small team meets officials at the block or district level, typically at the initial stage of action.

18. **Religious conversion**: Threats of religious conversion from Hinduism into Islam and into Buddhism were taken up by Dalits and in each case the first reaction of the government was to construct roads, and to create other basic amenities in the village. The threat of 'mass conversion' is obviously not just for availing public services. Issues of dignity, religious, and other aspirations are all important in such a process. Access to public services have also been an important consideration in these calculations.

19. **Picketing**: Court complexes and other major government offices are blocked and the volunteers 'court arrest' (willingly get arrested).

20. **Tuition centres**: Dalits have been particularly active in organizing coaching centres for children so that they can make use of educational facilities offered in public schools more effectively. A large number of these are organized under the banner of *'Ambedkar Manram'* (or Ambedkar Society). Such centres also play a role in ensuring that parents send their children to school, and also deal with school-related grievances. The centres also help the students by raising awareness about college options, and guide to make use of reservation and other benefits available. The most impressive of these centres that I saw coached over two hundred students at a time and had been running for more than twenty years. While others are less spectacular, they have provided extremely valuable service in ensuring that public schools are used to their best capacity.

A day goes by rarely when such a protest does not take place in the district. Organized public action like this combined with day-to-day protests have a huge impact on the framework of governance. There is constant pressure on the government and the administration to deliver, and to deliver to the common person as well. While there are corruption, elite capture of benefits, and other problems, it is increasingly difficult for the government to deliver to a small section of the population and get away with it. Such pressure also ensures that the government is responsive to practical problems in the design of programmes. Such problems can often be fixed with simple common sense solutions, but there is often little thrust to accomplish such changes. Public pressure creates that in the Tamil context.

Notes

1. This and other names are changed for their protection, unless otherwise mentioned.

2. I am relying on Parthasarathy's information on this. I did not cross-verify this information.

3. Negative news files going back to 1800s can be found in the archives in India.

4. In India all political parties have flags that are routinely used during party meetings. Reflecting the deeply entrenched political culture of Tamil Nadu, one can find flag posts with party flags in most villages, and often in habitations within villages.

5. I did not manage to cross-check this information.

6. The Panchayati Raj Act was not passed nationally at this time giving leeway for states in conducting Panchayat elections. The Dravidian parties that ruled Tamil Nadu since 1967 had a strong organizational base and did not want to undercut it by strengthening Panchayats, and thus Tamil Nadu never had a strong system of decentralized governance. Contrasting stories can be found in Madhya Pradesh and Karnataka where chief ministers without an organized following initiated strong systems of decentralized governance.

7. One interesting practice I encountered across Tamil Nadu is for people to refer to the Chief Minister or the Panchayat president who introduced a particular scheme or facility and by saying in 'her period' or 'his period'.

8. His claim that migration happened at their instigation was certainly an overestimate of the Mandram's role. Dalits have migrated from this

region for a long-time including to Ceylon before 1920s, and it looks like there was a substantial migration to Bangalore, Madras, and other towns in the 1960s, before the Mandram was established. That said, the claim on the political education associated with migration is a very reasonable one.

9. This is a kind of wrap-around skirt commonly worn by men in Tamil Nadu.

3

Changes That Enabled Action

In the last two chapters, I argued that there have been major changes in the nature of public action in Tamil Nadu, and that most social groups have been able to engage in action and voice their demands since the 1970s. This form of public action is decentralized, widespread, and is mostly initiated and sustained at the grassroots, with support from outside. While this form of decentralized public action is new, it is important to bear in mind that Tamil Nadu has a rich history of contention and there have been major social movements going back centuries. The late nineteenth and the early twentieth centuries produced several great social movements including the Dravidian, communist, Dalit, nationalist, and women's movements. These movements were powerful and have had impact—there is no doubt about that. That said there is an important difference between the kind of public action I talked about in the previous chapters and these powerful social movements: critically, public action today is much more widespread and is decentralized.

In the case of the large social movements the main agenda and most of the episodes of action were typically initiated from powerful leaders of the organization, and the impetus for action often came from outside the village. While some of the demonstrations drew large numbers of participants, the number of people who were actively engaged in these movements tended to be small.

Since the 1970s there has been a major increase in the episodes of contention that people participate in, including innumerable day-to-day struggles that are now commonplace.

During my discussions a set of factors came up again and again in explaining the change. Some of these were internal to the community such as the availability of educated youngsters to lead the action, increasing organization, greater willingness to assert themselves, and income to support action. These resources provided communities with the ability to engage in action more effectively than before. At the same time, there were also changes in external conditions that made it easier for people to do so. Children of dominant figures started residing in towns making it difficult for them to control people directly. Political competition made it necessary for the elite to accommodate the demands that they would have ignored or suppressed before. Such changes made it more likely that challenges would yield result—which was a motivator for action. These changes enabled widespread public action, which in turn is at the heart of Tamil Nadu's commitment to services. While I have divided them into different types of 'internal' and 'external' changes for the purpose of presentation, many of them are interrelated and tended to reinforce each other. I will start with a set of internal changes below.

Internal changes

I illustrated in the case of Erani how the education of one child had a chain reaction since he was able to get a stable job, which in turn enabled him to educate his brothers and one of them played a critical role in mobilizing in that habitation. Educated youngsters with the support of those with stable incomes were at the heart of the mobilization in Erani. As in that habitation, in almost every other case, educated youngsters proved to be the focal points of action. While some had gone to college and obtained professional degrees, many had only upper primary education. Even this basic schooling helped them read pamphlets, handbooks, and other materials that expanded their knowledge that was used in bargaining. This knowledge was socially valued and many would approach them on a variety of matters, laying the basis for their becoming influential locally. With practice these leaders also learned to write articulate petitions, complaint letters, applications for government schemes, etc. Since paperwork is the moving force of administration this basic skill was useful in dealing with the administration, and this made them even more valued in the community.

During the fieldwork I had the opportunity to look at files of petitions and complaints received by district and block officials in Tamil Nadu and also in a district of Rajasthan.[1] One remarkable difference was the size of the files in Rajasthan where the number of representations was minimal. In addition, the submissions in Tamil Nadu were of high quality in a sense that they carried all the details required for an official to follow up including the dates, locations, officials concerned, and the legal basis of their complaint. What was clear from these letters was that the complainants had engaged in the process earlier, and they also had the sufficient literary skills and knowledge of administrative processes to create strong submissions.

Since the demand for public services was so often contentious, the organizers required more than just formal education. These episodes required financial resources to print materials and organize basic things like food and water during a protest. Visits to various officials at the district and state level also involved costs, not to mention the lost opportunities to earn an income from a day of work. People who could incur these costs thus became valuable to mobilization. People with government jobs or relatives in white collar professions were an important source of such support. In addition, some people from marginalized groups became traders and contractors and this wealth became a source of support not just for the village but for mobilization of that community more widely. This wealth helped with political connections, ability to hire lawyers and also support mobilization in a large area. Some of them also ran gyms that became a space for organizing a set of youngsters who were willing to engage in violent conflicts.

In addition to income and wealth, connections in important places and the cultivation of allies also provided with critical resources. For example, many of the struggles required legal intervention, especially because the administration tended to treat them as a *law and order problem*. Legal and political support made a difference to how the administration and the police dealt with the protesters. People engaged in protests could be arrested, or protesters could be required to report to a magistrate every day until an issue is settled, which can take months together. Such forms of legal harassment helped the administration in maintaining a semblance of peace, while the injustice continued. Legal and political support reduced the costs of engaging in action and thus enabled protests. Even when the police were not involved, activists needed resources to navigate the complex structures of government. Protestors had to know which officials were responsible, what their powers were and how to approach them effectively. Dealing with the administration, especially a reluctant one, required a lot of practical knowledge. Some of this was provided by allies who worked with the administration who understood how it functioned and how to navigate it.

Given the long history of poverty, lack of access to schools, and other unfreedoms of caste, most social groups in Tamil Nadu did not have people with the income, education, connections, and other resources that were valuable for action. Gradual expansion of schooling, reservation of jobs in government, urbanization and other factors created a cadre of people who could support mobilization in most communities.[2] Barring a few highly marginalized groups in Tamil Nadu, most others had increasing access to such resources. This change had a telling impact on their ability to mobilize and engage in contentious action.

Thanks to spread of schooling I documented in the first chapter, there are now some educated people in every habitation of most villages. Thanks to reservation for the Scheduled Castes and Tribes introduced in the Constitution, and reservation for the backward caste communities introduced through legislation in Tamil Nadu starting as early as 1923, public employment and higher education opportunities have become available to all communities. While some lower caste communities have used reservation better than others, most communities now have at least a small cadre of people education in them.

People from oppressed communities have also started migrating for jobs in commercial agriculture and to low-end urban areas.

'We do not work under them anymore and so we do not have to submit to them' was a common refrain I heard from young lower caste interviewees, indicating a strong connection between livelihood opportunities and assertion. Their ancestors had to depend on a small class of landowners for their livelihood giving their upper caste employers tremendous power over them, and this was broken by alternate sources of income through new avenues of trade, migration, reservation, and white collar occupations. Simultaneously, land fragmentation and migration of children of large landholders to urban areas have further eroded the ability of the landlords to dominate.

The dominance of upper caste communities over others owed to the fact that they owned most of the land, and thus they were the main employers in what was a primarily agrarian economy. In this context of dependence, consequences for a protest were drastic, making public action difficult. Urbanization and the creation of industrial job opportunities created an alternative that those who were engaged in protest were able to avail of, and this choice has made a major difference to the context of rural mobilization. Among the major Indian states, Tamil Nadu is one of the most urbanized with almost half the population living in urban areas today. An interesting feature of urbanization is also that there are a large number of small towns that are dispersed in all parts of the state, so much so that it is possible to travel for an hour or two from most villages in order to reach a small town nearby (Rukmani 1994). The towns offered employment opportunities that are different and not linked to the opportunities in villages. Even when these were oppressive and low-paying, urban employment opportunities offered a choice of employment, which released people from dependence and thus enabled protests against dominance. While oppressed communities depended on those with land for employment, those with land also depended on the labourers to sustain their wealth. The opportunity to vote with their feet made it more difficult for landholders to sustain their oppressive practices, and it has enabled the labourers to discard servile behaviour that was expected of them for centuries before.

Opportunities for protest have also been shaped by the disappearance of large landholders in rural areas. Even though land reforms were barely implemented in Tamil Nadu, the threat of land ceiling discouraged older landlords from acquiring more land, and many gave up land to people who once worked under them. Further, many large landholders did not reside in the village anymore making it impossible for them to exercise day-to-day control. Though there are huge inequalities in landholding between castes, there are now some landowners from most castes, and BC people now control a larger proportion of land than before. Landless labourer communities have started migrating in large numbers to other parts of Tamil Nadu and other states for seasonal agricultural work. Harvesting sugarcane and other strenuous work attracted a high pay. As with Erani, Dalit leaders encouraged people in their community to migrate as a strategy of escaping domination. Thanks to the breakdown of the relationship of dominance, common people can now take up protests for public services, compete for political positions, argue for a share of Panchayat resources, and take action when their social access to services is prevented by the more powerful communities.

Economic inequalities continues to be high in Tamil Nadu and current pattern of economic growth led by large corporations, continuing land alienation of marginalized farmers and other factors are increasing inequalities today. While inequalities have not disappeared, there is now a choice of employment for people in rural areas that was unavailable only a few decades ago. Tamil Nadu's extensive social protection programmes including subsidized food grains that reach most households have further eroded the extreme dependence that families had on their employers before. The diversification of opportunities with social protection eroded dominance even in the context of increasing economic inequalities. This was an important background in which public action increased in Tamil Nadu.

A culture of assertion

While resources helped mobilization, it was not the only factor that motivated people to engage in action. In Erani's case, even though the material condition had not changed, one mother's decision to fight unleashed a set of changes in the decades to come.

In a society where people's basic freedoms are socially circumscribed by caste, gender, class, and other factors, people's decision to violate the boundaries imposed on them has the consequence of reshaping the boundaries, and thus reducing the unfreedom that is imposed not just on them but on others in society.

In her moving autobiography, Dr Muthulakshmi Reddy (Reddi 1964), the first woman surgeon of Tamil Nadu wrote about what it meant for a woman to go to high school. She was born in 1886 when a few girl children went to school, and there was no girl-child in her town who had ever been to high school. Her father insisted on higher education for his child, and under the circumstances he had to send her in a special horse drawn carriage that was covered in all sides to isolate her to minimize social criticism. Knowing who the passenger was, schoolboys often jumped onto the carriage to look at the passenger and this terrified the little girl who was doing something that no one else had done before her in her region.

Her challenges with education that started here continued throughout. To take an example, when she enrolled in medical school the best-known professor of paediatrics, an English man, was convinced that women were not capable of doing science, and so he refused to enroll her in his class. On one occasion he had to interview her for her oral exam in a different course and was impressed by her intellectual abilities, after which he relented and accepted her in his class. With this, she also paved the way for other women in the medical college to attend his course that they were not able to do so before.

Mere acts of going to school, drinking water, wearing footwear, sporting decent clothes, riding bicycles, entering a restaurant, finding a place to stay during travel, and other day-to-day essentials have been a challenge for an obscenely large proportion of the population in India, and this was particularly harsh in southern India, which had some of the most drastic socially imposed unfreedoms. The withering away of many of these unfreedoms has come about due to the bold activism of hundreds of thousands of people in their day-to-day lives, often at tremendous costs to themselves and those around them. The sharp social changes that one sees today are inconceivable without these individual sacrifices and determination to go through personal challenges to violate the norms of the day.

As I argued in the previous chapters, there is a sense that such acts of resistance have grown considerably since the 1970s, by the uncontrollable people. Some of this resistance comes from changing social conditions that allow them to resist, and a part of it also owes to profound changes in character of people, in a sense that the common person is much less willing to suffer indignities and other disadvantages today. Unfavourable treatments now can lead to arguments, formal complaints, protests, strategic voting, and other responses that people in positions of power have to contend with. Government officials often classified people as 'hard' and 'soft' depending on how far they would submit to the terms they found unacceptable. They argued that people in general have hardened, making it difficult for them to impose their rules on them. Most attributed this change in character to the great social movements of the nineteenth and twentieth centuries. In places where the communist movement was influential, the hardening was attributed to the fact that people had become 'communist minded'. Officials also argued that Periyar's influence through the Dravidian movement created a culture of insubordination. The hard people monitored, fought, argued, protested, disobeyed, and were unwilling to be controlled. This kind of uncontrollability made it impossible to enforce unfavourable laws, civic unfreedoms, political restrictions, and discrimination in services.

The idea of getting individuals to challenge the status quo has been at the centre of the cultural projects of most social movements in the state, and it was particularly so for the Dravidian movement. This emphasis is reflected for example, in the fact that it is also commonly referred to as the 'self-respect movement' given the emphasis of the movement in developing self-respect among the Non-Brahmin community, which was seen as an essential ingredient for social change. But the project of creating social change through individual transformation was not restricted to this movement. All the great social movements of the last century had this as a key strategy and this continues today with parties like the Dalit Panthers whose caption, *'Refuse to obey! Cross your limits! Rise up! Hit back!'* is repeated in party meetings on every single occasion.

The cultural project of emboldening people who have been long subjected to oppression was carried out in many different ways. Speeches, poems, movies, theatre, and other forms of public communication were regularly used to make a virtue of asserting one's dignity. Personal grooming in order to appear dignified has also been an important aspect of many such movements. Thus wearing pants, using hair oil, and in general being 'tiptop' has been emphasized upon. Naming of children, food, symbolic aspects of public festivals, posture, language, and all kinds of other details have been targeted by the movements in the quest for changing the relationship of oppression between groups.

Activists made it a point to demonstrate boldness in public ways to show that it is possible to do things that were socially considered impossible. A Dalit activist told me the story of how he was personally converted when he witnessed a Dalit lawyer who had come from the state capital.

At that time, we never entered police stations. The lawyer came wearing pants and 'boots' [when wearing even slippers was not allowed for the Dalits]. He went straight into the police station and seeing that he was well dressed, the police did not know how to handle him, and they treated him well [unlike the way they used to treat Dalits]. Knowing that he was a Dalit, a crowd gathered in front of the police station and we watched in amazement [the sight] of a Dalit man entering the police station and being treated properly. He then came out of the police station and went to a tea shop next to it. He was given a separate teacup that was reserved for Dalits. After drinking the tea, he got up and smashed it on the ground to everyone's amazement. He told the tea shop owner that discriminating against Dalits is illegal and he can be taken to court if the tea shop continued the practice of separate teacups. I realized at that time that all this was possible for Dalits.

The Dravidian movement in particular was noted for its aggressive style of raising uncomfortable questions in public and doing so relentlessly. Raising socially challenging questions was indeed the fundamental technique of the self-respect movement. As I discussed before, officials and Panchayat presidents complained regularly that leaders in the region had lost respect and that it was impossible to control people anymore. In most Panchayats there were a set of people who were willing to raise uncomfortable questions about the actions of leaders and other influential people. Decisions made by officials and Panchayat presidents that used to be accepted without protests a few decades ago were consistently questioned, and this has had a profound effect on the functioning of the administration. Even officials whose lives were made difficult by such questioning argued that relentless questioning had its merits, and many credited such a change to the self-respect movement.

The focus on subjective influence can be seen by the fact that self-respecters I spoke with dealt at length with terms like Periyar's ideals, ideology, religious myths, etc. For self-respectors, the most crucial way of bringing about social change was to get individuals who were oppressed to challenge the oppressive norms themselves. Questioning authority, ridiculing symbols of power and raising relentless questions against those in positions of power were key means of making people revise the way they think, and encouraging them to challenge their oppression. Given this strategy, the self-respect movement fought for the freedom of deliberation, and for challenging authority. Following Periyar's model many self-respecters insisted on the freedom to speak and to raise questions, as one of my interviewees put it, 'I would often discuss things deeply and cause bitterness among other people; I would tell people in advance that I will tell my opinion [which may contradict your deeply held beliefs], and you can say yours. I won't ask you to accept my opinion, that is your choice. That is what Periyar said, it is up to you to accept or reject my opinion and I followed the same'.

In my opinion, an important role that the self-respect movement played was to make it culturally acceptable to raise uncomfortable questions publicly and to transgress culturally imposed boundaries of a particular time. Having a set of people who question relentlessly can create a space for others by offering precedents as well a solidarity network to be public in their questioning. Even if this does not change individual attitudes, it can have an important social role in affecting the nature of public discussion and social action. In an atmosphere where the strategy of the self-respect movement has been continued by other social movements including communists, Dalit political parties, and women's movements, Tamil Nadu has seen a cultural transformation where a lot more individuals are now willing to engage in public action. Sustained action has also broken down many forms of social unfreedoms today with the result that one does not have to face insults or fight to go to school or access other services.

The cultural transformation may have been particularly effective in Tamil Nadu given the successful use of mass media such as movies by the social movements. Movement leaders from Periyar to contemporary leaders of the Dalit Panthers, such as Thirumavalavan, were powerful orators and were very skilled at creating high profile events that get widespread public attention. Literary giants such as Bharathiyar, Bharathidasan, and Pattukottai Kalayanasundaram among others created music that reached millions of people with calls for change. These efforts at cultural change sustained for decades and the demands for change have consistently been in the mainstream of public discourse. In the opinion of most of my discussants and mine, such cultural transformation was at the heart of the increasing assertion that Tamil Nadu has seen over the last few decades.

Expanding support network

In characterizing decentralized collective action, I mentioned that it is typically initiated at the grassroots but draws upon the support of allies externally. External support was indispensable in the early stages of mobilization, when opposition to it could be strong and even violent or when the issue was particularly divisive. The increase in decentralized public action we see today cannot be understood without taking into account the massive expansion of the support organizations created by the great social movements of the nineteenth and twentieth centuries. These movements started at a time when mobilizing was difficult and even dangerous for most communities. They battled adverse conditions and built a support network of leaders, repertoires of action for different conditions, political support, administrative connections, and other things to make public action safer and more effective.

The late nineteenth and early twentieth centuries saw the rise of three types of social movements that resulted in the support network we see today. These were (1) large scale social movements that had an impact across the region such as nationalist, Dravidian, communist, and Dalit movements; (2) socio-religious movements that challenged ritual and social status, and (3) caste associations.[3] The large scale movements had a sustained presence lasting decades and also a very large geographic presence giving them strategic advantages in the political arena among others. In contrast, the socio-religious movements and the caste movements built on strong existing social networks but had localized presence based on the social geography of the community.

The earliest large movement to create a Pan-Tamil Nadu organizational network was the nationalist movement comprising of the Congress party and a number of service organizations with an impressive reach across the state. The Congress was criticized for being dominated by Brahmins and for being socially conservative. While the critique has a lot of merit, it is simultaneously true that Congress also created a political space for other communities. In fact, many of the prominent leaders who went on to become strident anti-Congress activists started their political life with the Congress. For example, despite Brahmin dominance, Periyar was with the Congress and rose to the position of treasurer of the party in Madras Presidency before he broke up with Gandhi over caste issues. Similarly, many prominent communist leaders started their careers with the Congress, and the party also opened unprecedented political opportunities for Dalit leaders. Many Dalits of Tamil Nadu had their first experience with political mobilization through the Congress, however limited this opportunity was. The emphasis on social service and on removal of untouchability also inspired many teachers to reach out to Dalit children, which was reflected in my discussions with leaders of this community.

In the post-independence era, Congress sought to create a support base among Dalits in a competitive political atmosphere and in order to do this, it had to create a base of leadership among

Dalits themselves. This comprised of a network of Dalit leaders with some influence in districts while a few went on to become prominent state-level leaders. While the influence of Dalit leaders was circumscribed and they were often seen as tools to capture Dalit votes, there is no doubt that it created a network of local leaders who played a supportive role in Dalit struggles in their regions. It was less successful in attracting the support of BC leaders given the prominence of Dravidian parties since the late 1930s.

Other than the nationalist movement, the Dravidian and communist movements were most consequential in creating an organizational framework for lower castes and classes that were unavailable previously. The Dravidian movement has its roots in the late 1800s through socio-religious associations. In 1916 it got its first political organization in the form of the Justice Party. The Justice Party was based on a narrow social stratum of professionals, zamindars and others among the upper caste elite–but this changed dramatically in the 1930s with the induction of Periyar into the movement (Béteille 1996; Pandian 1994; K. Veeramani 1998). At this time the movement became a mass movement with a presence in most districts of the state, and this created an organizational framework for others to build on.

This network then became the basis for the foundation of the Dravida Munnetra Kazhagam (DMK) in 1949 when a section of leaders broke away from Periyar to found a political party. One of the objections of the breakaway group was the autocratic style of Periyar's leadership and this gave the impetus for DMK to create a party with decentralized membership and some semblance of intra-party democracy. Over the next few decades DMK created an impressive organizational base with party members that went down all the way to the village level. This party provided the BCs with the external support needed to mobilize and wrest political power from the local elite, who were traditionally members of the Congress party.

The DMK has since broken down into many factions and many of them have their own extensive organizations.[4] This plurality has been a factor in tempering the power of new challengers and in ensuring that the same culture of dominance did not continue under the new dispensation.[5] These organizations now compete for membership and provide individuals with options in almost every village. It also has implications for how responsive the leadership is to individuals who are confronted with some choice of associations.

The communist movement in India started with a few individuals who were radicalized through their travels to the West, many of them to the United States. The advances in Russia in 1919 excited a lot of intellectual discourse and this slowly led to the formation of organizations in the 1920s. The movement took off in Tamil Nadu and started becoming powerful from the 1930s in pockets of Tamil Nadu, especially in the Cauvery delta areas and in towns with an industrial base or railway junctions. Over the decades the movement has grown in presence and has created specialized organizations of industrial workers, agricultural labourers, government servants, and women. Even though communists have been electorally insignificant in Tamil Nadu, the movement has a strong organizational presence across the state, and with its strong focus on class it has provided organizational support for the most disempowered sections of the Tamil society.[6]

While the size of the three large scale movements far outweigh the others in Tamil Nadu, one should not overlook an impressive women's movement and a Dalit movement that also had large reach across the state.[7] In the pre-independence era, Tamil Nadu's nascent women's movement worked in close cooperation with women leaders in other parts of India, and from the 1930s onwards, this movement worked on expanding women's franchise, and bringing into public discourse women's education, health, and other issues (Basu and Ray 2003; Dietrich 1992; National Seminar on the role of Women in education in India 1975; Swaminathan 1999; Tilakam 1989). In the last few decades, an impressive network of NGOs focused on women's issues, women's networks associated with political parties such as the All India Women's Democratic Association (AIDWA) and the National Federation of Indian Women (NFIW) and one of the densest network of women's self-help groups (SHGs) in India have provided an organizational base for women. These organizations provide a support network for women who wish to take up a wide range of issues of concern to women from domestic violence to national policies that have an impact on women's lives.[8]

Women's public action also received support from most move-ment organizations, and women occupy prominent positions in many of them. The increasing presence of women in the admin-istration has also created important sources of solidarity. Socially speaking, there is a stark difference in the sheer social presence of women in Tamil Nadu compared to many of the socially con-servative North Indian states (Sinha 2014). That said, there are strange and strong dichotomies in the social presence of women in Tamil Nadu.[9] At the village level and perhaps up to the block level, one finds a strong presence of women in public action and also in the delivery of public services. Once we go beyond the block level, there are prominent women leaders including a strong Chief Minister, but there is a shocking absence of women mem-bers in district level meetings and above. Thus, even meetings organized by the relatively gender sensitized Communist Party at the district level or above could have no presence of women or a very thin sliver of women participants. Some of the organi-zational meetings of the DMK and other parties involved macho demonstrations that were intimidating to women with the result that one rarely found a woman near these meeting venues.

This strange mix of a high social presence at one level com-bined with a nearly complete absence at another can also be seen in other aspects of women's freedoms. For example, women in Tamil Nadu have a much higher level of physical mobility, con-tact with their relatives, control of income, and influence on major decisions in the household compared to women in other states of India. At the same time, more women in Tamil Nadu argue that it is acceptable for a husband to beat a woman compared to women in even socially conservative North Indian states. It is important to account for these since women's mobility and other freedoms restrict their access to organizational support. The network of support was particularly dense at the village and block level while there were a few women leaders who served as support networks at the district level and beyond. These leaders and their allies pro-vide critical organizational support over a wide range of issues including information resources, a support network to reach the administration, legal protection, etc. for women engaged in public action.

Unlike the great social movements, social-religious movements and caste associations had sub-regional presence. Tamil Nadu has witnessed several socio-religious reform movements over the last century. Prominent among them have been the Tamil Saivism, Ramalinga Adigalar and his anti-caste movement, and Narayana Guru's movement among the Nadar community. Other socio-religious reform m   ments including the Arya Samaj, Brahmo Samaj, and Theosophical Society, among others have had some presence in the region, though they never grew as prominent. All these movements created a strong cultural critique against social practices and the alternatives that they projected drew a lot of supporters. Apart from recruiting followers, these movements also collected finances for building temples, schools, feeding centres, and other social service organizations. Along with these, they also supported people who engaged in agitations over a wide range of civic and religious liberties. Followers of these movements not only supported action within these communities, but they also became available for recruitment by the great social movements.

Finally, there has been an explosion of caste associations serving the needs of specific castes. The most successful of them have been the BC groups, and some of which developed into independent political parties such as the PMK, Commonweal Party, Toilers party (all of the Vanniyars) and the Nationalist party (that was predominantly a Thevar caste party). In most other cases, caste associations represented the interests of caste groups with mainstream political parties. They also engage in conflicts as aggressors, defenders, and mediators based on the understanding of the interests of the caste group, and they also ensure that people of their caste are represented in the government at various levels.

The caste associations as we know today started in the 1800s but were given a major fillip during the caste-based censuses that were done during 1901–31. Several caste groups used the census as a linchpin around which they argued for a different caste ranking, with many of them seeking a higher status in the Varna system.[10] Seeking an official high status was given up with the introduction of caste-based reservations exclusively for the lower caste groups. For example, the Vanniyar associations that had a history of demanding a higher status in the Varna system during the 1930s started demanding the status of most backward caste (MBC) in the 1980s. Ensuring that their caste group is placed on a favourable caste category has been one of the major activities of caste associations both before and after independence.

Each BC group is mainly found in certain regions within Tamil Nadu, and so the caste associations tend to be strong only in those regions. Within these regions, they have provided a strong platform for public action for people belonging to that caste. While they have played an affirmative role for people belonging to that caste, associations of upper and backward caste people have played a regressive role for people belonging to other communities, especially those lower in the social hierarchy. Several BC associations have led the assault against Dalits and have actively resisted their political and social empowerment (Ravikumar 2008; Vikalp 2005).[11] While the overall impact of these associations in enhancing human freedoms is difficult to assess, there is no doubt that they have contributed significantly to the assertion of BC communities.

Given the strong antagonistic relationship between Dalits and Caste Hindus, Dalits rarely found the space in upper caste or BC led associations, even when the associations were meant to be caste-neutral. As I argued before, some of the large scale movements including communists, the Dravidian movement and the nationalist movement provided some organizational space for Dalits, but in no case was this equal. Along with these, there were several caste associations among the Dalits as well that have been mobilizing them since the late 1800s. Leaders like Rettamalai Srinivasan, M. C. Rajah and Iyothee Dasar were engaged in creating larger associations and organizing meetings that at times involved tens of thousands of people as early as in[12] late 1800s. Iyothee Dasar published a widely circulated newspaper called the *Oru Paisa Tamizhan*. Among the major Dalit caste groups in Tamil Nadu, Pallars and Parayars are reputed to have organized themselves better, while the Arunthathiyar community has not been able to do so as well until today. Like the BC groups, Dalits have also organized political parties in the form of Republican Party of India (RPI) and the Dalit Panthers of India (DPI). While both parties have enjoyed some level of electoral success, neither has been a major electoral challenge given the fact that Dalits are highly spread across electoral

constituencies. Even though they have not been successful independently, Dalit groups are sought as allies by the larger parties given
the intense electoral equations today. This has given them some
leeway in bargaining with the government, among other things for
extending public services. Even without electoral success, they have
both provided important organizational resources for Dalit mobilization. As I indicated before, public action and Erani was led by
people associated with RPI and the party provided valuable support
during negotiations. Similarly, DPI has a well organized network
and it is used widely by Dalits in order to take up their grievances.

Each of these movements created their organizational framework
for different purposes. But what all of them do is provide the support
that is required for public action, especially over contentious issues.
During protests these organizations provided a variety of support.
Many protests lasted several months, and protestors had to organize alternate means of temporary employment, which was possible
only through the allies that the movement had in other villages.
These parties also stepped up when there were threats of violence,
and external support was required to prevent violence through legal
means or on occasions organizing counter violence. Even though
Tamil Nadu has witnessed impressive social change without a
major civil war like one has seen in many other countries or regions
of India, it has not been without violence entirely.[13] In such cases,
broad social support has been critical to reducing the structural violence that communities suffer when they engage in public action.

Changes in individual capabilities and orientations, organization, and the availability of mobilizing resources among the
marginalized groups have enabled people of these communities
to take up public action much more extensively since the 1970s.
These changes that are internal to those engaged in action have
been accompanied by changes in the external environment that
have also affected public action. I turn to that next.

External conditions of action

The extent of public action can be affected by factors such as how
receptive those in positions of power are, the chances of retaliatory
violence, or other adverse reactions when someone chooses to

engage in public action.[14] It will tend to be greater if the social conditions permit people to take up assertive action safely and when the chances of success of action are reasonable. Since there was consensus that the conditions in which people engaged in public action have changed drastically in Tamil Nadu, I interviewed activists, officials, and other knowledgeable individuals who were engaged with mobilization since the 1940s. They discussed changes to the socio-political conditions that started well before independence and attained a critical mass during the 1970s and 1980s that unleashed decentralized public action.

At the crux of the change is the decline in domination by a narrow group of elites who once controlled all bases of influence. While inequalities persist today, the ability of a small group to dominate others has reduced considerably. This has come about in a number of different ways. Some bases of influence controlled by the elite have become less important today, for example religion and traditional conflict resolution mechanisms.[15] Those who had the ability to dominate owing to their control of land and other resources have migrated to urban areas, and the distance has made it less possible for them to exercise control. Intense political competition and adult franchise have forced the elite to let go of some of their oppressive practices in order to win the electoral support of the dominated communities. The most important change was the democratization of political institutions through India's progressive constitution. I will start with this and then discuss changes to the socio-economic bases of influence that interact with the formal political structures.

Democratization of political institutions

The most significant change that affected the dominance of narrow elite groups has been the democratization of political institutions, which has paved way for a much larger number of people to have a voice in collective decision-making, and has thus made public action much more meaningful. Prior to India's independence, political offices of importance were held either by the alien bureaucracy, or by a narrow section of elite in India including the princes. Within the East India Company bureaucracy, some form of local representation was introduced first in 1851 when it started nominating Indian members. These were without exception people who were known to be loyal to the alien administration who would not challenge the decisions made by the administration. In addition, the Indian members of the Legislative Council had limited powers, which consisted mainly of participating in the council discussions and offering opinion on these discussions. The members did not even have the power to ask for information from the district level bureaucrats on the actions they took.[16]

By 1892 this changed in a small but significant way with the introduction of elections at the district level. Given that religion was not a significant cleavage in the Madras Presidency, compared to other parts of India, the main challenge for the Brahmin dominated Congress came from the BC leaders. BC leaders such as Subba Rao, Panagal Raja, Thyagaraja Chettiyar and T.M. Nair started contesting in these elections starting with the very first election under the imperial administration in 1893. They went on to become seasoned politicians by 1920 when more broad-based representation was introduced. The electoral competition in the 1890s created a cleavage between the elite BC leaders and Brahmins who dominated Congress, and this led to solidarity among BC leaders from different castes, culminating in the foundation of the Social Justice Liberation Front, better known as Justice Party in 1916. The BC leaders were united by a common understanding that professionals, wealthy landholders and other elite from the Non-Brahmin castes did not have equal opportunity in government as the educated Brahmins did.[17]

The Government of India Act, 1919, paved way for the election of a much larger set of Indian representatives to the Legislative Council and it also vested them with more powers of decision-making. At this time, only propertied taxpaying male members were allowed to vote and to run for political office. The base for voting was expanded from the 1930s enabling more and more people to participate in the electoral process. The nationalist movement, women's movement, and others were active at this stage in pressing for the expansion of the number of people who could vote. With encouragement from the women's suffrage movement in England, a number of women's organizations in India started advocating for voting powers for women, which was finally granted to a limited number of women in the 1930s. The number of women who were permitted to vote expanded from the time, until universal adult suffrage was introduced in 1952. Today, any adult is permitted to vote and to run for office, which despite all its limitations, represents a remarkable transformation of power relations in the country.

Since formal political institutions are the same across all states, Tamil Nadu's exceptional performance cannot be understood by looking only at the institutional structures. By looking at institutions, along with the practices that determined how well they were used, significant insights into Tamil Nadu's performance can be gained. Two closely related and mutually-reinforcing factors enabled common people to use formal electoral institutions consequentially. One, there was organization among the marginalized groups that enabled them to use their numbers. Second, this created alternative political forces that made the political arena competitive—and competition forced serious contenders for power to pay attention to democratic aspirations more carefully.

Since caste has been central to political mobilization it is worth pausing here to consider how the upper castes were able to dominate politics in most parts of India until the 1990s even with the introduction of adult franchise in 1952. Even though the BCs and Dalits form the numerical majority in most states, the primary solidarity network is that of a specific caste and not a coalition of castes such as 'Backward castes' or 'Dalits'. While BCs as a category are numerically dominant across India, each caste within the larger category typically forms a small proportion of the population in a state. A single caste rarely amounts to more than 15 per cent of the electorate in most constituencies across India, and so their ability to sway the elections by themselves is limited (D. Gupta 2000). The creation of a coalition comprising of number of castes was thus central to capturing political power, and the Dravidian movement did precisely this (Béteille 1996).

The foundation for this was laid with the Justice Party, which was a network of leaders from various castes. Since the competition they faced was inevitably from the Brahmins, this translated into an anti-Brahmin coalition. Starting with the Non-Brahmin manifesto, the movement created a set of grievances against the Brahmins, and it constructed a story that the Non-Brahmins of Tamil Nadu were originally Dravidians who were invaded by the Aryans of North India. Brahmins of Tamil Nadu represented the Aryan invaders in this story, and this framing was used to create solidarity between the fragmented castes that represented the 'Tamil people' or the Non-Brahmins of Tamil Nadu. This identity was critical in forming a winning coalition (Jaffrelot 2003). The idea of the Aryan invader subjugating the original inhabitants of the land was created out of a number of different ideas that were prominent at the turn of the twentieth century. This included the works of European scholars who created the Aryan story, the work of Iyothee Dasar who first used it politically, and also the Tamil Saivite movement that had created a major Tamil revivalism with a strong touch of anti-caste sentiment in it (Geetha and Rajadurai 1993; Omvedt 2008; Vaitheespara 2009).

The Congress that was then dominated by the Brahmins and other upper caste communities in Tamil Nadu was pitted against the BC coalition forming under the rubric of the Dravidian movement. Until adult franchise was introduced in 1952, only propertied or educated people had the eligibility to vote, and the electoral competition between the two parties was restricted to an elite crust, in which the Congress had a clear advantage. The Justice Party was able to get elected only when Congress boycotted elections, but with the Congress re-entering the electoral fray in 1930, Justice Party lost its relevance and stopped functioning as a viable unit. It is in this context that the leaders of the Justice party appealed to Periyar, who had just broken away from the Congress protesting against Gandhi's support of casteist practices[18] to take over what was left of the Justice Party.

Periyar's imaginative leadership helped in converting the elite Justice Party into a mass movement that united most major BC networks and thus created a powerful political force against the entrenched power of the Brahmins in the government. This unity became politically formidable when adult franchise was introduced and voting was extended to all adults. Even though Congress was in power in Tamil Nadu until 1967, it had to contend with the challenge of the Dravidian movement from the very first election after India's independence.

India's constitution took the radical step of introducing adult franchise[19] and the first election of independent India was held in 1952. As a party that led India to independence Congress enjoyed legitimacy and it also had the organizational base to capture power across India, but it was unable to secure a majority in the Madras presidency.[20] The communists had significant electoral success in the Malabar region, in Telangana and in parts of Tamil Nadu, especially in the Cauvery delta region. Two Vanniyar caste-based parties won seats from their bastion. Given the demand for a separate Dravidian nation, the DMK did not compete in the elections but it supported many independent contestants, which enabled independent candidates to win 62 seats, as many as the second largest party in the legislature. The Dravidian movement also supported communists in the Cauvery delta region, among others.

Not only did the Congress find itself lacking a majority to form a government, many of the Congress stalwarts lost their elections and some in the Cauvery-delta region lost to people who were agricultural labourers in their own fields. There were concerns that the communists may be able to cobble support to form the government in the presidency. The Congress was able to form a coalition with the two Vanniyar-caste parties and thus form the first coalition government in independent India. The Madras Presidency was also the only large region of India where the Congress did not secure a majority.[21]

Communist Party of India (CPI) and other Left parties together had secured 127 seats against the tally of 152 seats by the Congress. In addition, there was a serious possibility of support from independent candidates who were sympathetic to Left politics. This combination of numbers was a significant threat to the Congress. While the electoral success of the CPI was not spectacular, the threat of the success went beyond the numbers. Many prominent landlords were defeated by communist candidates, indicating the possibility of challenging landed interests using democratic means. An armed uprising in Telangana by the communists had alarmed the government and the army was used to suppress the rebellion. In Tamil Nadu and other regions, many communists were armed and there were high profile incidents of landlords being forced to vacate their lands. As a result, there was intense animosity between local Congress leaders and communists, which prompted the banning of the Communist Party in 1947 in the presidency by the Congress government, and in turn communists considered the Congress to be their 'enemy number one'.[22] One of my interviewees who was with the Communist Party during independence even tried to assassinate the Congress Chief Minister in 1947, just before independence. Juxtaposed with this was the international context of Cold War with the increasing power of USSR. In this overall context, the electoral success of communists represented a serious threat for the economic elite of Tamil Nadu and the limited electoral success carried weight beyond its numbers.

The success of the communists posed a threat to landed interests and the industrialists. Under pressure from the communist movement, the Congress government was forced to legislate the tenancy reform bill, but this state law was made applicable only in two districts that were bastions of communist strength. Land reform and other 'class based' agenda was a difficult pill to swallow for the landed elite and the industrialists who played a dominant role in the Congress. But electoral competition created pressure on the government to do something to gain legitimacy and support of the masses. It is in this political context that far sighted measures on education, health, and village infrastructure were initiated in Tamil Nadu. This enabled the government to gain legitimacy with the common person without taking difficult measures like land redistribution.

In 1957 Madras Presidency was divided and some of the areas of communist strength became a part of Andhra Pradesh and Kerala. The DMK which had boycotted the 1952 election decided to contest in 1957 and these factors led to a steep decline in the strength of left parties in the Tamil Nadu legislature. Despite this, political competition continued to be intense since Congress had to face the rising power of DMK, which entered the electoral politics with reasonable success for a first time entrant. It grew in strength until it defeated Congress in 1967, and Congress never regained a dominant position in Tamil Nadu politics since. Even while it was in power, Congress had to contend with serious political challenges. Rajaji, who was the Chief Minister and the tallest Congress leader of South India, was forced to resign in 1954 when he tried to introduce the 'caste based education system'. Kamarajar, who replaced him, was conscious of the mass appeal of the Dravidian movement and he sought to gain legitimacy by appropriating some of the rhetoric of the movement (more on this in the next chapter). Both events would not have happened without the pressure created by the Dravidian movement.

Even though both Congress and Left parties lost their dominance in the legislature by 1967, the DMK was not able to gain a dominant position due to the split that occurred within four years of its forming the government. MGR, the most popular leader of DMK of that time, formed AIADMK and since then there has been a constant struggle between the two parties. In the last decade both of them have needed the support of smaller parties including the Congress to form a viable coalition. Since the margins of victory have been small and competition intense, it has become difficult for political parties to ignore even small social groups; thanks to this common people who could have been ignored when parties were unchallenged got a greater voice in the political system.

While discussing Erani, I mentioned that BC leaders reached out to Dalits in the context of increasing political competition. Dalit votes were traditionally taken for granted but competition between the backward and upper caste groups led to the clamour for Dalit votes among two parties. Since Dalits were organized at that time, it gave them the opportunity to bargain between parties through which they were able to secure services. The background of political competition thus created the space for more effective public action by once marginalized communities provided they were organized.

The Dravidian movement and the caste associations organized the BC communities early on, and they created a political contest at the grassroots with the forward caste communities. Since Congress was dominated by the forward caste communities, the newly assertive BC communities joined the DMK. Both needed votes from other communities in order to win elections, and this gave Dalits and other non-elite backward caste groups an opportunity to bargain with both parties. This enabled them to demand a share of offices, greater provision of services and a greater share of resources. Wherever political competition was intense and margins of victory narrow, candidates found it increasingly difficult to ignore any community, for that could easily lead to their political defeat. Thus, despite the sustenance of casteism and untouchability, serious candidates had to make accommodations, giving Dalits and other marginalized groups with numerical strength a bargaining power.

Local Dalit leaders recalled how those seeking votes before the 1970s would rarely step into the Dalit habitations to seek votes. It is not difficult to understand why Dalits would have had little political voice with people who did not even bother to canvas with them. Not only were Dalits ignored by candidates, but they were also intimidated to vote for the candidate of the dominant community or not to vote at all. The most notorious of such incidents took place in the Ramanathapuram district when a major riot broke after Dalits insisted on voting for the Congress against the candidate of the locally dominant caste (Béteille 1996; Chokalingam). While outright violence of this scale did not take place in other parts of Tamil Nadu, Dalits were intimidated not to vote in many other regions. Growing assertion among Dalits has made it difficult to prevent them from voting independently anymore.

The earlier Congress model of canvassing votes through influential families belonging to forward castes became untenable when they lost social dominance through which they could secure the votes without paying attention to people's aspirations. Instead of relying on upper caste intermediaries, parties had to start relying on intermediaries from the communities themselves to canvass votes. Even within communities multiple individuals started becoming influential giving people in these communities a political choice and a greater voice in the system.

Given that the elite class continued to control politics the class agenda was not attractive to the rulers, politicians have continued the Kamarajar strategy of using services to gain support (more in next chapter). The Congress and DMK were known for the creation of village infrastructure, the benefit of which did not always reach the poorest communities.[23] Recognizing this opportunity, MGR substantially expanded education, nutrition, and health programmes to create his electoral base. The image of MGR as a protector of the poor gave him a large following, and he consolidated this support base through the services. In the context of intense competition other parties have also been forced to cater to the aspirations of the poorest communities since.

MGR's screen persona was also immensely popular among women, and he consolidated this support through policies with a wide appeal among women voters. For example, when he converted the school meal programmes into *nutritious noon meals programme*, he made an appeal that his scheme would wipe the tears of millions of mothers who were not able to provide one full meal a day to their children.[24] He also increased the presence of women as service providers both as a form of direct patronage and as a way of increasing women's social access to services. For example, his health policy included an effort to ensure at least one female doctor in PHCs, which has helped to increase women's access to health services in the state.[25] Women's appointments in schools, the child care system,[26] and other services were also expanded significantly. By all accounts these policies helped to consolidate MGR's support base, and women's votes continue to be critical to AIADMK's electoral success even today. To counter the popularity of AIADMK among women voters, DMK started supporting women's self-help groups extensively and now Tamil Nadu has one of the most extensive self-help group networks among Indian states today.

The class angle was forcefully brought into the political discourse by communist leaders in the late 1920s, and by Dalit leaders earlier. Communist leaders and other intellectuals influenced by the movement sharply criticized the levels of poverty, hunger, and misery in the society and made these prominent political issues. Given the appeal of such rhetoric to a large number of voters, issues by the left intellectuals were routinely appropriated by other parties. Even if the policy prescriptions were not adopted, other parties and social movements have had to make a strong case that they care for the poor and work for their well-being.

The great social movements of the late nineteenth and early twentieth centuries created organizational networks and built social coalitions required for the formation of viable political parties. This created the social basis for political competition in the first elections in independent India and by 1960, the legislature had members representing the Congress, the DMK, the Communist Party of India, other Left parties[27] and a few parties representing BCs.[28] The sustenance of political competition in Tamil Nadu made it imperative for parties to respond to communities that were long ignored. Responsiveness made public action meaningful and provided the incentive for people to engage in much larger numbers.

In my assessment, political competition under adult franchise was the most significant force that empowered the common person in Tamil Nadu. It also explains why some communities, especially tribal people with a small dispersed population continue to suffer from serious political and social marginalization.[29] This marginalization is manifested in many ways, and in all walks of life. For example, it is not unusual even today for tribal people to be denied entry into buses, to be heckled in public, and to be discouraged from accessing government programmes. Even though the legal category called 'criminal tribes' has been abolished.[30] some of the tribal communities continue to be viewed as criminals due to their social background. I encountered several cases wherein the police arrested and physically abused tribal people without much outcry from the otherwise progressive Tamil society. Such marginalization would not be possible in Tamil Nadu if the population of tribal people were larger, or if they were concentrated in certain regions giving them a political clout.

Changing control of violence

In a large review of international literature on social movements, Sydney Tarrow identified violent repression as one of the four main external conditions that determined whether or not people engaged in public action (Tarrow 1996). As many other social scientists have argued, the possibility of violence can have significant social consequences even when there is a semblance of peace in day-to-day lives. The idea that people will refrain from engaging in an action that might result in bodily harm is certainly not too difficult to understand. As I argued in earlier chapters, the demand for public services often posed a challenge to existing authorities, and the use of public services by marginalized communities also represented a violation of caste–class–gender norms. In this context, attempts to access services by these communities were routinely met with violence. One cannot understand the growing public action without understanding the changing context of the use of violence.

Despite the fact that Tamil Nadu does not have the notorious repressive armies of places like Bihar or Chhattisgarh, violence was a constant theme among all my activist discussants. Two related ideas stood out in my discussions with activists on the issue of violent repression of public action: Marginalized groups faced threats of violence for even minimal challenges in the past, and the threat of violence has certainly not disappeared. On the contrary, there have been many recent episodes of violent repressions by powerful communities, and many have argued that this has increased in the recent decades. But, an important change is that groups that were once docile and did not respond to violence in the past have to now organized themselves and deal with violence through counter violence and make better use of legal and other institutional protections available to them. In fact, there are suggestions that the overt acts of violence that one sees today are a reflection of this challenge posed by the oppressed communities. The changing contour of violence was another key factor that led to the explosion of public action today.

The large social movements I referred to earlier in this chapter started at a time when violent suppression was common and the elite had considerable ability to inflict violence without a threat of sanctions. One of my interviewees was among the pioneers in establishing the Communist Party among agricultural labourers in the region and he was engaged with the movement from 1940 to 2008. Recollecting the challenges involved in mobilizing people prior to independence, TRV[31] argued that establishing an organization among landless labourers was a difficult task when landlords wielded tremendous power in society and in politics. His recollection of the period was peppered with words like *arajagam, adakku murai, aadhikkam, theendamai, othuki vaithal, pannai adimai,* and *kodumai* that translate into words like tyranny, suppression, ostracizing, domination, untouchability, slavery, cruelty, and violent control.

TRV argued that the society was sharply polarized between a few upper-caste people like the Reddiars and Pillais who owned most of the land, but were numerically insignificant. The BCs owned land in small pockets and were dominant in certain villages, and were numerically significant in his region. The other numerically significant set of people were the Dalits (TRV referred to them as 'Harijans', a term coined by Gandhi that is avoided by politicized Dalits who follow Ambedkar), who were mainly landless labourers or small tenants who cultivated two or three acres of land that belonged to the landlords. In a primarily agrarian economy, the landlords wielded tremendous influence since they determined who gets employment and who gets land to cultivate. Apart from economic influence, large landlords also controlled other bases of influence such as administrative positions, conflict resolution councils, and other offices — be they religious, cultural, or political.

The caste elite could tie a labourer to a tree and beat him even for minor infractions of norms or a challenge to their authority. Other forms of punishments included making labourers drink cow dung mixed with water (called *Kalli pal*), beating with reinforced ropes, burning houses, and destroying reserves of grains. The ability to inflict violence at will combined with the fact that policing and other state powers were vested with the elite and that gave them a firm control over the exercise of violence. Every major struggle TRV participated in encountered violence or the threat of violence. For example, a law providing basic protections to tenants who cultivated leased lands was extended to the South Arcot District in 1953. In retaliation, landlords started evicting the tenants with the help of henchmen from Ramanathapuram district. TRV argued that, 'At the time, Harijan tenants used to be afraid of

Ramanathapuram rowdies since they had large moustaches and carried things [weapons] with them'.

A local communist activist held two acres of land under lease from a local landlord, and he found out that the henchmen from Ramanathapuram would occupy his land the following day. A call was circulated to Dalits in nearby villages to assemble at his land, and many of them joined in ploughing his land. They were promptly arrested by the police. The next day, the land was occupied by the henchmen from Ramanathapuram and more Dalits were arrested when they tried to prevent the henchmen from doing so. In the ensuing struggle, police fired a few rounds of gunshots though without injuring anybody. Shortly thereafter, communist activists attacked one of the henchmen from Ramanathapuram killing him leading to further attacks and counter-attacks, leaving five people dead in the process. This was naturally followed by long rounds of court cases in which the communists were reasonably successful, thanks to the support base of lawyers that the party had.

This was among the early cases of retaliatory violence by the powerless in which they were only victims of violence. Violence was inflicted on Dalits not just in 'redistributive issues' when the elite had something concrete to lose; it was even inflicted in cases such as Dalits wearing footwear against the rules of caste. TRV recalled another campaign in Ponnanthattu village where communists organized a protest against the ban on Dalits from wearing slippers. When news reached Caste Hindus, the landlords warned the Dalits that they would 'break their hands and legs' if they were ever to enter the village wearing slippers. Despite the threats, the local Dalits made a triumphant march across the village wearing slippers for the first time in the main village.

The capacity for violence that rested with the landlords and other elite was supplemented by their control of state agencies. TRV recalled that even in places where they had a strong support, few people would turn up for the demonstrations that they organized.

100 people would tell us they would come but only 5 would turn up ... [and the] police will then come and arrest us. Even if 5 people

come, we would organize the march, [since] we should not leave the initiative. Only then will people start thinking about joining the march the next time. If we did not organize anything because only five people came, the struggle would come to a halt. When more and more marches happen, people would start joining us. It is a way of recruiting people [that is essential] for a mass party.

Many Congress leaders were suspicious of communism despite Prime Minister Nehru's orientation towards socialism. This was certainly true of large landlords and industrialists whose interests were diametrically opposed to the agenda of the communists. Since these elite controlled the Congress party, they were able to harness the violent power of the state to suppress communism. The party was banned in 1947 by the state government, and was made legal only after the High Court invalidated the ban. The government also used its policing powers to suppress the Communists. To quote TRV again:

> If people join the party, policemen may come at night to enquire what people are up to. They will make lists of people who are engaged in political activity and sometimes CIDs[32] may come to take notes about your activities and very often they would come to villages to make a list of all the communists in the village. When villagers gave them a list of people, those people would be summoned to the police station to find out how they joined the party, and the police threatened them by saying that they would lodge cases against them if they belong to the Communist Party.

Fearful of such suppression in the initial stages, communists made a tactical decision not to enroll people in the party. Instead they decided to enroll people in the All India Trade Union Congress (AITUC)—the trade union of the party. Further, they carefully avoided using the flag of the party wherever possible and would instead just hoist a red flag with the name of the union written in white. Apart from such symbolic measures to keep the party in the background, activists also tried to cultivate allies. Some of the initial meetings and protests were organized along with progressive members of the Congress party. For example, the first major protest was organized in a village called Keezhanatham in which 96 people were arrested, and that included many Congress members including Venkatraman, who later became the President of state Congress, a prominent minister in the state cabinet and finally the President of India. While the Congress had a small core of progressive thinkers, it was by and large dominated by large landlords and industrialists. Thanks to this, there was only a limited possibility of building alliances with the Congress party to further the communist agenda.

The communists also sought to prepare the groups that they organized for violent confrontations. A teacher of *silambattam*, a martial art, would assist TRV as a part of the campaign preparation to the villagers. Lessons in martial arts were strictly prohibited among the Dalits, and even if such lessons did not provide them with adequate skills to defend themselves, it emboldened them to stand up to violence. Such strategies of counter-violence were used by many other groups that were engaged in action either by organizing themselves or by seeking the support of external groups for this purpose.

For example, one of the Dalit leaders that I interviewed ran a gym that became a training ground for a set of youngsters who were bold and willing to participate in retaliatory violence. The group became (in)famous when they retaliated in a riot and subsequently their support was sought by Dalits around the district when they feared violence. At times they would send a reinforcement of trained youngsters during tense situations, thus stopping violence. In addition, this group was based in a major town that the elite from the offensive villages had to visit periodically. It was impossible for the offenders to have a protective shield around them when they moved from the comfort of their villages–and this vulnerability gave an opportunity for retaliatory violence against them. This possibility of retaliation gave Dalits a strategic advantage in diffusing violence.

These examples illustrate the centrality of violence in sustaining oppressive norms and the fact that such violence was overcome using organized resistance. The power of the mercenary rowdies was met with the collective force of labourers who were emboldened by the strength of association. Similarly, organization also provided critical resources such as lawyers, progressive notables, strategists, and people who could influence the administration to provide justice or prevent victimization. This form of organized resistance to violence was relatively rare before the 1960s, but it has increased dramatically in the last few decades.

The result of organized resistance has not been uniform. In some cases, resistance has worked akin to a MAD or Mutually Assured Destruction strategy that has made the elite more cautious about inflicting violence. In other cases, the resistance has led to increased levels of violence that have manifested in the form of large and small riots in Tamil Nadu. Even today, Dalits continue to be disproportionate victims of violence, but their submission to violence cannot be taken for granted.[33]

The quest to balance the disproportionate use of violent power against marginalized groups was strengthened by the introduction of a strong and protective legal framework especially for the Dalits in the Indian constitution. The Constitution enabled the legislation of protective laws like *Scheduled Caste and Scheduled Tribe (Prevention of Atrocities) Act, 1989* that provided stiff penalties for violence against Dalits. This law made violence against a Dalit person a non-bailable offence and so if a complaint is registered against someone who inflicted violence, she had to be arrested immediately by the police without the protection of bail. Where Dalits were organized, there was at least the real threat that it could be invoked against the offenders, which made them cautious about beating Dalits, burning their houses and committing other violent crimes. Not surprisingly, the removal of this protective law has been one of the demands of the dominant Vanniyar community (Anand 2013).

With organization, oppressed communities are now better able to use state institutions to protect them from violence. Lower caste police officers, lawyers, and seasoned activists knew the correct provisions in the law that would afford them protection, and such knowledge was critical even to register a complaint using the correct wording to secure legal protection. When people were organized, allies in the administration could balance the tendency of the elite to benefit from the power of the state in a disproportionate manner. These factors changed the nature of social bargaining fundamentally. During times of conflict, communities have started using legal provisions strategically in order to fight against the unfreedoms that are imposed on them. It is not unusual for Dalits who bargain against a ban on using public services to argue that this ban is punishable under the 'SC-ST Act'[34] and this threat of legal punishment significantly changed the calculus of the bargaining.

The changing balance of violent power across social groups has had a major impact in relaxing the oppressive norms of caste, and this is true even in places where there is continuing violence between communities. Violent punishments meted out at will are much less common and this has allowed people to mobilize, demand their share of public resources, access prohibited services and engage in democratic politics. This has been so effective that many of the unfreedoms that were immediately punished have now disappeared, and the nature of caste in itself has been transformed in Tamil Nadu.

While caste and class based violence have changed, it is not clear if there has been a change in the nature of gendered violence in the Tamil society. Survey evidence points out that there is a high level of domestic violence, higher than some of the other Indian states, and an acceptance of domestic violence even by women.[35] Women's freedoms have also been adversely affected in the context of caste-politics since interactions between men and women of different castes tend to be treated with greater scrutiny than same-gender relationships across castes. Such sensibilities increase in the context of caste-based mobilization and lead to further restrictions on women.[36] Lack of security was cited as a reason as to why many women do not travel to participate in public action outside the village and this is a serious limitation to women's engagement in democratic decision-making.

With regard to caste and class, it was clear that the level of severe violent repression without a challenge has changed before the 1970s. Without this change, public action would have been an option only for those who were tremendously motivated or organized. The widespread decentralized collective action and day-to-day resistance would not have been possible with the continued culture of repression that TRV discussed and fought against. While the voice of the common person cannot be ignored, it is by no stretch of imagination an equal society where all citizens have an equal voice. Dominant castes and classes continue to wield a significant amount of power. A class of political 'rowdies' and others do terrorize people through the use of violence. There is tremendous systematic violence upon Dalits, women, tribal people, and others—but unequal power now coexists with increasing democratic challenges.

If one were to judge Tamil Nadu exclusively through contemporary history, there is much oppression and inequality today. But if we expand our view and examine the last six decades or more, the context of violence, oppression, and marginalization have changed significantly. These changes have been fostered by the changing nature of livelihood opportunities, expansion of education, organization, the use of counter violence, and a number of other strategies used by the once marginalized communities. The changes within communities were in turn supported by the democratisation of formal political institutions, the institution of supportive laws and other factors. Thanks to these changes, the number of people who are engaged in some form of public action has increased dramatically in Tamil Nadu, with the consequence that their voices cannot be ignored in making policies, laws, and institutional arrangements today.

Notes

1. This was in Jalore district where I was able to look at the letters in the Collector's office and also in a block office.

2. I documented Tamil Nadu's success in spreading education earlier. Tamil Nadu also has one of the highest shares of people with 'regular jobs' in India (B. Paul et al. 2009).

3. Selected references to these movements can be found in the following works: (Baliga 1962; D. Washbrook 1989; Ganeshan 2003; K. Veeramani 1998; Ma.Pa. Gurusamy 2006; Mohan 1993; Miran 2007; Natarajan 1959; Sarkar and Sarkar 2008; Sivasubramanian A. 2001; Tamizhvanan 1985;Valarmathi 2008; Valarmathi 2008).

4. Among them, AIADMK is the most formidable. A history of this party can be found in the book by Tamizhvanan (1985).

5. Subramaniam (1999) deals with this issue extensively.

6. For an excellent overview of the movement see Ganeshan (2003).

7. Balasundaram (1997), Gorringe (2005), Kshīrasāgara (1994),Omvedt (2008), Patankar and Omvedt (1979), and Vikalp (2005) provide a useful account of this phenomenon.

8. For an account on women leaders and their work see the following: (Miran 2007; Muthulakshmi Reddi 1964; Raman 2004; Valarmathi 2008).

9. Comparative indicators of women's freedoms are available in National Family Health Surveys and Human Development Reports of India. Sen and Drèze provide a good overview of these surveys and also make an argument linking women's freedoms and the performance of public services (Drèze and Sen 2002). Dipa Sinha's PhD (2014) looks at this in a comparative perspective between the states of UP and TN.

10. This has been discussed in works including (Radhakrishnan 1990; Radhakrishnan 1998; Juergensmeyer 1982; Frankel and Rao 1990) among others. Ambedkar also provides an interesting picture of the politics of the process (Bhimrao Ramji Ambedkar and Moon 1979).

11. Despite Periyar's espousal of the Dalit cause, Dalit leaders have accused him of being partial to the BCs as articulated by (Ravikumar 2008). One visible manifestations of this conflict can be seen in a series of protests that Periyar led by burning India's new constitution in order to protest the special privileges given to Dalits (Tiruchy Selventhan 2007).

12. Given the poor development of the transport infrastructure, even more acute poverty of the community at that time, and poor communication facilities overall, mobilizing must have been a great challenge in the late 1800's. To be able to bring a large number of people must have taken an incredible amount of organizational effort.

13. The following works provide insightful accounts of political violence in TN (Chokalingam; Narula and Human Rights Watch 1999; Vikalp 2005).

14. The social movement literature since the 1970s has paid a lot of attention to these factors (Koopmans 1999; Kreisi and Weisler 1999; McAdam, Offe 1987, Tarrow 1996; and Tilly 2001).

15. While religion continues to be very important in the social life of India, the ability to use religion as a way of imposing unfreedoms on people has reduced significantly.

16. Markandan provides a useful overview of the evolution of the council and legislative powers (Markandan 1964) and for an account of politics of the period, see also Sadasivan (1974) and D. A. Washbrook (1976).

17. Articulated in the founding document of the party i.e. the *Non-brahmin Manifesto* (K. Veeramani 1998).

18. Gandhi was ambivalent in his support for the anti-caste struggle at Vaikom in Kerala and he also supported the system of separate dining of Brahmin children in the Gurukulam school funded by the Congress party in Tamil Nadu. These incidents led to Periyar's resignation from the Congress (K. Veeramani 2002).

19. While it does not look radical today, adult franchise was a bold idea for a poor country with little literacy in early 1950s (Guha 2008).

20. The Madras Presidency at that time consisted of parts of Malabar region currently in Kerala and of the Telangana and the Andhra regions as well.

21. Hyderabad and Travancore–Cochin were the other two regions.

22. A term used by my interviewees who were engaged with the Communist Party at that time.

23. Narendra Subramaniam distinguishes this in his work as 'Bureaucratic clientalism' and 'Populist clientalism' (Subramanian 1999).

24. This was a part of his speech in inaugurating the Nutritious Noon-meal Scheme on July 1, 1982 in a school at Papakudi village of Tiruchirappalli district (Chand 1988).

25. In an interview with Mr. Hande, the longest serving Health Minister under MGR.

26. It is true that women's appointment in services such as preparation of meals and child care does extend gender stereotypes. That said, TN thankfully appoints women in leadership positions in these departments unlike many other states of India where managers, trainers and supervisors are typically men. The entire leadership and training team of the child care system in Tamil Nadu is comprised of women, and so are the 'organizers' of the mid-day meal scheme.

27. The Kisan Mazdoor Praja party, with a presence in Malabar region, the Socialist Party, the Forward Block (Marxist group), and the Krishikar Lok Party got a total of 65 seats (Suri 2005). The Left parties in this list were prominent in areas that became part of Andhra Pradesh and Kerala in the first reorganization of states—but not without leaving a mark in Tamil politics by that time.

28. The Nationalist Party comprised primarily of Thevars, and Toilers Party and the Commonweal party of the Vanniyars were prominent.

29. Tribal people form less than 2 per cent of the TN population, and they are dispersed geographically—making them electorally powerless.

30. This category was introduced by the British administration, and this legal fiction was used to unleash mass oppression. This included, for example, a rule that all adult male members have to spend every night in a police station—just because they belonged to a community labelled as a 'criminal tribe'. This was restricted not just to the population categorized as Scheduled Tribes today. For example, a section of the Thevar community was subjected to this rule leading to a campaign which propelled Muthuramalinga Thevar to popularity.

31. TRV or T. R. Vishwanathan is his real name, and I have used it instead of a fake name. I interviewed TRV in the last month of his life, and we had a long interview despite his failing health since this gave him an opportunity to talk of his life's work. He did not want me to mask his identity in my writing.

32. Officials from the central intelligence agencies.

33. Narula and Human Rights Watch (1999) and Vikalp (2005).

34. This is the familiar name for the Prevention of atrocity against Scheduled Castes and Scheduled Tribes Act.

35. International Institute for Population Studies and Macro International (2008) discusses this issue.

36. M.N. Srinivas argued about the loss of women's freedoms along with the improvement in caste states in his work on Sanskritization in the 1960s (Srinivas 1987).

4

Normative Challenges
in Tamil Nadu

In the last few chapters, I argued that the voice of the common person has increased and that dominance by the elite has declined in Tamil Nadu. This made the government more responsive to the aspirations of the common person, but that response can take many different forms. Large scale industrialization, land redistribution, nationalization of private property, religious agenda, reservation, and other competing visions have shaped policies across India. In this chapter, I will look at how basic public services became a collective priority in Tamil Nadu amidst many possible options. In order to understand this, we have to look at major social movements that reshaped cultural norms in Tamil Nadu (starting in the 1850s), and also at decentralized pressure from the grassroots for extending public services.

Since I have discussed decentralized collective action in detail, let me start with a discussion on the role of major social movements in shaping collective priorities. Starting around 1850, Tamil Nadu witnessed an incredible range of experiments with social transformation which lasted over a hundred years. Associations were formed, newspapers started, and debates continued intensively on how the predominantly Hindu society could be reformed. Ideas from around the world were explored by large and small groups leading to experiments for social change. Gandhian notions of social reform, idealized visions of a class-less Tamil past, inspirations from women's franchise movement in England, adaptations of the Tuskegee school model, commu-nist ideology, Arya Samaj branches, and multiple other experi-ments took place with the view of creating a new vision for the society.

This period led to several major social movements that had a profound impact on the Tamil society. In this era of intense debate and experimentation, it would be difficult, if not impossible, to isolate the impact of specific movements. Movements talked to each other, criticized, fought, and also drew inspiration from each other resulting in interesting positions that developed continu-ally in this process. It would be impossible to understand social change in Tamil Nadu without taking into account the diversity of thinking and the cross-pollination of ideas that took place in this fascinating period.

These movements together reshaped norms in two important ways. One, they argued against the fundamentally unequal norms that prioritized the freedoms of a narrow section of the society, and vehemently denied even the most basic freedoms to the majority of the population. Two, they created a vision in which public ser-vices were an important vehicle through which the well-being of the common person could be improved. These two visions had to interact since norms of caste, class, and gender regulated who had access to services. Infrastructure for education, basic health care, mobility, participation in collective decision-making, and other social arrangements were made for the benefit of the narrow elite. Services were created mainly in the habitations of the dominant sections of the society and social barriers prevented others from accessing them. Services such as subsidized grains, scholarships, or school feeding that were demanded mainly by the poor were given less priority than large infrastructure, higher education, gov-ernment jobs, and urban amenities demanded by the elite. Social movements in this contentious century challenged these unequal norms, and this challenge was a critical element in creating the commitment to provide public services for all.

These normative changes were fostered during the contentious century when arguments were rife and movements competed with each other to shape widely held ideas, identities, understandings, values, norms, and other aspects of cultural life. What is fascinating about Tamil Nadu is the intensity of the cultural transformation; in fact, it is my contention that cultural challenge was one of the most significant forces in Tamil Nadu's transformation. Many different kinds of cultural tools were used for the challenge including movies, theatre, establishment of libraries, oratory, challenging established understandings through research, violence,[1] and the organization of spectacles.[2] Cinema became a major vehicle for new political parties, and the Dravidian parties were singularly successful in using it.[3] The impact of cinema on politics is so entrenched that aspiring politicians try to act in movies in order to get their names and their message across, while popular actors often nourish political ambitions.[4]

Almost all the powerful Tamil politicians of the last century were great orators, writers, or actors, and this is certainly true of all Chief Ministers (CM)s so far, barring one.[5] Apart from career politicians, there has also been a deep cultural impact through the poetry of people like Bharathiar, Pattukottai Kalayanasundaram, Bharathidasan, and Ramalinga Adigalar who reached millions of people, which continues to be a part of Tamil life and society today. Apart from these well-known figures, poetry, writing, and debating were also practised by common people who did not have the opportunity to publish their work on a mass scale. For example, many of my interviewees have run manuscript magazines. Debates are commonly organized in schools and colleges, and on major holidays the prime-time television on all the mainstream channels includes a debate on social issues. Many speakers, poets, street theatre groups, and other artists are invited in schools and other venues across rural Tamil Nadu. These people have carried the messages of social movements deep within society. The ubiquitous tea shops with their supply of free newspapers serve as common places (especially for men) to gather and discuss public issues. Such an active culture of deliberating on public issues by common people is essential to understanding the depth of normative change in Tamil Nadu.

Together, the people of Tamil Nadu raised serious questions about entrenched inequality and socially imposed unfreedoms on BC people, Dalits, women, and others. The effective use of cultural media ideologically prepared both the elite and the oppressed people for social change. This facilitated local agitations for public services and made social change smoother. Leaders of such mobilization also articulated policy visions for a free India that framed what are legitimate policies for a government to do. With the legitimate policies articulated, a government under threat from political competition had to resort to these policies for its very survival.

Another important role that these intellectuals played was to act as bridges between the ideologies of multiple movements which enabled cross-pollination of ideas across ideologies. The most important of such figures is undoubtedly Bharathiar. Born in an orthodox Brahmin family, Bharathiar was recognized for his poetic genius even at the age of ten. The process of travelling and meeting new people exposed Bharathiar to radical ideas from many different perspectives. Sister Nivedita, a disciple of the famed Saint Vivekananda, is said to have impressed upon young Bharathiar the need for equal rights for women. He also came to deeply disdain the unequal caste practices of Hinduism including untouchability. Simultaneously, the well-read Bharathiar was exposed to the revolution in Russia and the communist ideology. His poetry and essays discussed the need to combat social, political, cultural, and economic unfreedoms together without prioritizing one over the other.[6]

To take an example, his iconic poem *Pallar Kaliattam*[7] celebrates the arrival of freedom. In this poem written two decades before India's independence, he describes the celebration of the arrival of freedom not just from the alien oppressors, but also from exploitation and poverty. It is freedom not just for one section of the society, but for women, for the untouchables and for others from the shackles of the society. In this and in other works, he fervently asked for a society that is classless, casteless, and free from exploitation. In doing so, he adroitly combined ideologies from multiple social movements, each of which focussed on specific forms of unfreedoms.

As I argued before, cultural challenges were spearheaded in Tamil Nadu by multiple social movements that were simultaneously active during 1850–1960. This period witnessed the rise of new Dalit movements, multiple caste movements, and the Tamil Saivite movement that became the precursor for the Dravidian movement. The nationalist movement gained in strength and became a major mass movement after Gandhi's influence over the Congress party, during World War I. Communism became a major force in the 1920s, and women's movements started advocating for women's education, access to health, voting rights, and other issues. The cultural transformation in Tamil Nadu cannot be understood without paying attention to each of the movements and the questions they raised, but also the interaction between them and the way the shaped each other. I will start by providing a brief description of the movements and the cultural transformation each sought.

Dravidian movement

The Justice Party, which was the first organization of the Dravidian movement, began in 1916 with a 'Non-Brahmin manifesto' that focused on privileges enjoyed by educated Brahmins that were not available to educated Non-Brahmins. The emphasis of the Party was on government jobs, which was seen as the most important means to social mobility. It is not surprising that the Justice Party focused on problems of the educated elite among the BCs; the party, after all, was comprised of the elite among the BCs including zamindars, doctors, lawyers, and other professionals. Government jobs and higher education were the social priorities of this group, which was taken up vigorously. The party had an early success in the election of 1920 thanks to a political opportunity that was disproportionate to their actual electoral strength. Indian National Congress, which had the greatest electoral strength, had abstained from the election across India in protest of some of the provisions of the Government of India Act, 1919. In most other parts of India, the Congress factions broke away from the main group, contested the election and won them easily. Unlike in other areas, the Congress had completely abstained from the election in the

Madras Presidency enabling the Justice Party to come to power. Congress continued to abstain from elections until 1927, during which the Justice Party was able to return to power.

While in government, the Party introduced the 'First communal G.O.' in 1923, which was the earliest attempt in India to institutionalize a system of affirmative action in government jobs for the lower castes in India.[8] This government order was followed by other attempts by the Justice Party to regulate the process of hiring people into the government with the view of creating a preference for Non-Brahmins. Since this time, reservation in jobs has been a major aspect of politics in Tamil Nadu, culminating with over 69 per cent of all jobs and seats in educational institutions being reserved for Non-Brahmins by the 1980s.

When the Congress decided to compete in elections again in 1927, the Justice Party was voted out, and it quickly faced oblivion given that it had no mass base. Around this time, Periyar had quit the Congress and the leaders of the Justice Party requested him to take over their party, which he accepted. Periyar transformed the Justice Party and made it an organization with a mass base. In the process, he also withdrew from direct electoral engagement and renamed the movement as the Dravidar Kazhagam (DK). The DK also came to be known by other names based on the issues that it emphasized. The most popular among them was the 'Self-respect movement' given the emphasis of DK on cultivating self-respect among the lower castes. It was also called the 'Godless party' based on its strident atheism, and the 'Rationality movement' given the emphasis of the party on developing rational thinking as a means of social change. For many self-respecters (as the members of DK were referred), the key message of DK was atheism and the challenge to the Hindu religion. This message also coincided with the strident opposition of the party to Brahmin domination considering that religious positions were controlled by the Brahmins and that hold gave the Brahmins tremendous influence on society. Opposition to religion was thus seen as a means of challenging Brahmin domination.

The opposition to religion and to the discrimination sanctioned by Hinduism took multiple forms. DK encouraged its followers to give up Hindu rituals and the use of Brahmin priests in them. New rituals were created instead, the most popular of which is the 'Self-respect marriage' that started in 1928. These marriages involve no priests or other brahminical symbols and they are based on taking vows by the bride and the groom in a public function. Such marriages are common even today among political families not just in the Dravidian parties, but also among politicized Dalits and communists.

The DK argued that religion's hold and its use for oppressive practices could not continue unless people accepted it willingly. Arguing that the myths of religion were used to subjugate people, the movement argued for dispelling myths and for cultivating rational thinking. This lay at the heart of the DK's cultural project. Many of the DK spectacles involved deliberate violations of deeply held beliefs. Plays, talks, poems, and other media were used to further the questioning of caste practices and the elevated status given to Brahmins.

One event illustrates the fundamental method of the DK's work and Periyar's genius. In 1971 Periyar asked members of the DK in Pondicherry to organize a fire-walking festival by the self-respecters. This is traditionally done for religious purposes in temples where a pit is dug in front of the temple and a fire is lit on which devotees walk barefooted. The event by the DK was organized in front of a well-known temple of the goddess Draupathi Amman that hosts a major fire-walking festival every year for its devotees. The popular myth (itheegam) is that those who walk on fire in front of the temple should do so only if they completely respect the goddess, and are pure. If one is, the goddess will protect them from harm. Sundaran teacher's grandmother told him a popular story that those who walk on fire in the pit are actually walking on the skirt [Pavadai] of the goddess and so they will not be hurt if they are true devotees. The story goes that one Englishman tried to observe this through his binoculars, but since he was not a devotee he was promptly punished for seeing this and his eyes were burned. Periyar's call for people who were non-devotees and antireligious to participate in this fire walking was precisely to challenge such myths.

The DK was popularly called 'the godless party', and the news that people who do not believe in God were going to walk on fire in front of the temple sent a wave of interest through the surrounding region. Sundaran teacher was one of the self-respecters who participated in the event. Describing it he said,

> News spread far and wide that members of the godless party [*Sami illathavanga katchi*] were to walk the fire, and a huge crowd had gathered to watch ... even the temple festival did not get this kind of a crowd. Normally, they used to bring water from the nearby river [to cool people's feet after they walk the fire] and we did not even organize that. We also purposefully carried slippers on our hands just to indicate that we had no respect for God, and we wanted people to understand that. Carrying the slipper we walked the fire.

The event was carefully orchestrated to challenge widely held beliefs, and the symbolism of nonbelievers walking the fire with deliberate disrespect by carrying slippers in their hands was powerful and disruptive. Like many other events organized by Periyar, this too captured people's imagination and drew a large crowd to witness a spectacle that would challenge their own beliefs. This event also illustrates an important aspect of the DK's technique that was used by Self-respecters in Villupuram widely, which is one of raising contradictions within people's understanding in culturally situated ways. Let me illustrate this with a few more examples.

Sundaran teacher cultivated the habit of maintaining paper cuttings extensively on religious issues and especially on religious leaders. 'There is the famous story of Karaikal Ammaiar who said that it would be insulting to God to use her feet when she goes to worship him. She would crawl on her hands when she went to a temple so that she is respectful. While devotees like her went through such pains for God, the modern day saints need A/C cars, milk, fruits, and all kinds of luxuries', he argued building a contradiction between a widely held belief that Godly people have to be self-denying. Talking about this tactic the teacher said, 'I collect a lot of paper cuttings and constantly compare what people do in the name of God with what people ought to do. This is my main task'.

The idea of a saint using modern comforts may not be a contradiction in some cultural contexts, but in rural India where air conditioning is seen as a major luxury, combined with the expectation that saints should live a life of material self-denial, drawing attention to such examples can lead to a devaluation of religious practices. Similarly, a set of people who deny God while walking on a fire pit with slippers on their hands would provoke nothing but wild curiosity in most cultural contexts, but it had a powerful meaning here. The impact of the self-respect movement cannot be understood without accounting for the fact that it was able to frame discussions on religion and deliver them powerfully in ways that were resonant with a large section of the population. This could be achieved only by being culturally situated, and by challenging cultural practices by raising contradictions and questions from within.

Given that rationality was seen as the key means of social change, education was given a high social priority by the DK. One of Periyar's demands while supporting the candidature of Kamarajar as Chief Minister in 1954 was that Kamarajar would work towards universalizing education and making it free for all children. The DK had a major impact on making mass education a social priority and this factor was critical to the expansion of education that started in the 1950s. The DK was also instrumental in the demand for education in the vernacular to enable most children to access the educational materials.

The impact of the DK could be seen in two major episodes of contention over education policies, both led by the Congress strongman, Rajaji. The first instance was DKs opposition to making Hindi compulsory in schools based on the argument that it would privilege Brahmin children, and also enable the domination of the North over the South (more on which below). The intense protests over the issue forced the reluctant Rajaji to withdraw the programme. The second instance was more detrimental to Rajaji's political career. As the first Chief Minister of Madras Presidency after India's independence, Rajaji introduced the 'caste based education system' based on the argument that most children follow the occupations of their fathers, and so teaching them the craft of the parents in school will enable them to take up the profession more effectively. In this system, children would learn mainstream lessons during the morning, and in the afternoon, they would focus on a craft practiced by their fathers. DK mounted a strident opposition to the programme by arguing that it would sustain inequalities in the society. The agitations resulted in the resignation of Rajaji, who would never become a Chief Minister again, and the removal of the caste-based education scheme supported by him.

DK also created support in the community for affirmative action and for removing caste-and-gender-based unfreedoms. It supported the eradication of untouchability[9] including various unfreedoms imposed on Dalits. One of the early caste-based struggles that Periyar undertook was at Vaikom Satyagraha, which started when a lawyer belonging to the Ezhava community was denied the use of a public road to travel to the court in Vaikom, now in Kerala. As in this issue, the DK has taken up the question of equal social access to public amenities such as roads, water, schools and other services for all groups including Dalits and women. The movement also made women's rights a central part of its campaigns. As early as 1929, the movement resolved for a set of rights for women in the famous Chengalpattu conference including women's right to: education, property, remarriage, equal access to jobs, consensus in marriage and the increase of the age of marriage to at least 16. As a practical step, the movement also demanded an increase in the intake of women as teachers in the school system.

There is just criticism of the Dravidian movement and of Periyar that their actions did not match their rhetoric. There is a lot of evidence that the Dravidian movement prioritized the freedoms of BC people and was not as militant on the issue of untouchability or women's rights.[10] Seen from the perspectives of women's rights movements, one could also say that the Dravidian movement had a deeply gendered element to it. In my opinion, such criticisms have their point, and I take them to be valid. At the same time, movements cannot be assessed exclusively on the basis of current rhetoric. The Dravidian movement and Periyar himself created powerful arguments against untouchability and for the rights of women that have had a long lasting cultural impact on the Tamil society. The fact that the movement had a deep cultural impact in itself is important because it paved the way for social change, even if the practices that they called for were not consistently followed within the Dravidian movement itself.

To get back to the question of the Dravidian movement's impact on creating an agenda for public services, the movement made mass education a priority, and it advocated for education to be accessible to all—physically, socially, and economically. Apart from education, the movement also sought equal access for all groups to public services. The idea that public services were created for a small section of the society was criticized severely, and this has had an impact on the nature of policy making in Tamil Nadu. Finally, since the movement considered that 'modernity' was a way of securing social change and escaping from debilitating traditions, it also supported the expansion of electricity, transport, and other amenities to villages in order to modernize them. Thus, public services came to occupy a very important part of the vision of the movement, and the strength of the movement ensured that it would be made a major social priority.

Socio-religious movements

While the approach of the Dravidian movement was to challenge religion per se, there have been a few prominent social movements that have used the religious idiom, and a change in the nature of religious practices as a way of attaining social transformation. Prominent among such movements were the Tamil Saivite movement, Ramalinga Adigalar and his movement for a casteless society, Narayana Guru's leadership of the Nadar community, and the movements within the church in Tamil Nadu.

While these movements had different goals, all of them demanded the removal of socially imposed unfreedoms on the community that they championed. In some cases, such movements were focused narrowly on their own community, without demanding a larger structural change and equal freedom for all people. Other social reformers including Ramalinga Adigalar, challenged inequalities of caste per se and argued for the removal of some forms of inequality for all. For example, Ramalinga Adigalar rebelled against exclusionary practices in temples and founded his own temple where he took up major symbolic efforts to ensure that it was open to people of all communities. He radically transformed worship in the temple by not employing Brahmin priests who could act as mediators, and allowed people to offer prayers directly to god by lighting a lamp at the temple. Instead of giving the rest area for pilgrims a typical Hindu name (that excludes people of lower castes), he called it *salai* that literally means a 'road' that could be traversed by all people. He also made issues like hunger central to his work, as reflected in some of his famous poems.

Adigalar's work and also the Tamil Saivite movement challenged mainstream Hindu practices attributed to the brahminical order. They argued against the inequality inherent in this order wherein a small community had the control over ritual practices, while others had to depend upon them for religious needs that were important in a deeply religious society. Many communities were also barred from entering temples or receiving ritual services, symbolic of the larger discrimination in other spheres of the society.

Similarly, the social unfreedoms imposed on lower caste people, especially the Dalits, were criticized by the Christian church, often leading to an impetus for social change. At the same time, in its quest to attract members of higher castes into Christianity, many churches also started practising caste-based discrimination within the church, even though caste did not form a part of the religion. Having services at different times, priority seating for upper caste people within the church, different burial grounds and other forms of discrimination were incorporated into church practices in order to attract a following, thus replicating the unequal social structure within the Christian religious practices in India (Balasundaram 1997; Caplan 1980; Oddie 1975; Sivasubramanian A. 2001). The tension of Christian critique against the Hindu caste system, along with the need to incorporate caste within Christianity for its own expansion, has led to struggles within the church. The rhetoric of equality in the eyes of God propelled lower caste people and Dalits in particular to question discrimination within the church and larger social inequalities.

In such cases, while religion was the main focus of the debate, it simultaneously became a symbol of questioning inequalities in the social structure at large. The idea that certain communities should not be barred from accessing temples, churches, or other religious amenities has thus had a broader implication in terms of questioning why any community should have special access to any public service. Socio-religious movements including the Tamil Saivite movement provided the rhetorical framework for challenges against caste by the Dravidian movement that followed. The power of these movements thus cannot be understood merely by looking at their impact at changing religious practices within their religious establishments.

Given the broad diversity in socio-religious movements, their impact in creating a normative agenda also vary widely. One common factor between many of these movements is the emphasis on education as a mode of change, which is also reflected in other identity movements such as the Dravidian movement. The Pure Tamil movement, among others, placed tremendous emphasis on vernacular education. While the intention of this movement was the return to purity in Tamil, the emphasis on vernacular education coincided with the demand by others to expand local language education to ensure that all children have equal access to education.

Many of these movements had what one could call a 'social work' mind-set that led them to provide public services themselves as a part of their work, and they have run schools, hospitals and other services. This is particularly true of the Church which was deeply engaged in providing services. Reform movements thus brought a vision of services as something that could contribute to well-being, and they were leaders in creating the agenda removing civic unfreedoms in the society. Thus, they created a demand for services and sought to make them accessible to all.

Cultural influence of the communists

The communist movement had tremendous influence in shaping the intellectual landscape of Tamil Nadu. Not surprisingly, the communists focused on class issues and forming new solidarities among the lower class. It had strong roots among the poor and raised issues that mattered to them but by interpreting these problems along class lines. For example, early communist activists working with Dalit agricultural labourers framed the fundamental problems of the Dalits through the class lens by arguing that landlords do little work on the land but get most of the share of production. Apart from extracting the product of their work, Dalits are made to live in separate and squalid quarters, labelled as untouchables and their freedoms are severely curtailed. It is not difficult to see why such messages would have resonated and helped to build solidarity in this population. Having framed the problem as a class issue, the communists then argued that the problem could be solved only through the 'class agenda,' involving reforms in land, wages, and other issues. Since the current regime of private property rights and lack of protection for the working class was at the root of their exploitation, the movement demanded the redistribution of land, nationalization of large industries, and protective measures from legislation to organization of workers in order to tackle exploitation. Until the 1970s, the communist movement in Tamil Nadu focused on the core class agenda described above and public services did not feature prominently as a solution. As a result, there were very few campaigns by the communists in Tamil Nadu on issues such as education, the PDS, health care, roads, or other services.

Even when the movement did not seek the expansion of public services, it had an impact on shaping the debate on that subject. Most importantly, it raised problems faced by common people including tyranny, hunger, and poverty. By bringing relentless attention, they forced other social movements and political parties to address them. Not everyone agreed with the class solution, and some offered public services as an alternative. To take an example, the communists were at the forefront in raising the issue of hunger which arose out of the increasing prices of food grains in the early 1960s. It is in this context that the DMK offered highly subsidized food grains as an electoral promise.

The popularity of the communist rhetoric and the growing strength of the movement from the 1920s to the 1950s forced major political players to formulate ideas focused on the poorest in the society. In a predominantly poor country, social movements seeking a mass base had to contend with the issues raised by the communists, and offer alternatives that were attractive to the poor. Despite this competition, many social movement leaders engaged with communist leaders on a regular basis, and were deeply influenced by some of the issues raised by them. In fact, most of the major leaders of this period had extensive engagement with communist thinkers, including those in the Dravidian movement and the Congress party.

Periyar, for example, had regular interaction with communist leaders such as P. Radhakrishnan and was even inspired to visit Russia in 1932. After this visit, he worked on an agenda for the Dravidian movement that included many class demands and even invited Radhakrishnan to preside over a public meeting on these demands. Periyar at one point of time endorsed major land reforms as an essential step for social transformation. Later, C. N. Annadurai, the founder of the DMK, went on to claim that the party was 'genuinely Communist' (Hardgrave 1964). The party manifesto for the election of 1962 claimed that the ultimate aim of the party was to create a 'Dravidian socialist federation', and it called for the nationalization of banks, transport, movie theatres, and large commercial chains. While the DK and the Dravidian parties borrowed from communist thinking, they also criticized the communists for ignoring caste issues, and thus differed in terms of the specific policy understandings. As I mentioned earlier, the Congress party also had a long engagement with communist ideology, and was the original home for many of the communist leaders prior to independence. Prominent Congress leaders continued to be sympathizers and allies of communist activists, and carried some of this influence within their own party.

The communist movement started in the 1920s in Tamil Nadu and grew in strength until the 1950s. The 1950s is perhaps the time when communists had the greatest influence in Tamil politics directly, both from their electoral performance and the general sense of threat with which the party was perceived. During this period, the most significant achievement of the communists was to demand legal protection for tenants, which was grudgingly granted by the Rajaji-led government by promulgating the 'Pannaiyal padhugappu sattam' or the tenant protection law. The impact of communists in getting this law passed can be seen by the fact that it was originally extended only to the Tanjore district, where the communists had the greatest strength, even though the law was created by the state government.

Following their success, the communists fought for the law to be extended to other areas based on massive mobilizations of labourers. The law sought to protect the rights of tenants, who were the main cultivators in many parts of Tamil Nadu. The tenants leased land from the landlords, and they contributed all the inputs and labour needed to cultivate land. During harvest, up to two-thirds of the produce could be taken by the landlord even though he contributed nothing more than the land for production. The law sought to increase the share of the tenants as a way of protecting their rights.

Not surprisingly, the law was not implemented by the landlords leading to an opportunity for mobilization by the Communist Party. Leaders working with agricultural labourers and tenants focused on mobilizing in order to enforce the law. This was the major issue under which mobilization happened in the 1950s in rural areas. Apart from that, communists also fought for a land reform bill with a suitably low ceiling, and for higher wages for the agricultural labourers. All of these were classic class issues, and the overall mission of communists was to achieve a revolution through democratic means. The primary agenda was for radical reforms of the property rights regime.

Communist critique played a critical role in furthering land reforms and the introduction of the land ceiling act in most parts of India. Even though land reforms were barely implemented in Tamil Nadu, the land ceiling law created an impetus for families of large landlords to reduce their landholdings over decades, and in the process changed the nature of social domination in rural areas. One aspect of the land reform agenda that was spearheaded by the communists has now become a major aspect of contention - namely, giving the landless a right to homestead land. Even when these laws were not implemented automatically by the state, they provided tools for those engaged in collective action.

The appeal of the communist ideology among the general public, and the fact that the communists were a significant threat in the 1950s created a condition wherein the ruling Congress had to forge an agenda that appealed to the vast majority of the poor. Without competing mobilization, it may have been possible for the Congress to avoid addressing issues relevant to the poor. Thus, even though the Congress came up with an agenda that had nothing to do with the communist prescriptions, the influence of the communists in shaping this agenda cannot be mistaken. Most importantly, the trenchant class critique of the communists meant that the government had to institute a policy with conscious reference to the majority of the poor. Without this appeal, any alternative policy would not have had legitimacy.

The Communist Party of India split into two in 1964 and it was weakened in the 1960s due to internal dissent. In any case, the party was never able to achieve mass appeal like the Dravidian parties, and never again had the electoral success that it had in 1952. Unlike West Bengal, Andhra Pradesh, or other states, the Naxal movement based on a philosophy of armed revolt did not take root in Tamil Nadu.[11] Communism also declined globally, which further contributed to a weakening of the perception of 'communist threat' to the ruling elite in Tamil Nadu. Thanks to these factors, communism is a much weaker force today than it was in the 1950s. Despite this weakening, communist parties continue to wield influence disproportionate to their electoral strength. This is primarily because of the fact that unlike many of the mainstream political parties that mobilize mainly mainly around elections, the communists tend to mobilize at all times—and thus their impact far exceeds other parties with similar electoral clout.

Since the 1970s, communists have also started taking up issues beyond the traditional class agenda, and public services have featured more actively in their campaigns. There are different reasons for the shift in agenda. In the process of expanding to new areas, young leaders found it easier to start by focusing on public services, which is not as divisive an issue as land reforms, or a demand for increasing wages. As one communist leader succinctly put it, he established the local branch of his party starting with a campaign for mosquito control in his area. After all, mosquitoes do not discriminate between the rich and the poor, and so he got the support of all sections of the society for his campaign. A focus on public services provided an easier entry into politics, and there was also a clear demand for it among the public. Many communist activists also started entering politics at the Panchayat level.

Since Panchayats are responsible for delivering water and other services, they naturally had to focus their attention on these services.

Changes in production relations including low margins of agricultural production, the disappearance of large landlords and other factors also made mobilization more challenging along traditional class issues. For example, many communist leaders recognized that farmers who already had low margins would find it difficult to increase agricultural wages while maintaining a viable farm. With increasing population, the urgency for basic public amenities including housing increased. All these factors led to the emergence of public services as a major agenda for action even among the communists. Apart from advocating for it in the assembly and in the policy arena, party chapters in rural areas mobilized actively on grievances related to roads, schools, health centres, water facilities, and other issues.

The communist influence is difficult to evaluate in the Tamil context since they have never occupied political power in the state, and core communist issues including land reforms were never really implemented in the state. At the same time, there is no doubt that they have had a major impact in shaping the intellectual landscape of the time, and have been a force that shaped the ideologies of other movements. The communist movement had strong roots among the poor and thus was the forefront of raising issues of the poor. Communist activists constantly talked about acute poverty, hunger, ill-health, and other issues suffered by hardworking poor people and sought to argue that these problems were faced by the poor irrespective of caste. At least in the initial days, these problems were highlighted with the view of demanding a change in the property right regime, but they also had the unintended effect of strengthening the government's commitment to address them directly by providing public services.

Caste associations

As I pointed out earlier, Tamil Nadu developed an intense network of caste associations that have been the main backbone of political mobilization in the state. Caste associations have worked on numerous issues such as affirmative action in education and employment, removal of social unfreedoms and re-categorization of their caste status, etc. and the agenda has varied at different points of time. Many of these organizations started by demanding a higher categorization in the Hindu Varna system during the censuses of 1901–31 when caste was recorded in the census. They sought to be categorized at a higher Varna level, more specifically a reclassification from Shudra to a Kshatriya status. The demand for upward categorization did not make sense in an era of affirmative action because there was a significant advantage to claiming a backward status. Some castes have since fought to categorize themselves as 'Backward' and 'Most Backward', so that they can avail of better reservation quotas in education and employment.

Caste-based organizations have generally led the struggle for social mobility following the popular strategies of the day. Many caste organizations favoured *Sanskritization* as a means of achieving upward mobility. This process involved the appropriation and use of the customs of the upper castes while making the claim that they too belonged to a higher caste. Simultaneously, caste organizations also created social arrangements to help their communities with education, starting businesses, getting jobs and accessing other opportunities. This was accomplished by creating facilities such as schools, banks, tuition centres, libraries, sports facilities, and access to social networks. The popularity and the continuing strength of these caste associations reflects this work and the fact that many individuals belonging to these communities rely on the caste network at critical times.

Given that caste organizations take up multiple issues for the benefit of their caste, they have a broad range of demands. Among them, public services have been taken up as an agenda, as an avenue of creating jobs for their constituents and also as a tool of social mobility. An important aspect of their work has been to fight socially imposed unfreedoms for members of their community pertaining to accessing public services. Caste networks thus provide a mechanism for social bargaining for better amenities, fighting for the removal of social unfreedoms in accessing amenities and also in preparing people belonging to these communities to make better use of the public services created by the government.

While the caste associations of the BCs have been politically powerful, Dalit associations have been particularly successful in fostering social change. This rich history is often underplayed thanks to the general marginality of these castes and also due to the fact that the Dalits have had very few prominent leaders since independence. Despite the relative lack of prominence, the movement has a rich and interesting history. In keeping with the broader trend of caste-based mobilization, Dalits also started mobilizing in substantial ways in the late nineteenth century. Many of the Dalit leaders of this period had fathers who had worked with the British, thus enabling them to get wealth and education that helped with mobilization. The list of major leaders includes Iyothee Dasar, M C Rajah, and Rettamalai Srinivasan.

Iyothee Dasar ran a newspaper called *Oru Paisa Thamizhan* that was widely circulated across Tamil Nadu, and it framed many of the grievances of the community. He framed the argument that Dravidians were the original inhabitants of the land and that they were defeated by the Aryans from the North. In doing so, he was among the earliest people in India to use the argument that the marginalized population of the region was the original inhabitants of the land, and thus deserving of greater rights and a claim to power.[12] He also framed an argument that Dalits were originally Buddhists, and upon their subjugation by the Aryans, the Brahminical system was imposed on them and they were labelled as untouchables and enslaved. This argument was taken up and refined later by Ambedkar, who realized that conversion from Hinduism could be one of the many mobilization tactics for the Dalit community (Omvedt 2008).

Other leaders, including MC Raja and Rettamalai Srinivasan, led impressive mobilizations of the community and some of the conventions held by these leaders attracted thousands of participants from across the presidency. Mobilization of such numbers in the nineteenth century is particularly impressive given the fact that the communication infrastructure was poorly developed, Dalits were extremely poor and that they also suffered from severe oppression by the dominant communities. Both these leaders were nominated to the Madras Legislative Council in the 1920s as representatives of 'depressed classes' by the colonial administration.

A brief look at the Legislative Council debates indicates that Dalit leaders brought a different perspective. For example, in the first council (1920–23), M. C. Rajah was among few who would foreground his speeches by pointing out that his community was poor and if policies are to reach them, their poverty should be taken into account. In a memorable petition of 1923, he along with other untouchable leaders argued that if the benefit of education was to reach Dalit children, measures needed to go beyond just subsidized tuitions. The petition argued that there should be school feeding during the break if poor children were to obtain the full benefit of education and that there should be scholarships to compensate for their labour so that parents living in crushing poverty can afford to send their children to school. They also made a point that apart from making tuitions free, the scholarships should take care of all educational expenses (Radhakrishnan 1990). The farsightedness of this petition is absolutely remarkable in a sense that education policy has evolved exactly in this way in state after state in India. It is my contention that the farsighted agenda set by these leaders served as the cornerstone of progressive policies in the years to come.[13]

The political genius of Ambedkar and his dominance of the Dalit politics of our era have undermined the role of Dalit leaders in Tamil Nadu prior to India's independence. Following independence, there have been fewer large-scale Dalit movements in the state. The Republican Party of India started by Ambedkar has some presence, and in recent years, the Dalit Panthers have created an impressive presence in parts of the State. The shape that the Dalit movement has taken in Tamil Nadu since independence has been primarily in the form of local mobilization, often with the support of political parties and other leaders. I described one of the examples of the movement in detail in the second chapter, when I discussed Erani.

Over the years, the Dalit movements have taken up numerous issues of socially imposed unfreedoms. Freedom to vote, to dress according to one's choice, freedom of mobility, freedom to access public amenities, freedom from violence, and the ability to run for political offices are among the civic and political freedoms that the Dalit movement has advanced. Dalits have also organized service centres on a mass scale. These take the form of Ambedkar societies to assist Dalit children with tuitions, scholarship support, finding jobs, ensuring that reservation quotas are fulfilled, and in other ways that prepare young Dalits for opportunities opened up through reservation and otherwise. Apart from running their own services, the Ambedkar societies take up grievances on various public services and represent them to the administration. They also enable Dalits to fight for social access to existing amenities, and for a non-discriminatory treatment within these amenities.

The focus of the Dalit movement on basic civic and political freedom and for political power has led to a consistent focus on public services. Given the level of political oppression of the community, Ambedkar societies also found it expedient to take up public services as their main agenda rather than more contentious agenda such as the demand for land or political positions. Given the crushing poverty of Dalit communities, and the pathetic conditions in which they have been forced to live, access to water, basic health care, roads, cremation facilities, electricity, street lights and other basic services can make a huge difference in their lives. PDS and other measures of social protection go a long way in protecting them from hunger. Dalits also view education as one of the key means of social advancement, given the fact that they have practically no property on which they can build their fortune. All of these factors have made public services central to the well-being of poor Dalits, and it is no surprise that it has been the central demand of Dalit activists in the state.

Women's movements

The women's movement, along with its broad base of supporters in the nationalist, Dravidian, communist, and other movements, has focused on women's unfreedoms in different domains. One of the early successes of the movement was to expand the political participation of women by campaigning for voting rights for women. Despite consistent resistance from the alien government to offer voting rights to women, the movement succeeded in obtaining voting rights for educated women in the 1930s, only a few years after voting rights were extended to women in the UK. The women's movement also challenged norms that prevented women from getting education and also took up issues of women's health, mobility, property rights, the role of women within a family, domestic violence and a number of other issues.

In the last few decades, NGOs and party affiliated women's organizations have focused on a broad range of issues of concern to women including: domestic violence, safety in the streets, livelihood and social protection. In order to understand women's role in shaping public priorities, one has to go well beyond the agenda articulated by social movements and NGOs. The social presence and assertiveness of women at the grassroots level has had tremendous implications in shaping policies at the state level. The fact that women could follow policies and vote independently based on their priorities forced Tamil politicians to offer an agenda that would be attractive to women in order to secure their support. Traditionally, women have supported the extension of public services including education, nutrition support and health care policies, and this has been instrumental in shaping political priorities for these services in Tamil Nadu. Many of these services expanded dramatically under the tenure of MGR, who consciously sought to cultivate a voting base among women. The need to secure women's support has forced other parties, including the DMK, to extend policies matching women's priorities including self-help Groups, smoke-free gas stoves, and sustaining the entitlements in the PDS.

Kamarajar and the public service agenda

Having discussed the role of many of the major social movements in Tamil Nadu, it is now appropriate to get back to the politician who played the most instrumental role in making public services the political priority: Kamarajar Nadar. Kamarajar came to power in 1954 after Rajaji was forced to resign following protests to his caste-based education scheme. Unlike Rajaji and other prominent leaders of the Congress who were mainly upper caste, Kamarajar belonged to the Nadar community that was marginalized and discriminated against at his time. As an astute politician, Kamarajar secured the support of Periyar for his candidature and in the process promised Periyar that he would make education accessible to all children in the state.[14] He followed this promise by expanding the school system with the view of creating one school in every Panchayat. Even today, he is widely considered the 'father of education' [*Kalvi Thanthai*] in the State.

Kamarajar was placed in a peculiar position through his stint as the Chief Minister of Tamil Nadu. He had to battle the challenge of the communists who had a strident class agenda and consistently critiqued Kamarajar as not doing enough for the poor. This critique was also advocated by the rising DMK, which had a strong base among the BC groups. While these parties consistently criticized him for not doing enough for the poor, the Swatantra party started by Rajaji complained of taxes, an expanding state and other issues in order to create a constituency among the rich. His own party, the Congress, was comprised of some of the leading landlords and industrialists, who were sympathetic to Rajaji's arguments.[15]

Buttressed by strident critique from the left and the right, Kamarajar created a strategy for securing broad social support. This involved avoiding drastic land redistribution or other measures demanded by the communists. He argued that the class agenda of the communists required violence, and that communism was incompatible with the democratic framework. Kamarajar wrote many articles during his tenure as the Chief Minister in which he argued that democracy was the most important form of power wielded by the common people. He argued that communism is incompatible with democracy, and so the class agenda demanded by the communists would ultimately disempower the common person. At the same time, he argued that the point of independence was for the government to create a good life for the citizen within a democratic framework. The government's way of doing so was to create basic public amenities including education, health care, and other forms of support so that people are able to develop their capabilities (Kamarajar 2003).

Given the broad support for mass education created by the Dravidian, Dalit, and women's movements, he started a massive expansion of the school system. Along with this, he articulated a vision that the educated child must be able to avail him or herself of productive employment, which was possible only by the expansion of industry and agriculture. Using this argument, he sought to expand the opportunities for private industries and to create infrastructure for both industry and agriculture. This involved the establishment of power plants, dams, roads, and other basic infrastructure. He also argued for creating a tax base in order to expand social programmes, while creating a space for private industry to expand. This vision prioritized public services along with the growth of industry and agriculture.This vision of Kamarajar, the product of his political contingency created by strong social movements with differing perspectives, has been the policy in Tamil Nadu.

Unmediated grassroots pressure and decline of ideology

The era of strong social movements with coherent ideologies came to an end in the 1960s. Social movements were superseded by political parties. Public action that was mainly led by social movements has since been taken over by decentralized collective action, often by people who do not have a strong and well-knit ideological foundation. The pressure from the common person unmediated by ideologically bound organizations has shaped collective priorities. It is more likely that grassroots action of this sort is based on concrete needs and problems demanding immediate solutions, rather than the abstract possibility of revolution, economic growth, structural adjustment and other forms of salvation through indirect means. In other words, a group of people confronted with ankle-deep mud to reach the nearest road are more likely to demand an all-weather road than structural adjustment policies.

With the decline of social domination, immediate needs that could be solved have become the major focus of public action in Tamil Nadu. As a result, the dominant proportion of representations, petitions and other forms of assertive protests have been on public services. In this atmosphere, political parties find it expedient to offer an agenda in which services are central. Such a response to democratic aspirations has been called derisive names including 'populism'. The massive expansion of public services during the tenure of MGR was roundly criticized both by the left and the right. Thankfully, good politics won over bad economics, be it the economics of the left or the right, and led to the massive expansion of public services in the state. Let me review the history of that expansion in the post-Kamarajar era since we discussed his role above.

Kamarajar resigned as the Chief Minister to take up an active role in national politics in 1963. The DMK came to power shortly thereafter in 1967. As I argued before, the communists had brought relentless focus to poverty and hunger, which the DMK started focusing on heavily. They offered heavily subsidized food grains as a poll promise, but could not fulfill their promise beyond two years citing fiscal problems. Education continued to be a political priority that the DMK could not ignore. In keeping with the socialist rhetoric, the DMK nationalized some of the major private transport corporations in Tamil Nadu. This also had a tactical advantage in that some of the large private transport corporations that were privatized belonged to Brahmins who were known to be supporters of the Congress party. In any case, public transport has since been a major policy priority. The DMK set up transport corporations across Tamil Nadu which led the creation of an excellent public transport system in the state. Along with this, the party has also focused on road connectivity up to the village level by what are called as 'feeder roads' to villages with a population of at least 1500. The party has also focused on the electrification of villages.

The DMK started developing internal dissensions when Karunanithi became the Chief Minister following the death of C N Annadurai in 1969. The party split in 1972, and MGR created the AIADMK based on his personal appeal. The personal appeal and the wide recognition that MGR had were developed during his career in the movie industry as a lead actor, and the politics of MGR is closely associated with his screen persona, which was incidentally crafted by the Dravidian literary machinery. Unlike some of the versatile actors who tried many different characters, MGR sported a persona that was common to most of his movies. The persona was one that consistently challenged the injustice meted out to the poor and vulnerable by those in positions of power, and MGR was always the hero who extended a helping hand to those in need. His character focused on social inequalities and many forms of injustice suffered by the poor and by women in the hands of the elite. His movies have thus had a strong political content, and to a certain extent he continued to maintain an off-screen persona of being modest, approachable, and caring that fostered his widespread popularity especially with the poor, women, and Dalits.

Since his electoral chances rested on the popularity that he enjoyed with these groups, it became imperative for him to sustain the image of his persona as a protector of the poor and of women in his political life. He started by criticizing the DMK for going back on its promise to provide subsidies for grains, and made hunger one of the key elements of his politics. When the AIADMK came to power in 1977, it led the most impressive expansion of food programmes in India's history. School feeding had been a part of the education system, but it was available only to a part of the government schools before this era. The quality of food was basic and infrastructural support for the programme was inadequate, leading to disruptions and other problems with its implementation. MGR converted the 'noon meal' programme into the 'nutritious noon meal' by improving the quality of the food, and he also extended school feeding to all children in government schools up to class ten. Recognizing that a lot of children under six suffer from malnutrition, he also initiated a massive expansion of the Integrated Child Development Services (ICDS) and provided substantial support for supplementary nutrition for children who came to the child care centre. The PDS was extended by introducing a wider variety of goods, and he provided the political support to ensure that the system reached the poorest people.

Politically, MGR is best recognized for his nutrition support, especially through the mid-day meal scheme. As I mentioned earlier, in his inaugural speech, while extending the mid-day meal scheme, he made a rhetorical appeal that the programme was being extended so that women do not have to watch their children go hungry, and that he would do anything even if he could only wipe one tear off the mother's eye that had to watch her child go hungry. This kind of rhetorical appeal connecting nutrition programmes to women has since created a political necessity for other parties to sustain the programmes, even when there were strong neoliberal pressures and the withdrawal of central financial support for extensive food programmes.

Officials and politicians who had served in the government during MGR's tenure as Chief Minister consistently argued that he was open to ideas for programmes that would contribute to social justice and uphold the image of MGR. This openness created a space for the bureaucrats to suggest new programmes that went beyond poll promises or demands by social movements. Thus, enthusiastic bureaucrats and ministers found a willing ally to extend an assortment of social programmes during his era. As an astute politician, MGR recognized that his persona could only be sustained by the delivery of programmes that would reach and be appreciated by his main voter base: women, Dalits and the poor in general. This required a massive expansion of public services with a keen eye on making them universally available to all communities. The AIADMK regime thus laid the foundation for the expansion of a number of public services addressing the needs of the poorest sections of society. More importantly, it introduced a system of delivering these programmes universally across the state and across all social groups.

The most impressive and the least talked about expansion during his tenure was the primary health care system. The number of primary health care centres more than doubled within the first seven years of the AIADMK rule, and it was also accompanied by impressive improvements to the centres. The number of doctors, basic facilities, and the availability of drugs in each PHC improved dramatically during the process. A policy was created to ensure that women doctors were available in most of the health care centres to cater to women's health needs. These improvements helped Tamil Nadu make impressive progress in combating infant mortality and other health outcomes that were discussed in the beginning of the book.

Interestingly, MGR is best recognized for his role in the noon meal programme even though it was one of the less impressive expansions of a public service during his tenure. The school feeding programme was already in place while MGR expanded the coverage and improved the quality of the programme. There were far more impressive expansions in school facilities, primary health care centres and to public health programmes during this period. While some of these immensely impressive expansions and improvements to services have been practically unnoticed in the academic literature or in the media, MGR has been made an icon of school feeding both within and outside Tamil Nadu.

The popularity of MGR with women forced the DMK to come up with alternatives to attract women voters. The most significant step taken by the party was to create extensive self-help groups for women in 1989. Since then, Tamil Nadu has had one of the most extensive SHG networks in India. The political environment has been extremely competitive since the death of MGR with incumbent parties being defeated typically by huge margins of seats, but typically with much smaller margins of votes. In this competitive political atmosphere, parties have found it difficult to remove popular programmes instituted by others,[16] while creating new ones with their own branding. The DMK is better known for extending infrastructure including transport and electricity while the AIADMK gave a priority to education, nutrition, health, water, and other public services. Between them, they have contributed substantially to the expansion of public services and in making these services a key part of the political agenda.

Finally, it is important to note that not all programmes that are taken up are based on responses to mobilization and strategic calculations to get votes during elections. There are many programmes in the state that are conducted without any reasonable expectation of political gain. These include programmes addressing Adivasis or tribal people, and those addressing disabled people in the state. The population of Scheduled Tribes in Tamil Nadu is less than 2 per cent, and they are widely dispersed across the state making them electorally insignificant. While the number of disabled people is considerably larger and could potentially be a voting base, there is no political identity or political mobilization

based on disability in Tamil Nadu. Disabled people and tribal people are among the most marginalised in Tamil Nadu today. Despite
the electoral insignificance of these two groups, Tamil Nadu has
put forward more programmes addressing these groups than most
other states in India.

The rollout of these programmes is a direct result of motivated bureaucrats with the support of NGOs that work on behalf
of these two social groups. There is now an impressive network
of NGOs that work with disabled people in Tamil Nadu, and the
knowledge of these groups has been a significant force in shaping policies towards disabled people in the state. Many of these
NGOs have an advocacy wing that seeks to influence policies,
which has had a significant impact in policy-making. That said,
it is important to note that the advocacy strategy of these NGOs
rarely includes an electoral strategy based on mobilization of
votes. As this indicates, support of political masters can often
be obtained for programmes that do not have direct electoral calculations. It is true that some of these programmes contribute
to the overall image of the government as one that stands in
support of the common person. But, it is not the case that electoral considerations are the basis of every important decision
respect to public services. Good intentions in the presence of a
largely effective bureaucracy can go a long way in creating effective programmes, but these are more likely to happen in places
where services, rather than other approaches, are seen as a way
of addressing the well-being of these groups.

This brings me to the discussion of an important factor in Tamil
Nadu's performance which I have not yet discussed. People who
have interacted with the bureaucracy in Tamil Nadu and in other
parts of India often find that there is tremendous enthusiasm and
dynamism among a set of bureaucrats in the state. It is not uncommon to find principal secretaries in charge of government departments taking an active interest in the design of programmes. Many
other officials at different levels are highly motivated, hard-working and have shown tremendous personal commitment to implementing public service programmes in the state. Some of my most
joyous moments were spent with trainers, mid-level officials, and
Anganwadi workers at lower levels of the administration without

whose inspiration, imagination and hard work, Tamil Nadu's performance would be impossible.

The picture I paint here is completely different from the broader public perception of government workers. The public perception and the literary portrayal is mostly of corrupt officials or lethargic government offices where nothing is accomplished. There is certainly a partial truth to that perception in the sense that there are many offices that people go to only to find unmotivated government officers or those with tremendous personal motivations. Along with this truth, there is a parallel truth of hard-working and motivated government workers doing thankless work in which positive aspects of their work is mostly ignored and only mistakes get highlighted in the public arena.

Tamil Nadu's performance on a wide range of indicators is well documented, and I wish to emphasize that hard work, creativity, and other resources have gone into the programmes, whose results we see in these indicators. This raises the question as to why there is a strong qualitative difference in the performance of bureaucrats in Tamil Nadu, as well as in other states where there is strong government performance. I do not have answers to that question, but I can safely say that the enthusiasm of the bureaucracy would be meaningless without the requisite political space. Such political space would not have been created without the social and political dynamics that I discussed in the previous chapter. The electoral pressures and constant public action from the grassroots creates pressure on the politicians to deliver. The political compulsion of the elected officials creates a situation wherein they have to make bureaucrats deliver. This inspires them to recruit officials with a good reputation to programmes that enjoy a political priority, and once recruited, it makes sense for the politicians to give these bureaucrats the space for them to perform.

I believe that this space and the pressure to perform provide an important part of the explanation as to why committed bureaucrats are selected to run programmes that are a political priority. The fact that they are supported and provided resources is likely to contribute to the motivation of these officials, not to mention the fact that their work can have a positive impact on a large number of people. At least in the top level of the bureaucracy in India, the selection is made on an all India basis through the Union Public Services Commission (UPSC). UPSC is the centralized organization that selects top officials for all positions in the administration, police, railways, accounting services and all other major government programmes.

Typically, half of the officials in any state are from that state while the rest are chosen from other states. Selected candidates are allotted to different states without any reference to their state of origin. Thanks to this, there is no reason to believe that at least as far as the top bureaucracy is concerned, the quality of the candidates does not explain the level of motivation that they have in different states; the space they work in offers a much better explanation than the selection mechanism. That argument does not hold for lower level government services where candidates are almost exclusively chosen from within the state, and thus the culture of the state could matter for their performance. While I cannot answer if that is true, I hold the opinion that what matters most is the space in which they function, and that this space has been shaped by the political and social dynamics that we discussed so far.

Summing up

The priority for services in Tamil Nadu cannot be understood without taking into account the multiplicity of social movements and their cumulative impact in shaping the government's agenda. Among them, social reform movements played a special role in making a case for public services as a principle tool of development. This vision was subscribed to by the Dravidian, Dalit, and women's movements. These movements arose by questioning the unequal norms of the past and they criticized laws and policies that favoured the elite. These moral arguments have become the touchstone for evaluating laws and policies—and governments risk losing their legitimacy by adopting laws or policies that are contrary to them. Through this, the movements today have forced governments to opt for universalistic policies that could reach the most people, and to create programmes that are relevant to the common person. The vision of development through services created by the reform movements coincided with the demand for services at the grassroots level by the people, and in a context of intense political competition, governments have found it expedient to secure people's support by delivering these services in a nearly universal manner.

Notes

1. Violence is often used to secure change by terrorizing people into accepting or creating that change. Here I am talking of the use of riots to secure attention for an issue and often to create a stronger sense of identity and solidary among a group. I would call such a use 'cultural'.

2. By 'spectacles', I refer to visually striking events that deliberately draw huge public attention.

3. One account of MGR's success is presented by Dickey (2005). Not everyone appreciated the success arising out of cultural means rather than traditional organization. For that perspective, see Pandian (1992).

4. While it is not uncommon for actors to try and get a political role, successful politicians have also tried to act in movies. For example, Thol. Thirumavalavan, the current chief of the Dalit Panthers party acted in the movie *Anbuthozhi* as a militant fighting for the Tamil Elam cause.

5. When Kamarajar started focusing on national politics, Bhaktavachalam took over as a CM. He is the only CM so far who was not a popular artist of some sort.

6. His contribution is discussed in Ganeshan (2003), Pe. Maniyarasan and A. Marx (2007) and Raj Gauthaman (2005).

7. See *Pallar Kaliattam* (Bharathiyar 2000).

8. There have been 'reservation' of jobs for others in the meanwhile, including reservation of all army jobs to people belonging to 'Martial races'.

9. For Periyar's view on this, see Ramasamy (2005).

10. See Ravikumar (2008) for this critique.

11. There were groups though that referred to themselves as 'Naxals' and they engaged mainly in cultural struggles and organizing outside the electoral framework. One such case has been written about by Gorringe (2005).

12. While he was no doubt among the earliest, it is not clear as to who was the first in making this case. Some have claimed that Iyothee Dasar

was the first person to make this argument, while similar claims have been made by other 'Adi' movements of the North (Juergensmeyer 1982).

13. One of the Dalit conferences led to such resolutions even earlier in the 1890s (Geetha and Rajadurai 1993).

14. The DMK had broken away from the Periyar-led DK in 1949 protesting his marriage with a young woman of 28 while Periyar was in his 70s. This break created the opportunity for the Non-Brahmin Kamarajar to secure the support of Periyar against the DMK. Thus, in a strange turn of events, Periyar ended up supporting the Congress, which had been his main foe for many years.

15. His struggles with various parties and the efforts toward creating a policy agenda is reflected in his essays (Kamarajar 2003).

16. There is a popular perception that policies created by one party are removed by the other when the competitor comes to power. This perception is supported by the fact that there are major reversals that are politically prominent. While such reversals are constantly in the news, the fact that most of the programmes in the social sector do not get touched is much less talked about, lending to the perception that what is done by one is undone by the other.

Section II

Beyond Tamil Nadu: A Tentative Argument

I mentioned in earlier chapters that the communist parties were active in mobilizing around public services. Pointing this out, some of my discussants drew analogies with the movement's impact in Kerala. This analogy made me question how far Tamil Nadu's history might resonate with Kerala. It also made me ask why services did not become a priority in West Bengal where the communist parties were in power for a much longer time than in Kerala. During other meetings, comparisons were drawn to identity movements in Bihar and UP and the Dravidian movement. In other words, even though my work was on Tamil Nadu, comparisons were constantly made to other parts of India and these were instrumental in shaping my understanding of Tamil Nadu. Inspired by this process, I would like to examine whether Tamil Nadu's performance could give us insights into the performance of other parts of India. The attempt here is not to generalize Tamil Nadu's performance, but to ask if its history has a resonance to histories elsewhere. As I mentioned in the introduction, this account is not based on systematic fieldwork, and it is offered as a tentative account. While I did not conduct fieldwork as a part of this research, I have had many long discussions with activists, officials, and journalists working on issues such as health, education, social reform, land reforms, and other issues over the last 15 years. I also have the benefit of secondary literature. These have convinced me that there are important analogies between the experience of Tamil Nadu and other states. Even though I am not in a position to provide an authoritative account of it, there is merit to offering a tentative account of the phenomenon. The chapters in Section Two should be read with this cautionary note.

When it comes to the performance of states, there is now a broad agreement on the exceptional performance of Tamil Nadu and Kerala on a wide range of basic public services. There is also widespread agreement on some of the worst performers including Bihar, Orissa, Rajasthan, and Uttar Pradesh. The performance of most other states is tricky to assess since there are significant differences in how they are assessed across studies. For example, Punjab has consistently featured at the top of the human development index (Planning Commission 2001, UNDP and Jolly 2000) among Indian states, but it has been ranked among the worst performers by the Public Affairs Centre survey (PAC Survey) on public services (S. Paul, Balakrishnan, and Public Affairs Centre 2006). Unlike the top performers who tend to provide a broad range of public services exceptionally well or the poor performers who tend to deliver most services badly, other states tend to provide some services well but not all basic services. Thus, studies tend to rank states differently depending on which services they focus on. To go back to the previous example, the Human Development Index calculations are based on education, health and income levels in which Punjab has been a remarkable performer. The PAC survey looked at PDS, water, public transport and other services in which the state has a poor record of performance. If differences in assessments arose only on the basis which programmes are covered in each survey, it would be possible to combine data from multiple surveys to make a broad based assessment of performance. That is unfortunately not possible since there are differences even how a given programme is assessed by different surveys.

For example, there are different ways of ranking the performance of states in each service. Official statistics tend to measure the performance based on current policy priorities, which tend to be thin indicators of performance. For example, basic infrastructure and accessibility have been the main policy focus in education and health care and so the government has been collecting statistics on whether there is a school and health care centre within a pre-scribed distance from every village. Such a dataset will help us to understand what proportion of villages have a school within 1 km and the health sub centre within 5 km, which is useful, but provides little insight into their performance.

Like the statistics collected by government ministries, a lot of surveys also look at the mere availability of the service in the vil-lage. Thus, the presence of a school building with a teacher who comes once a week will get equal weightage as a well-functional school in another. Even in looking at availability, most surveys tend to concentrate on large infrastructure such as buildings, hos-pital beds, or other infrastructure that are easily measurable in a large-scale survey. Given that easy accessibility of services and the availability of basic infrastructure form a critical part of delivering such services, these surveys do give us an important perspective but it is important to go beyond basic inputs in order to understand how well a program functions.

To some extent, one can read the input measures along with surveys that focus on the outcomes including life expectancy, morbidity, reading levels, death rates, etc. Since the outcome mea-sures are co-determined by a variety of factors beyond the inputs recorded in other surveys, we cannot assume that the mere avail-ability of services has resulted in the outcomes recorded in the other surveys. That said, having access to a broader range of infor-mation about the provision of services and well-being outcomes provide us with a slightly better picture of a state's performance in public services. These can be complemented with a few surveys that also look at user satisfaction.

In the absence of any widely agreed upon index of public services that I could rely on, I have consulted a set of surveys and reports that shed light on the performance of various states. Very few studies look at the extent and quality of services in the Indian context, and the most detailed among them are the Public Affairs Centre's survey of public services (PAC) and the India Human Development Survey of 2005 (IHDS). IHDS covers a wide range of services and provides a thorough understanding of the availability of the services in each state at the village level. It also evaluates some of the services by looking at qualitative aspects of their performance. In addition, it also measures several outcomes including the status of health, education, poverty, and gender parity. The PAC survey looks at primary education, childcare centres, primary health care, the Public Distribution System, transport and water in detail. The survey looks at the availability, regularity, and user satisfaction with the services.

I have consulted a few other surverys such as the National Family Health Surveys (NFHS), Human Development Reports,[1] ASER survey, FOCUS Report, and the PROBE Report which look at the performance of specific services. The first three are extensive and they cover most states, while the PROBE and FOCUS reports look only at a selection of states in regards to one service. Finally, I have complemented these indicators by adding information compiled by the Government of India.[2] Based on this rather long list of sources I have created a set of performance categories discussed below. As I mentioned earlier, there are differences in the evaluations of states across these indicators, so there is room for interpretation. Given this possibility, I have created three very broad categories of consistently good performers, consistently bad performers and states with varied performance across services, so that the room for interpretation is minimized.

Large scale surveys typically take a lot of time to compile and are not made available to the public quickly, and the IHDS conducted in 2005 is among the last large survey that provides information on a broad array of services. This does not reflect important changes on the ground in places like Bihar and Andhra Pradesh that have created some impressive programmes in the recent years. Given this predicament, I have also offered some reflections towards the end on states in which there are credible reports of changing performance.

Consistently high performers

The exceptional performer without any doubt is Kerala, which is iconic for its ability to deliver a wide range of public services including health, education, nutrition, sanitation, and child care to most people in the state. Kerala's performance is widely known and does not need much repetition here. Another state whose performance has been exceptional in past 20 years is Himachal Pradesh. Himachal has dramatically expanded its roads, electricity access, water, immunization, education, and an array of other public services. Himachal was the top performer in full immunization (NFHS III), had the fourth highest life expectancy in India (66.8 years at birth), had a low infant mortality by the standards of Indian states, was among the lowest proportion of children out of school with reasonable educational achievements of children in school (ASER and the IHDS also records that most of the villages had road access).

The performance of Himachal Pradesh is acknowledged consistently across reports,[3] and it is likely that these have contributed to the third position this hill state had in the Human Development Index. Low gender disparity in the state is a major contributing factor to its performance, among other things, by ensuring that women have access to a large range of basic public services. While HPs performance is strong in these areas, the IHDS records a relatively poor presence of the PDS, banks, and police stations in Himachal villages. With a consistent performance across a range of services, and in a number of different evaluations, HP scores as an exceptional performer among Indian states in the recent years.

Largely urban states like Delhi, Puducherry, and Goa also have a strong performance across a broad array of the services. Considering that road, water, electricity and health care are easily available in a larger proportion of urban areas compared to rural areas, it is difficult to compare these states with other large states that have large rural areas. Further, income levels in urban areas tend to be higher, enabling people to access many of the services through private sources as well. Given this factor, I have not looked at urban states in this work.

Varied performance

Southern and Western states of India have generally outperformed the Hindi heartland and the states of India's east. While Tamil Nadu and Kerala have been consistent in their performance across public services, states like Karnataka, Maharashtra, Gujarat, and

Andhra Pradesh have performed above the national average. They normally do not feature in the bottom across all basic public services, but they rarely feature as exceptional performers. The IHDS and the PAC indicate that Andhra Pradesh and Karnataka have made an array of public services available in most villages. Karnataka and Andhra have a strong PDS, programmes for sanitation, water, road connectivity, transport, street lights, and social protection programmes based on cash and food transfers.

AP has an impressive programme of Self Help Groups for women through which the state offers financial support to women. It also has an extensive coverage of the Indira Awas Yojana, a free housing programme. Karnataka is noted for its road connectivity and for ensuring that roads are usable even during heavy monsoons. It is also a forerunner in extending electricity connection to villages, with a larger proportion of Karnataka villages having electricity connection prior to 1975 as compared to other Indian states.[4] The PAC survey indicates that Karnataka's health system is widely used and citizens expressed 'full satisfaction' with doctors in Karnataka more than anywhere else in India. Karnataka's water supply is also relatively reliable compared to other states. In other areas like citizen satisfaction with the PDS, literacy, or the number of children out of school the state lags behind many others.

Maharashtra has focused on road connectivity, the availability of credit and ensuring electricity for a good part of the day, along with an above average performance in the ICDS. The relative priorities of Maharashtra clearly indicate the power of the farmers in the state, especially the larger farmers who tend to use infrastructure such as electricity and credit more extensively. The ASER survey indicates that Maharashtra's school children do better in reading and arithmetic than in most other states, including Tamil Nadu. It also has a reasonable performance in gender disparity. At the same time, it has a very low ranking in terms of full immunization and the provision of water, sanitation, and housing.

The much discussed state of Gujarat does very well in making public transport widely available and in extending water facilities and health care. It was also one of the earliest states to make school feeding available across all schools. According to the IHDS, a large proportion of anganwadis in the state provided supplementary nutrition, immunization and growth monitoring services. Gujarat's notable performance in milk cooperatives and in creating infrastructure for agricultural operations is not covered in these surveys, and thus they mask an important aspect of the state's performance. Despite its considerable wealth achieved through sustained economic growth, the state has lagged behind most others in extending monetary and food support to aged people, pregnant women and disabled people. The food for work programme was also not implemented widely, and the state had very low numbers of women's self-help groups. In other words, Gujarat offers very little cash or food support for vulnerable groups even when most of the financing for these programmes is offered by the Government of India, requiring only a small proportion of matching contributions by the state government, with the exception of the PDS and the ICDS. Gujarat also lags behind in extending sanitation facilities to houses, even when it does reasonably well in offering housing programmes across most villages.

The most interesting case is Punjab, which as mentioned earlier, had the second highest human development index in India. High life expectancy at 69.82 and high levels of income have been major contributing factors to Punjab's performance in the HDI. In a range of other indicators pertaining to public services, Punjab rarely features among the top few states in any indicator. It has a moderate performance when it comes to immunization, infant mortality, and sanitation availability in houses.[5] While the proportion of villages that are connected by pucca roads is high in Punjab, it also has among the highest proportion of villages that are not connected by any road at all.[6] It has a relatively high presence of banks and post offices within villages. It performs well below the national average in terms of the presence of NGOs in villages, basic infrastructure for Panchayats, and in offering housing programmes, old-age pensions, maternity benefits, drinking water programmes and other aspects of the PDS. While Punjab ranks second in human development, it ranks a distant 17 in terms of gender disparity among Indian states. It also has among the poorest performance in the PDS.

Punjab's higher level of income explains in part the low numbers of people having access to pensions, the PDS, and other forms of social support. Many of these programmes are financed by the Government of India, and each state gets its allocation based on the number of people below the poverty line in the state. This automatically results in a lower number of people receiving social protection benefits. But higher income levels do not explain the poor records in immunization, public health and other such issues. Many states in India have gone well beyond the entitlements mandated by the government of India for social protection programmes based on the priority given to these programmes in such states.

Punjab's human development can be attributed to the economic performance of the state. It is one of the few states that has had tremendous investment in agriculture starting from colonial times, continuing into the green revolution era in India. This has contributed to high levels of income in the state and also one of the highest wage rates for agricultural labourers in India. Punjab has also had a long history of movements for social equality. While there are continuing inequalities in the state, there is no doubt that these social movements have had a major impact on the social access to the available services, especially for the Dalits in the state. Overall, the fact that Punjab rarely features as an exceptional performer in providing any basic public service despite historically higher levels of income in the state only indicates its low commitment to services.

The IHDS, among others, argued that the North-eastern states have performed remarkably in regards to education and an array of social protection services. Compared to other states, India's North-eastern states have a greater number of children going beyond class 12, and a larger proportion of students in the Northeast also have basic skills to handle computers and speak English, both of which have become a major means of accessing better paying jobs (HDR 2010).

Many of the North-eastern states have a high life expectancy, low infant mortality, and other favourable human development indicators. It is clear that governments have been playing an important role in extending education in the region, and it is also probable that these indicators have been supported by extensive social protection programmes including pensions, maternity benefits and other forms of cash transfers. The region has a relatively poor record in extending basic infrastructure such as roads, electricity and public transport. When it comes to other programmes such as the PDS or the ICDS, there are sharply divergent assessments by the IHDS and the PAC surveys. For example, the IHDS indicates that Tripura ranks among the best in India with regards to sanitation, the ICDS, drinking water and an assortment of social protection services available in each village. The PAC survey indicates that the reliability of these services is low and the user satisfaction over services covered in the survey is among the lowest in India. Since a lot of large-scale surveys do not cover the North-eastern states in sufficient depth, assessing the performance of this region in itself is challenging.

Glimmers of hope

Orissa, Uttar Pradesh, Madhya Pradesh, Rajasthan, and Bihar have consistently been among the worst performers across most studies pertaining to public services. Bihar, Uttar Pradesh, and Madhya Pradesh were bifurcated and predominantly tribal areas were separated to become states of their own. These states: Uttarakhand, Chhattisgarh, and Jharkhand also have very poor indicators across most public services. While there is no doubt that the performance of these states is abysmal, there has been a general improvement in access to certain basic amenities including schools, immunization, physical infrastructure of health care centres, school feeding, electricity access and roads. These improvements are often led by national efforts with programmes heavily funded by the Central Government. While there is much room for improvement today, the improvement over the last decade has certainly been substantial. For example, most children today enroll in schools today even though the quality of education and rates of completion in the school system leaves much to be desired. Similarly, there is now an accessible sub-centre and a wide network of primary health care centres, but there are wide disparities in the availability of doctors and other facilities across states. While the poor quality of services is a cause for concern, it should not be overlooked that the expansion of the services is a result of conscious policy options and a consistent push from the civil society to ensure that such services are available to all. The attention has now shifted firmly towards the quality of services, and I remain hopeful that with sustained attention there will be substantial improvements in the quality of the services in the years to come.

While the improvements mentioned above have been led by the efforts of the Central Government, there have also been a few remarkable programmes led by state governments. The rapid expansion of schools in Madhya Pradesh using the Education Guarantee Scheme, Rajasthan's success with NREGA, Chhattisgarh's experience with the PDS and the recent improvements in education, roads, health, and crime in Bihar are some examples of this phenomenon. I will argue that the improvements are not accidental, and that some of the dynamics that drove the performance of Tamil Nadu can give us insight into these glimmers of hope.

What makes these changes impressive is the fact that they happened at a rapid pace with the backing of their chief ministers. They indicate how far political will can go in transforming regions that are considered hopeless, and that change can happen at a remarkably fast pace. While these changes have been impressive, they have not fundamentally transformed the states, which continue to be among the poorest performers in public services. But if such improvements continue for a few decades, then there is a strong chance that the performance of these states would catch up with the rest of the country. In the following chapters, I will argue that there is a chance that the performance improvements will continue in some of the states given that they are based not just on the personalities of certain chief ministers, but on deep-rooted social changes that demand better performance from governments.

In keeping with the basic structure of my argument, I will first look at some of the powerful agenda setting movements that different states have had, and how they shaped the policies of governments. Following this, the last chapter of this book will look at the different levels of voice that common people have in different states of India, and make the argument that common people have had a greater voice in the better performing states.

Notes

1. The India Human Development Report, 2010, is based on the IHDS 2005. This report did not include a human development index that could help compare the performance of Indian states, and so I have also used previous HDRs for this purpose.

2. These include data on (i) Roads, gender disparity, households with toilet facility and kacha houses from the National Human Development Report 2001 by the Planning Commission (ii) Literacy level by state from the census of 2011 and (iii) Life expectancy and Infant Mortality rate during 2001-05 by the Office of Registrar General of India.

3. NFHS, ASER, Focus, PROBE, IHDS.

4. IHDS 2005 has questions regarding when the service is available in the village. The inference is based on this data.

5. This need not be a result of government programmes. In general, Punjab has a lower number of 'kacha' houses, and this could contribute to the availability of sanitation in houses.

6. These villages are connected only by paths, and not even by Kacha roads.

5

Setting the Agenda: India

I have argued so far that when common people have a voice in the society, the society is likely to put in place collective arrangements for the well-being of a broader section of the population than just the elite. This work recognizes that voice need not translate into a demand for public services. There are many different ways of achieving well-being, and each will translate into different social priorities. For example, one major understanding today of how to advance human well-being comes from neoliberalism which argues that economic growth of countries overall is the most critical means of advancement. In this conception, there is some support for public services, but overall the focus is on a set of fiscal, monetary, and institutional measures that have little reference to services. Left ideologies, on the other hand, have prioritized 'structural reforms' of a different kind involving the reform of land, wages, and the conditions of work. Both the left and the right ideologies have tended to de-emphasize public services and have even considered the extension of public services a harmful measure for the overall goals that these ideologies support. It is also possible that societies develop political priorities that do not put human well-being at the centre of the agenda; after all, wars, riots, and other forms of destruction have taken place so often with the backing of popular will, even if they were not for the sake of advancing well-being of any of the parties involved.

Understanding how collective priorities emerge requires us to look at both the dynamics of power and the shaping of agendas. In this chapter, I will focus on the contest of ideas and look at some of the major ideologies that have shaped policies, laws, and institutions in different parts of India. The landscape has been shaped by a rich array of ideologies and movements including different communisms, market centred ideologies, socialisms, social reform, human rights, religious movements, caste groups, ethnic movements and others. Political priorities are naturally shaped by the specific mix of ideas that are advocated in any particular region at particular points of time. Unfortunately, this book does not offer me the space to discuss these in detail. Instead, I will make the broad argument that there were few streams of thought in which public services were seen as an important way of advancing human well-being, and that services have become a priority where such ideologies have been influential for sustained period of time.

While most mainstream economic ideologies did not make a case for public services, there have been a few key sources of support that have consistently supported it. Social reform movements were early advocates and they were powerful from the early nineteenth century up until the 1960s. This theme was taken up later by a few identity movements, some of which had their roots in social reform, and in the last few decades, rights-based movements have been the most forceful advocates. A lot of thrust for services has come from decentralized public action not mediated by ideological organizations. These movements have not had a uniform presence across India and so the impact that they had on the policy agenda has depended on the specific mix of movements in each state. I will start by looking at some of the influential agenda setting movements that favoured services and then discuss their regional impact in determining state-level policy priorities.

Socio-religious reform movements

Socio-religious reform movements[1] were the earliest advocates of services and many of them saw them as a critical tool for achieving social reform and contributing to the welfare of historically marginalized communities. They thus advocated the expansion of services and the removal of social restrictions on women, Dalits and other vulnerable groups in accessing them. Both aspects are critical in understanding the evolution of the commitment to services for all. Socio-religious reform was pursued by a wide variety of organizations and thus there were competing visions on development and social change. While most groups engaged with some services, a few advocated the radical expansion of services for all. Where such movements were powerful for a sustained period of time, they were able to make a powerful case for expanding education, health care, and other amenities for the benefit of all.

Reform has been a theme among social movements in India for centuries, and many of these movements have had a profound impact on the society. In the nineteenth century, the expansion of travel, income, education, and also the critique of Indian society from the West led to intense social ferment, and made some of the social and religious issues salient for public debates, which in turn created the impetus for several social reform movements. These movements were active from the early 1800s and they became powerful towards the end of that century. Some of the prominent movements include Brahmo Samaj, Ramakrishna Mission, Arya Samaj, Prarthana Sabha, Social Reform Congress, and the Dravidian movement. Protestant missionaries were also prominent in creating a thrust for social reform.

Even though colonial presence started in India in the 1600s, social reform became a prominent theme only in the 1800s. This is due to the fact that the English East India Company did not encourage missionary activity in India for fear of antagonizing local powers and thus disrupting trade. This attitude changed with the renewed Charter Act of 1813 that required the company to permit and encourage missionary activity (Robinson 2010). This led to an increased presence of missionaries, among whom Protestants were particularly active in criticizing local traditions and demanding social reform. This critique and the resultant discussions around it had an impact in fostering reform movements both within and outside the Hindu society (Oddie 1969).

Caste and caste-based unfreedoms became central to this demand for social reform; after all, the missionaries brought with them highly conservative Victorian morals in regards to gender, but they did not share the local caste prejudices which enabled them to create powerful arguments against the caste system. Missionaries played an important role in framing caste as the most debilitating aspect of the society in India, and the arguments they framed have persisted. They argued that the caste system was tyrannical, that it suppressed feelings of empathy towards others, and that it consigned the bulk of the population to slavery. They argued against the fact that an individual could not work to improve his social status through wealth, character, or other aspects of individual effort, and thus that caste retarded economic development, perpetuated injustice, and suppressed the development of patriotism.[2] Overall, they made the argument that in order to improve the human condition in India it was essential to reform society and the caste system.

Different visions were put forward on how to achieve this reform and it was through in this process that universal access to services was framed as a solution. The most important link between services and missionary work lies in the fact that many of the Missionaries directly provided services to marginalized communities and they saw it as an important tool for the improvement of their condition. Another important link was that the caste system created barriers for missionaries to expand their activities since higher caste people who sought to convert were ostracized by their communities, making it costly for them to convert to Christianity. Converts were often denied their ancestral property and many of them also found it difficult to access public wells and other amenities. This prompted the missionaries to take up campaigns against communal restrictions on the access to public services. This was codified for the first time in the form of the *Caste disabilities removal act (Act XXI of 1850)*.[3] While the missionaries led these efforts, there is also the history of missionaries incorporating caste practices within the church to facilitate conversions. But the discourse within the church created a space for lower caste people to protest against civic unfreedoms within the church, and in south India, they were able to take up this protest in the church much before they could do so in Hindu temples or other social spaces (Sivasubramanian 2001). Churches thus provided the space for the politicization of lower caste people on the issue of civic freedoms, which became a major political issue over the next century.

The popularity of services provided by the missionaries led to the fear of mass conversions among Caste Hindu organizations, a fact that was supported by many group conversions from the last quarter of the nineteenth century. The work of the missionaries also found resonance with many in India and led to intense debates on social reform. Hindu social reformers such as Jyotirao Phule were products of mission schools and were deeply influenced by missionary work. These factors together created a thrust to provide services among oppositional Hindu reform movements. That said, one should not make the mistake of assuming that service orientation was central to all reform movements. Each reform movement prioritized certain problems and created strategies to address them (Divekar, Kulkarni, and Kantak 1991; Natarajan 1959; Sen 2005).

Brahmo Samaj, for example, prioritized the reform of Hindu religious practices and wanted to create monotheism and abolish idol worship. The founder of the Samaj, Raja Ram Mohun Roy, was also one of the earliest crusaders against *sati*, the practice of immolating the widow in the funeral pyre of the husband. Opposition to sati gave rise to questions on the well-being of Hindu widows, leading to the creation of welfare homes and other basic services for widows. Women's rights, in this narrow fashion, was prominent among other reform movements of that time. As many scholars have pointed out, these practices were prevalent mainly among the upper caste communities, and so the campaigns were directed at a very small community.

The Arya Samaj sought to tackle the differences by performing 'Shuddi' or purification of the lower castes, after which they were welcomed into the higher caste society by the Samajists (Jaffrelot 2003; Juergensmeyer 1982). Others sought to retain the Varna system of four major categories, while eliminating the large array of castes within the system. Gandhi was among the prominent intellectuals to have advocated this and he stood against the destruction of the caste system overall.[4] Some of the radical positions on the caste system came from reformers who themselves were untouchables or BC people, the most prominent of them being Ambedkar and Periyar.

These movements borrowed some techniques of change from the missionaries including legislation, education, social work, and cultural change. For example, Ramakrishna Mission and Arya Samaj started a large number of schools, and they created some space in them for lower caste people. Many of them operated hospitals and engaged directly in creating an array of basic public services. Transforming people from marginalized groups has been at the centre of most social reform projects, and education was seen as an important means of achieving it. Similarly, such movements also keenly realized the need for the individual to have a supportive environment for change. Recognition of the role that services could play in people's well-being and the service orientation that many reform movements had made public services a major aspect of their work and politics. Given that the reform movements were predominantly led by people who had received university education, it was not surprising that education was a major demand. At the same time, these movements also demanded a series of other measures including agricultural support, health services, occupational support, welfare homes for the destitute, etc. In doing so, reform movements presented a vision for the improvement of human condition through the delivery of public services. Services have rarely occupied such a central position in the vision for development in most ideological frameworks, and by doing so, reform movements have been critical in developing a social commitment for services. Unlike neoliberalism, communism, or socialism, socio-religious movements do not necessarily have an inbuilt economic ideology. Given the engagement of many reform movements in providing services, it is not surprising that they sought the expansion of services in response to felt needs, rather than argue for economic growth or revolution to solve these problems ultimately. Reform movements also created strong arguments for extending services beyond the preserve of the elite which laid the foundation for universally accessible public services. For example, a resolution inspired by the social reform Congress in 1917 read, '*the necessity, justice and righteousness of removing all the disabilities imposed by religion and caste upon the depressed classes ... Those disabilities being of most vexatious and oppressive character, subjecting those classes to considerable hardship and inconvenience by prohibiting them from admission into public schools, hospitals, courts of justice and public offices and the use of public wells, etc'* (cited in Jaffrelot 2003, 14). Similar fights were waged on the right of women to access schools, hospitals, and other amenities without which it is inconceivable that today's governments will seek to put in place broad-based public services that are available for all.

While reform movements had a footprint in most parts of India, they were particularly influential in some regions for a sustained period of time. I argued earlier that Tamil Nadu was one such state. Another region in which social reform movements had an impact was Kerala (Aiyappan 1965; Desai 2005; Mathew 1999; R. Jeffrey 2001). In the early 1800s, Kerala was known for some of the worst forms of caste- based unfreedoms in India. Reform movements in Kerala challenged these practices successfully, resulting in a remarkable transformation of the society. Communities from the relatively dominant Nairs to the highly oppressed Dalits created their own organizations to spearhead social reform. In addition, they started service organizations in a large scale. These movements created pressure on the princes that ruled the Travancore and Cochin areas of Kerala to expand services and to open them for all communities.

While there was a relatively clear agenda to obtain greater freedoms for people of lower castes, the agenda for women's freedoms was more complex. The critique of the gender conservative church led to decreasing freedoms for women in the social space, and it also led to the breakdown of the matrilineal system of this community. At the same time, there was also a demand for women to become teachers and to enter other professions and the presence of women in these services made them more accessible to women. The presence of women leaders including two Maharanis (who held brief tenures in Travancore), a woman surgeon, women teachers who mobilized their communities, and others served as examples of what educated women could achieve and how they could contribute to family income. This created a powerful argument for women's education, and for their entry into a range of services. It is not surprising that by independence, Kerala also had the largest cadre of women teachers and health professionals, far surpassing other parts of India (R. Jeffrey 1976; R. Jeffrey 2001).

By independence, Kerala also had the most impressive record in education, health care, food programmes and other services, while undergoing a remarkable transformation in social relations in the region that enabled most groups to access these services. This transformation in turn has influenced Kerala's politics in a democratic context, wherein elected governments have been forced to expand services and make them universally available. It is important to remember that the communist movement of Kerala was in its third decade at India's independence, and while it was becoming a significant force, Kerala's achievements at this time could not be attributed to the communist movement. The agenda for public services was created mainly by social reform movements, and it is the success of the reform movements that forced the communist movement to make services a part of its agenda.

The impact of reform movements in creating a commitment to services varied in other regions depending on how central services were to the movement's vision in that region; not all reform movements were service-oriented. It also depended on whether they had a sustained presence without much competition from alternate ideological movements. Within the reform movements, there were considerable differences in the service orientation, and thus, even in some areas where reform movements were prominent, they did not contribute to the public service agenda. While protestant missionaries Arya Samaj, Ramakrishna Mission, SNDP and a few others were highly engaged in providing services, others prioritized religious issues or focussed on narrow slices of the *women's question* that paid attention to services focussed on upper Caste Hindu widows.

Christophe Jaffrelot argued in *India's Silent Revolution* (Jaffrelot 2003) that the reform agenda of prominent movements differed substantially in their content between North and South India. He argued that reform movements of the South, especially the Dalit movement led by Ambedkar and the Dravidian movement, were radical in their agenda while the prominent movements of North India situated themselves within the religious framework, and thus were not radical in their demands for social change. I disagree with his reasoning that reform movements of North India did not develop a radical content due to their engagement with religion, given the fact that there are many cases in which religious movements have been radical in their demands. That said, there is no doubt that the reform movements of South India were far more radical in their demand for social transformation, whereas the prominent North Indian counterparts of this time sought to preserve several social distinctions and did not call for far-reaching change. The radical content of the Dravidian movement among others played a critical role in demanding that the government should provide certain services *to all* in order to ensure that the domination between communities comes to an end. The lack of similar radicalness among the Samajist or by Gandhi led to a weak critique on government policies and institutions. Even when they had a service orientation, they did not demand that the governments provide universally available services. This distinction is critical. One thus finds radical service-oriented reform movements in the South, while there were strong service-oriented movements without a radical touch in places like Punjab and Bengal.

In addition to the absence of a radical touch, reform movements were not dominant for a sustained period in most of these states. Tamil Nadu and Kerala were important exceptions wherein reform movements dominated for decades, and were successful in influencing the agenda of the movements that followed. They have thus had a lasting impact in setting social priorities in the post-independence era when administration expanded rapidly. In other areas such as the North East, Bengal, Maharashtra, and Punjab, reform movements became powerful but faced intense contests in determining social priorities from other movements.

For example, reform movements in the North East[5] were powerful until the 1940s, and thus were able to make a case for public services for several decades. India's independence created a sense of threat that the local culture could be undermined by the mainland which resulted in ethnic movements that became dominant by the 1960s with an emphasis on issues like autonomy. In Bengal, the powerful Brahmo Samaj declined towards the end of the nineteenth century. By the time the communists came to power, the reform movement had ceased to be a force and thus had no influence on the class-agenda of the communist coalition. In the West, Tilak challenged the reform movements of Maharashtra by arguing that political reforms should take precedence over social reform. Thus, despite the fact that Maharashtra had some of the most impressive reformers including Ranade, Phule, and Ambedkar, they had to share the social space with the strident Nationalist movement that diluted their agenda (Pandit 1979). The reform movements of Punjab (Juergensmeyer 1982) faced stiff competition from peasant mobilization with the support of the colonial government, a militant left movement and different shades of religious cleavages.[6] Social reform did not attain the same level of prominence in other parts of India, even though there have been some such movements in most parts. Since the mid-nineteenth century, there have been some reform movements in the Hindi heartland states such as the Triveni Sang of Bihar, Ravidasis of Uttar Pradesh, new manifestations of Sufism in Rajasthan and Madhya Pradesh. While these movements have made substantial contributions, they have never been dominant in their regions.

To sum up, reform movements with a radical touch were much more prevalent in South India, and they were successful in fostering a remarkable social transformation in Tamil Nadu and Kerala. As a result they were able to make a powerful argument for the state governments in independent India to provide basic public services extensively with the view of reaching the most marginalized communities. Reform movements had a substantial presence but lacked the radical touch and thus had a more limited impact in the North East, Punjab, and Bengal. This helps us to understand not only how reform movements helped create an agenda for public services, but also why they had a differential impact in different parts of India. Even though reform movements per se have ceased to be powerful in most parts of India, these ideas have been carried forward by other movements that became powerful in the regions of their influence. Dravidian and caste movements absorbed some of that agenda in Tamil Nadu and the vision has been accepted by all the major movements of Kerala including the communist movement. Thus the vision of the movement has been sustained even when the movement itself ceased to be influential.

Unmediated grassroots pressure
and 'populist politics'

While the large social movements created an agenda for services in Tamil Nadu, it is day to day demands for services at the grassroots that created the greatest thrust in recent decades. In the context of growing political competition, leaders such as MGR found it expedient to expand services dramatically as a way of sustaining support. Given sustained grassroots pressure, services have been expanded by other chief ministers of Tamil Nadu as well. As in Tamil Nadu, some of the most impressive instances of expanding services occurred through chief ministers who did not have rigid ideological leanings and were open to democratic demands from the grassroots. In many instances this was used as a strategy to gain new bases of support, going beyond the traditionally dominant families or a strong party organization capable of mobilizing support. Such a circumstance forced such Chief Ministers to appeal directly to common people based on popular aspirations in order to win elections. In the academic literature and media, such leaders have been labelled as *populists*, and it has been argued that populism leads to the expansion of services.

Despite the wide use of the term, 'populism' is analytically unhelpful as John Harris points out:

> [Populism] is one of those terms which is widely but loosely used and perhaps little understood, so that some scholars have been led to question its value altogether for political analysis. It is rather confusing when the same term is applied to a farmers' movement in the US in the late nineteenth century, to a movement which was in opposition to the Bolsheviks in Russia at around the same time, to a regime like that of Peron in Argentina, which involved a form of corporatism, and to a political leader such as MGR. Populism, indeed, is not an established political philosophy like socialism or liberalism or even fascism, associated with particular programmatic texts. (Harriss 2001)

What is common among populist leaders is that they appeal to the common person as part of their core political strategy, but as Harris points out, there is little reason to believe that this will translate into any particular set of policy prescriptions, including the demand for public services.

In the Indian case, it is productive to move away from populism as the analytical framework in order to understand why leaders like MGR and NTR promised services as a way of gathering political support. What is common between so-called populist leaders of India is that they all struggled to win elections when they did not have adequate support from the dominant families or powerful party organizations needed to mobilize votes. Indira Gandhi had broken off from the party organization and she never built the party to use it for mobilization. MGR and NTR were founding new parties, and were confronted with weak organizations. Nitish Kumar and Y S Rajasekara Reddy, among others sought to secure the votes of social groups that were no longer under the control of dominant local families that once provided the backbone for mobilization. In the absence of any organized or network to reach voters, they had to appeal to people's sensibilities directly, which could not be done without paying close attention to people's aspirations.

As I argued earlier, a lot of grassroots demands and public action are based on localized demands, and in general, is rarely oriented towards abstract policies. For example, despite the fact that globalization and liberalization have been at the forefront of debates at the national level, very few people have heard of these terms and have little idea of what they represent (Mooij 2005). People relate to political priorities that have a concrete and direct impact–and among them, services enjoy tremendous democratic popularity today. In cases where voices from the ground are able to penetrate the corridors of power without mediation, they have an impact on creating a political commitment for services.

The fact that such policies do not stem from powerful ideological frameworks has made it easy for commentators from the left and right to talk of such policies derisively, even if they have broad democratic support. To take an example, MGR's effort at expanding school feeding and other nutrition support programmes were roundly criticized by the left and the right through his lifetime, and it is only recently that some of his programmes have started gaining legitimacy thanks to the influence of rights-based campaigns. While strongly ideological organizations have criticized the expansion of nutrition support, these measures enjoyed tremendous democratic support. It would have been inconceivable that MGR continued to be elected through his lifetime against competition from the Congress and the strong DMK in Tamil Nadu without this support.

Taking a cue from MGR, many other politicians have made food support an important part of the political plank. The other icon who got immense political support by the promise of highly subsidized rice through the PDS was N.T. Rama Rao (NTR). Like MGR, NTR also realized that he got tremendous support from women voters, and this spurred the expansion of women's self-help groups in the state. After his party, the TDP, abandoned the popular plank, it was taken up by its main rival in Andhra, the Congress under the leadership of Y S Rajasekara Reddy (YSR). YSR used the strategy of sustaining support by massively expanding programmes such as the NREGA, health, pensions and other public services that made him an icon with popular support even after his untimely death in a helicopter crash. Similarly Nitish Kumar's popularity in Bihar and Raman Singh's popularity in Chhattisgarh also owe much to promoting certain services in their states.

Providing work during times of distress, meagre pensions, subsidized food, and other simple forms of support mean a lot for people who have little to fall back upon, and the tremendous support base of politicians like YSR, MGR, and NTR points to the fact that they were able to make a substantial difference in the lives of many through the expansion of public services. In recognition of this, politicians who have a record of expanding public services with the commitment to reaching a large number of people have generally been able to get sustained political support, and have often been re-elected with significant majorities.

Given the fact that there are very few cases in which politicians with a good record in expanding public services have not managed at least one successful re-election,[7] what is really interesting is why public services did not become a more integral part of the political agenda in India. The answer to this question lies in the fact that common people have not had a strong voice in government given the sharp inequalities. Thanks to social dominance, public action by the common person was rare and the elite also had the opportunity to quash or ignore it. In this context, the voice of the common person was not felt in the corridors of power. With the breakdown of dominance, this voice of is more readily heard in power centres, and it has created a greater thrust for delivering services.

An interesting corollary of this is women's votes. The traditional approach to securing votes was through appeals to dominant families, caste leaders, and ultimately to families. Some of the politicians described above sought to create a support base among women without the mediating influence of the family or caste. The dominant method of doing so has been to promise services of greatest concern to women. These include education, nutrition support, social security, water, and other basic services that matter to women's lives and their families. Some governments have expanded micro credit for women's self-help groups precisely with this intention. Governments have also sought to make existing services more amenable to women by appointing more women workers in services, and by creating safe spaces (such as ladies' special buses). Services have been so central to securing women's support that we find very few alternative approaches which appeal to this constituency in India.

Accessing services in most parts of India has required struggles on the part of the local communities even when budgets and resources have been allocated from the top. Thus, without assertion from the grassroots, mere attempts by chief ministers or other top politicians and bureaucrats will have little chance of reaching people in the first place–and thus cannot become a part of a strategy to win political support. In the context of persisting dominance, such programmes do not get created or they can get hijacked by the elite. This has been the dominant history in India and this explains why services have not been used as a political strategy more widely despite their popularity.

This also explains why regions with earlier social transformation were more committed to services. South India with its early history of social transformation thus has a better record with these services. Similarly, the expansion of services in Himachal Pradesh happened in a context of relatively greater gender equality (Citizens' Initiative for the Rights of Children Under Six

2006; Drèze and Sen 2002; Planning Commission 2001), and also following the breakdown of oppressive labour practices (Negi 1995). Social transformation is now happening in a set of other states, especially in the Hindi heartland. Given the fact that major ideological movements of this region, including communism and socialism, have started waning, unmediated voices are reflected more directly in governance resulting in the improvement of public service delivery in states like Andhra Pradesh, Bihar, Chhattisgarh, and others.

Socio-economic rights movements

While Tamil Nadu's experience can give us insights into understanding how reform movements and grassroots pressure have both created public support for services elsewhere in India, there have been other ideological sources of support that have not resonated in Tamil Nadu. Prominent among them are the socio-economic rights movements which started becoming influential in the 1980s. These movements arose in an environment in which an assortment of services existed but they did not reach large sections of the population. By using the language of rights, these movements advocated the expansion of services in a way that anyone who desires it will be able to avail of it. It also makes the state the ultimate duty bearer who should step in to provide when people are unable to avail it through other sources for any reason.

The earliest instance of discussing a public service as a right in India goes back to the late nineteenth century when education was discussed as a right, inspired by the passage of the Elementary Education Act in Britain in 1870. This led to an impetus to create right to education laws in different provinces in the early 1900s, but most of these laws were weak, partly due to the belief that the state did not have the capacity to fulfill this and other rights. This attitude also shaped the drafting of the farsighted Constitution of India. Based on the idea that socio-economic rights are highly desirable but may not be feasible immediately, the framers adopted a set of *directive principles*, following the Irish constitution. Unlike rights, directive principles are not legally binding, but the framers hoped that they would provide a guideline for governance.

Until the 1970s, there was no serious example of a public service with an embedded right, but since then, there has been an expansion in creating concrete legal entitlements around issues such as employment, education, nutrition, child care, and health. The earliest programme in the rights mode was Maharashtra's innovative *Employment Guarantee Scheme* (MEGS) that guaranteed unskilled manual employment upon demand to any of its rural residents. This is perhaps one of the most ambitious programmes based on a legal guarantee in any state.[8] After a two decade gap, another such programme was initiated in the form of the *Education Guarantee Scheme* of Madhya Pradesh.[9] This scheme guaranteed that any habitation without school facilities will be provided with a school within a month of demand by the inhabitants. This scheme has been criticized rightly for extending ill-equipped schools; while there is merit to that argument, there is no doubt that EGS increased schooling significantly in Madhya Pradesh and there is evidence that these schools have performed on par with the regular schools in terms of children's basic skills. These are the only two notable rights-based schemes created by state governments.

When it comes to socio-economic rights, the Government of India did not have a direct role in the original draft of the constitution since health, education, rural roads, and most other subjects were the preserve of the state governments. But due to a variety of reasons, including the fact that state government finances were not increasing rapidly, the GoI has been playing an increasingly active role in socio-economic issues. The first major impetus for the GoI to take up a programme in the rights mode came with the Unnikrishnan judgement by the Supreme Court of India,[10] in which the court declared that the government has the duty to extend education to all by a creative reading of the directive principles with the fundamental right to life in the Indian constitution. The judgement provided a major impetus to right to education campaigns in India. Pressure from these groups led to an amendment of the Indian Constitution making education a fundamental right in the Constitution itself. The amendment was introduced in 1997 but it was not passed until 2005.

Pressure from right to education campaigns has been critical to an increase in education spending by the GoI, and to a renewed political commitment to expanding education for all, which has led to a major expansion of schooling in India over the last two decades. Along with this, other campaigns such as the Right to Food Campaign (RFC) and campaigns for the rights of disabled people have been shaping education laws and policies over the last two decades. The RFC led to the rapid expansion of school feeding in India starting in 2002 and groups working on disability have been trying to ensure that the school infrastructure is accessible to people with differing abilities. Free lunch at school is now a reality in all government schools, and it is also widely implemented in government -assisted schools.

Another landmark programme in the rights mode by the GoI is the NREGA, which was inspired by the MEGS. Along with the NREGA, there has been pressure on the government to undertake other food programmes in the rights mode including early child-hood care, old age income support, and other forms of support for people vulnerable to hunger. Many of these became legal rights in November 2001 through a direction by the Supreme Court of India, some of which were consolidated through the Food Security Bill passed by the Parliament of India in 2013.

The impact of the rights-based campaigns go well beyond the handful of laws creating legally backed entitlements. Rights-based arguments are now prominent in fields such as housing and health even when they are not codified legally. By evaluating policies from the framework of a right, campaigns have been able to frame a line of critique on what the budgets and rules should be for a variety of policies–and even when they are not followed, such critique has an impact on the direction of the budgets and policies. These campaigns cover a wide array of subjects includ-ing land, housing, education, nutrition, health, child care, liveli-hood, care for the aged, and other issues that are fundamental to people's well-being. The ideas of these campaigns may have a large impact on policy making in India in the years to come. There are no regional trends within India when it comes to creating legal entitlements around public services and the strongest thrust of the movement has been to create legal entitlements through nation-al legislation. Since these programmes are implemented at the state level, there are marked regional differences in how they are implemented, and public action has made a difference in converting legal entitlements into a practical reality.[11]

Other ideas and ideologies

Reform movements, unmediated voices, and rights-based movements have been among the three most important sources of support for services as a means of development. While these three are by far the most important sources of support, some vision for public services can also be found in other ideologies. As I mentioned above, some prominent identity movements have absorbed their vision from reform movements. Identity movements among historically oppressed communities had the tangible benefit of removing restrictions in accessing services even when other issues such as dignity or reservation policy have been at the heart of these movements.

Another source of support has been regional movements. In many cases regional identity became politically salient around questions of culture. For example, the threat of ethnic identities being marginalized by mainland India provided the impetus for mobilization in India's North East immediately after independence. Questions of justice including armed repression became salient subsequently. In other regional movements, cultural affinity was much less of a concern compared to socio-economic concerns. A powerful illustration of this in the recent past is the Telangana movement which demanded separation of the Telangana region from the state of Andhra Pradesh. This movement argued that the coastal districts of Andhra got a disproportionate share of benefits through the state, and only a separation from Andhra Pradesh would enable the people of the Telangana region to get the benefits of state programmes. This kind of a perceived injustice based on a regional identity has been a powerful factor for mobilization in many parts of India, and it started immediately upon independence.

Politics based on regional identity lends itself to demands for a separate nation, state or greater autonomy from the central government. Such demands have led to the division of states, the creation of new districts, and other arrangements to increase the range of issues over which the regional group has self-governance. While autonomy is the prime demand of regional movements, the need for self-governance has to be articulated in terms of what they wish to do with it, and this discussion tends to create a social consensus on an agenda for the government, which can be substantially different in each case. To take some examples, the socialist ideology of the NC leaders combined with the political exigency of a large Muslim population that worked under predominantly Hindu landlords led to the demand for land reforms in Kashmir early on. This is a rare case of identity politics demanding a class solution. The demand for statehood in Himachal Pradesh was made on the premise that people's aspiration for 'development' was not being met effectively since the central government, which governed this region, was far removed from the concerns of Himachal Pradesh. In this case, the movement led by Virbadhra Singh articulated a vision in which the government could play an active role in creating public services such as roads, electricity, and schooling for the development of the state. The division of Assam as well as the creation of Jharkhand, Chhattisgarh, and Uttarakhand were based on tribal identities and the demand for self-rule, in which cultural issues and economic oppression were both important. In some cases, the preservation of the tribal way of life became the dominant concern, while at least in Jharkhand and Chhattisgarh, the dominance of tribal people by outsiders was an important motivating factor. Among these cases, it is fairly clear that the mobilization for statehood in Himachal Pradesh in the 1960s had an impact in creating a social commitment for public services, and the state has seen one of the most impressive expansions of services since it was granted statehood in 1971.

Similarly, women's movements have also been champions of services, and have contributed to the agenda in two major ways. They have been an important voice in demanding health services, expansion of education, child care programmes, and other services. This is not surprising since women are very closely engaged with public services for children, and a basic service such as water has huge consequences for their lives —after all, it is women who traditionally had to walk a long distance and fetch water for the household.[12] The second critical contribution has been the introduction of gender element in public services delivery. For example, without the efforts of women's movements from the nineteenth century onwards, it is inconceivable that the schooling rates of girl children would slowly catch up with that of boys, as is happening state by state today. Women's movements have played a critical role in demanding that women have equal access to services, in ensuring that public services cater to women's special-needs, and also by incorporating women as service providers. All of these have had consequences for women's access to services.

I have argued so far that identity movements that were based on some form of perceived historical injustice tended to focus on inequality by design, and in the process they tend to create a social commitment for redressing these grievances. In some cases, redressing grievances involved a massive expansion of public services and the removal of restrictions on access. I argued that movements of lower caste people, some regional movements, and women's movements have all contributed to creating a commitment for public services. In discussing the impact of identity movements, it is important to recognize that not all identity movements focus on inequalities and unfreedoms suffered by the community in question. Many identity movements have been led by dominant communities based on concerns that were important to them. Such movements tend to protect privilege and so they undermine discussions on human unfreedoms and inequalities—and thus undermine the effort at creating a social commitment to address them.

Such movements have sought to preserve unequal privileges either directly or indirectly. The notorious Senas of the Rajputs and Bhumihar Brahmins of North India have become a force for the historical privilege enjoyed by these caste groups. These Senas have quashed dissent and attempts by lower caste communities to assert themselves, and thus, they sustained the unfreedoms of these communities directly. Other movements with a strong social base of supporters from the dominant communities have taken an indirect approach to undermine challenges by appealing to religious or national identities which can overwhelm the discussions on inequalities and unfreedoms in the society.

Identity politics of this sort has recourse to cultural toolkits that help with making nationalism or divisive politics the salient political issue. These include highlighting conflicts between communities or nations, orchestrating violence, shows of chauvinism and the relentless focus on divisive symbols as a way of dominating the discursive space with that agenda. By drawing attention to some common 'enemy', such discourses are able to make it difficult for oppressed communities to raise their issues and thus create the demand for remedying their grievances. The most prominent of such issues has been the Hindu-Muslim divide in parts of India which has enabled the elite of both these religions to undermine movements for social justice within them.

While caste and other forms of inequalities became the dominant idiom in South India as early as 1920, Hindu-Muslim cleavage was the most prominent aspect of politics until the 1990s in North India. It is not that caste was not at the centre of politics in these states. Party tickets for contesting in elections, appointments of chief ministers and selection of people for jobs and for popular bureaucratic positions have happened on the basis of careful caste calculations, except that these were the preserve of certain elite castes in each region. While the politics of appointments and of power were based on caste calculus, culturally salient issues have been about religious cleavages, which is helpful in sustaining the politics of upper caste dominance. By making religion, rather than people of a religion, the main focus of cultural debates, North India was unable to create public debates that were supportive of progressive change.

No discussion of agenda-setting movements in India can be complete without discussing communist movements and neo-liberalism. The link between communist movements and services is complex and so I will treat it separately below. As far as the neo-liberal vision for India is concerned it has been consistently criticized for undermining public services in favour of minimizing the role of the government. This core agenda had its side note, often labelled as 'reforms with a human face'. Human capital theorists among others had created a space in the mainstream economic thinking for 'investment' in education, based on the argument that investment in basic education provided high returns.[13] There has also been support for public interventions in public health and minimal social security in mainstream economic thinking of the era. Based on this ideology, organizations like the World Bank have supported increased funding for education. While there were differences in the vision for education, both camps tended to support increased funding at least for basic primary education.

The World Bank and other multilateral agencies have also played a role in some areas of health policy, early childhood nutrition and education, sanitation, access to water, and other services. But the vision of multilateral agencies with a strong neoliberal agenda has differed sharply from that of the rights-based campaigns on the extent of commitment that the state should have, and also the range of services that the state should create. While there has been some support for expanding state commitment to public services among neoliberal ideologues, the support is circumscribed based on a deep ideological mistrust against the state and its ability to deliver efficiently, not to mention an uneasy relationship between economics with questions of justice.

The support for the market along with a deep suspicion of state's ability to deliver has resulted in a specific vision for public services. There is on one hand a commitment to expand education, health, and social security. At the same time, there is a strong argument that this has to be limited by 'targeting' the poor. Unlike the rights-based campaigns that put a priority on reaching everybody, the neoliberal commitment has a sharp eye on the fiscal deficit and government expenditure in general. In education, there is thus a strong pressure to undermine state funding for higher education and to focus on lower primary education. In the health sector, much attention and finances have gone into creating 'vertical programmes' that target specific health issues such as tuberculosis, malaria, polio, and other dreadful diseases but without creating a public health system that is capable of addressing a multiplicity of basic health needs. The support for social security has been nominal at best.

An apt symbol of the neoliberal vision for social security and its contest with democratic aspirations is the PDS. Based on pressure from the World Bank, the GoI changed its policy of broad-based food support to a targeted system called the Targeted Public Distribution System (TPDS). This led to the division of the population into those above and below the poverty line (BPL), with only the BPL families being eligible for food support. Targeting based on a draconian definition of poverty combined with highly ineffective means of identifying families living in poverty has led to continued opposition to the TPDS system since its inception in 1997. States like Tamil Nadu and Andhra Pradesh, where the PDS has broad political support, quickly abandoned targeting or relaxed the draconian poverty standards, in effect expanding the PDS. This has since been followed by many other states such as Chhattisgarh, Kerala, and Himachal Pradesh where food support has become a political priority (Khera 2011a). The space that the technocrats sought to carve for themselves was eroded by democratic forces, and it is likely that it will continue as socio-political transformations deepen.

Communist movements and class critique[14]

Ideologically speaking, there has been no influence comparable to that of communist movements in India. The struggles of Russia at the end of the First World War, and the revolution of 1919 captured the imagination of many intellectuals in India. Since then, various shades of communist ideologies have shaped every conceivable public debate in the country. The movement has had an impact on policies not just directly through communist governments, but also indirectly through the influence of communist ideas over other parties and among public intellectuals. 'Communism' does not represent a single body of well-articulated ideas in India, and there are substantial differences in the vision and strategy of different communist movements. Dealing with the entirety of it would require a separate book in itself. In this case, I have taken up the limited task of trying to assess the influence of the movement in creating a commitment for public services in India, while ignoring other aspects of its rich history.

A useful starting point for this discussion would be the experience of Kerala, which saw the first elected communist government, not just in India, but in the world. Many scholars have argued that the exceptional performance of Kerala in providing public services can be attributed to communist influence. Considering that the communists have been at the forefront of progressive politics in the state, this idea sounds credible at the outset. Upon closer examination, this idea is problematic because if the influence of the communists is what led to the priority for public services in Kerala, it is surprising that West Bengal, where the Communists have been in power for a much longer time, has a poor record with respect to public services. The key to understanding the paradoxical outcomes is that public services have not been a part of the ideological core of the communist parties. The focus instead has been on a narrow, yet important, class agenda based on property and labour rights. The core ideology traces all societal problems to the way property and production relations are organized, and it offers communalization of property, redistribution of property to the worker, and labour rights as solutions to these problems. In a situation where complete abolition of private property was not feasible, the core demands have been for expansion of public production, abolition and redistribution of large property and expansion of the rights of labourers. In the rural context, this meant support for abolition of Zamindari lands, redistribution of land to farmers and gaining better returns for tenants and labourers. The fundamental cultural project of communism was to reframe all problems discussed by people through the class lens, and in the process, offer class solutions for all problems. Thus, when education, hunger or other issues were taken up, these were used to frame the need for a radical change in the regime of property rights, rather than to frame a demand for public services. It is thus not surprising that public services did not become a policy priority in West Bengal where the communists were in power for over three decades.

As I argued before, public services became a priority in Kerala as a result of social reform movements in specific princely states. Education, food support, and health were already important political issues in Kerala by the time the communist movement started in the 1920s. Social reform movements had started ushering in a major change in the social structure by breaking down the strict caste hierarchy, and services were seen as the key to social reform.

The reform movements also provided the initial cadres and orga-nizational framework through which communism grew in Kerala, and communist activists borrowed some of the repertoires of their predecessors. For example, the party used a strategy of creating libraries and organizing education for the illiterate as a mobilizing strategy during its period of growth. During World War II it was active in organizing food committees and campaigned for state-led food distribution to address the food shortages of that period. The party thus engaged with issues outside the classic class agenda even in its early stages, and it would have been impossible for the movement to grow without addressing the issues that were already salient in the society. Thus, the public service agenda was thrust on the communists in a way that they could only ignore it to their peril.

The Kerala experience, in other words, is not just a result of the strength of the communists; it is also a result of their vul-nerability. Unlike in Bengal, communists were in power in Kerala for much shorter durations, and the social space in Kerala was highly contested by different social movements. Since indepen-dence the communists fought consistently for political power in Kerala, coming to power several times, but also losing power to the Congress regularly. By 1980, when the Kerala model of develop-ment was well established, the Communist governments had been in power for only a little over half the duration since Kerala was established. The Congress and the other non-communist groups were conscious of the extensive political support and legitimacy that the communists enjoyed and, as in Tamil Nadu, these parties had to offer an alternative set of policies to gain support. Services had become a major social priority and these parties were able to gain public support by providing them extensively. Thus, even the policies that were put in place by the Congress-led governments of Kerala have to be understood within the context of the trenchant class-critique of the communists.

The experience of Kerala and Tamil Nadu cannot be understood without accounting for the confluence of social movements that took place in these regions, each shaping the other. Unlike these states, cultural dominance of the communists was institutional-ized effectively in West Bengal, which stifled the space to form other agendas. The cultural dominance and stable tenure of the communists enabled them to take up land reforms, extensive unionization, and other aspects of the core class agenda, within the rubric of the Indian Constitution. In the absence of other competing social movements or political parties with different ideologies, communists in West Bengal did not face the same intense pressure as did their Kerala counterparts in extending public services or taking up other policy measures that enjoyed wide public legitimacy.

The strong ideological party organization may have helped the party to achieve substantial land reforms. But the same party organization and institutionalized cultural dominance has made it difficult for the party to go beyond the core agenda. Even leaders with a long record of service within the party have struggled with articulating new ideas, and thus have never found the space to discuss an alternate agenda, which is a prerequisite for creating public support for it. The party was also insulated in West Bengal from external critique which was stifled by the immense intellectual machinery of the movement. In this atmosphere, it is ironic yet understandable, that the recent defeat of the left coalition of West Bengal was accomplished by using a class critique against communist parties.

Left Parties have not come to power in states other than Kerala, West Bengal, and Tripura but they have had a presence as in Tamil Nadu. Through this presence they have been able to shape policy priorities in other states, without being able to dominate the agenda setting process. Such a presence has led to impressive policy measures in different parts of India. For example, the path-breaking Employment Guarantee Scheme of Maharashtra was legislated when the minority Congress government depended on the support of left parties for its survival in the state in the late 1970s (Jadhav 2006). Nationally, the most ambitious programmes to expand public services were legislated during the first United Progressive Alliance government (UPA) (1999–2004). Just as in Maharashtra in the 1970s, the UPA government was led by the Congress Party, which did not have a majority in the Lok Sabha and it was supported by the Left Parties who then had the largest number of MPs in their history in the Lok Sabha. The relatively lacklustre performance of the second UPA government on social policy followed the exit of the Left from the coalition.

Since the 1980s, the communists have taken up more campaigns on public services moving away from classic class agenda. Unions, women's organizations, and other bodies affiliated with the parties have been active in mobilizing around public services, and the parties have also been major supporters of laws and policies related to services in the Parliament of India. Communist parties have lent critical support in the parliament to campaigns on the right to education, the NREGA, the right to information, the food security bill, public health, and the universalization of the PDS. The engagement of the communist parties has thus varied with time and space, with more attention being given to public services in recent decades. They took different stands in Kerala which had strong alternate movements, than in West Bengal where they were in power unchallenged for decades, and in the parliament where they functioned as an opposition. This diversity in positions was best represented in an ironic moment in the late 1990s when the Left Parties were offering tremendous support in the Parliament to make education a fundamental right, while the same parties in power in West Bengal had not appointed a single teacher for more than five years–despite a weak record of schooling in the state.[15]

To summarize, when it comes to commitment to services, the contribution of the communists was to provide a class critique that forced other parties to ensure that they extended the services to the underclass. Ensuring universal availability of services gave other parties a legitimate agenda, and it also protected them from the critique that these services were being created only for the elite. In other words, while the communists cannot be credited with making public services an agenda, they played a critical role in ensuring that the services were offered in a more extensively in places where public services were already in the policy agenda.

Regional impact

So far, I have been looking at different agenda setting movements that have been powerful in India with some sense of the regional prevalence of these movements. Let me now map this more clearly to states that have been consistently good, moderate, or poor performers with respect to public services, starting with the most impressive performers: Kerala, Tamil Nadu, and Himachal Pradesh. Among the three, Kerala and Tamil Nadu had similar beginnings and trajectories. Both states started with high levels of civic unfreedoms based on caste, though Kerala had a stronger history of women's freedoms. A number of different social movements became powerful simultaneously in both states and it was the culmination of their ideas that resulted in the public service agenda.

The key drivers of this demand were strong social reform movements in which lower caste people played significant leadership positions themselves. Both states also achieved remarkable social transformation that has led to a much greater participation of the common person in politics. Both Kerala and Tamil Nadu are known for high levels of political awareness among the population, highly entrenched political cultures, multiple forms through which people can mobilize, and also a closeness of the political classes with the common person. These factors ensure that the voice of the common person is more readily heard in the corridors of power. All of these factors are conducive to making public services a social priority. While Kerala and Tamil Nadu have seen some amount of Hindu-Muslim politics, it has only been marginal in the politics of these states. In other words, caste and class, with their inherent focus on historic disadvantage, have been the focus of political action which is more conducive to progressive change. Finally, both states did not fall prey to large scale violence–either by social movements or by the state–that inevitably turns the attention of the society to human right abuses and other issues. Thus, Kerala and Tamil Nadu have had a combination of factors that were favourable for an agenda of public services, and these have not been superseded by the intensity of other issues within the society.

Unlike Kerala or Tamil Nadu, Himachal Pradesh did not have the same level of caste-based unfreedoms that led to a strong focus on civil rights during the colonial era. Instead, there were extensive campaigns on forced labour and the forced sale of commodities at a low price to the rulers—called *Begar* and *Beth* (Negi 1995).

A large part of what is Himachal Pradesh today was under princely states, and so the campaign against *Begar* and *Beth* quickly
translated into a demand for self-rule. In the initial phases, the
campaign was for absorption into the Indian Dominion, later
it transformed into a demand for statehood rather than being a
union territory under the direct control of New Delhi. Himachal
Pradesh also had a set of social reform movements, some of which
demanded greater literacy and education. It was also influenced
by the Gadar movement of Punjab with its strong left leanings,
though no communist movement became powerful in this region.
In that sense, Himachal Pradesh had a confluence of movements
with none dominating the social space. As I mentioned above,
Himachal Pradesh started with a higher level of social equality
and in particular women's freedoms that typically enables people
to have a voice in the scheme of governance. This was articulated
during the movement for statehood in Himachal Pradesh and created a social consensus that an important duty of the state would
be to provide services extensively.

Some of these enabling conditions were present in the moderate performers in the South, West and Northeast of India. Many of
these states did not start with the same kind of civic unfreedoms as
in Kerala or Tamil Nadu, and the North-east in particular is known
to be a relatively egalitarian region. But unlike the South, some of
the Western states including Punjab are known for greater levels of
gender disparity. These factors have an influence on how responsive politics is to the common person. For example, states like
Andhra Pradesh and Karnataka have had extended periods with
politicians who were highly responsive to popular demands. These
politicians have made significant expansions to public services during their tenures. There are also examples of popular movements
displacing established parties from power, such as the student's
movement that captured power in 1978 in Assam or the communist movement that has consistently been successful in Tripura.
There have been many episodes across these states of governments
being highly responsive to popular aspirations, but it has not been
as sustained as it has been in the southern end of the country. It
takes several years to roll out a high quality programme, and the
high performers have been consistent in creating new programmes

over decades. This gave them an edge over the moderate performers who have rolled out impressive services, but not on a consistent basis across all tenures.

Most of these states had their share of social reform movements that brought an emphasis on services. Among them, Maharashtra has a particularly impressive history with leaders like Ambedkar, Ranade, and Phule. Along with Maharashtra, Bengal was the seat of early reform movements led by people like Raja Ram Mohun Roy and Rabindranath Tagore. Many of the north-eastern states too had impressive reform movements, and no student movement in India has been as powerful as in this region. While the reform movements, student movements, and the relatively low levels of caste-based dominance in this region created a ground for demanding public services, almost all of the states have also been witness to other powerful agenda setting movements that have diverted attention to issues such as agricultural investments, land reform, Hindu nationalism, political reform over social reform, separatism, and human rights abuses. In the recent years, neoliberal visions of development have also been powerful in states like Gujarat and Punjab.

States like Andhra Pradesh and Punjab have an impressive history of communist movements. In Andhra, many of the communist activists took arms, and the long history of armed revolt and violence by the state, had a consequence on agenda setting in the state. The communist movement was focused heavily on the capture of political power and on class agenda such as land reforms. Unlike in Kerala where the response of non-communist parties to the communist struggle was to roll out an alternate agenda for popular support, the response of the state in Andhra was to repress the armed revolt. It is important to remember that the communists of Kerala gave up arms in the 1950s and entered electoral politics, which created the space for other parties to create an agenda for governance that would gain electoral support. That was not required against the Naxal movement which was concerned with warfare more than in trying to secure popular support. It is only in recent years, with the success of suppressing the Naxal movement, that the state government in Andhra has been more conscious about extending public services as a way of securing greater support in once Naxal strongholds. In case of Punjab, the communist movement was contesting in the public space not with caste movements that had a greater focus on public services, but against landed farmers who had become a powerful force in the state from the middle of the nineteenth century under the colonial rule. As a result, wage struggles and other class issues became reinforced, and one of the responses of the elite to undermine the struggle was to make religious cleavage more dominant in the region.

Thus, some of the influences that have traditionally demanded public services have had a powerful presence in these states, but they had to compete with other strong agenda setting movements. The attention of the governments in these regions have thus been divided between public services and other issues, some of which have contributed to broad-based human well-being, while others have been divisive and destructive.

States that have been consistently poor performers such as Rajasthan, Madhya Pradesh, Orissa, Bihar, and Uttar Pradesh have been dominated by elite-led politics for a long time. The continued effective dominance of the elite in these regions made it difficult for the common person to have a strong voice in electoral politics. Reform movements have traditionally been weak in these regions, and those that existed did not take as radical tone as those in the South. Non-elite identity movements have become strong only in the recent two decades, much of their efforts have been spent on gaining political power and basic civil and political freedoms. It is only recently that these movements have shifted their attention strongly to public services, which has led to glimmers of hope in what has been a desolate region.

These states have also been dominated by politics over a range of other issues such as the Hindu Muslim cleavage, land and forest rights of tribal people, peasant movements against the Zamindari expropriation, and strident nationalism. Not only have these made it difficult for an agenda to emerge over public services, the situation has made it difficult for any progressive agenda to become salient. The dramatic social and political changes that have been happening in the region over the last few decades provide us with some measure of hope.

As I have maintained through this book, we cannot understand policy priorities only by looking at the framing of issues. It is also important for us to understand the nature of social domination and whether any agenda facing the common person could become salient at any given time. This offers an explanation as to why unmediated grassroots voices did not become salient or why movements with any progressive agenda did not become dominant in this region. I turn next to varying levels of domination across Indian states and how the voice of the common person is becoming more powerful across India, but at varying rates.

Notes

1. Given the fact that these movements were very powerful for nearly a century, there is a large body of literature on them. Here is a small selection of books that informed my thinking on social reforms: (Devarajan 1990; Juergensmeyer 1982; Natarajan 1959; Sen 2005; R. Jeffrey 2001; R. Jeffrey 1976; Roy 1998).

2. Oddie writes that there were some who argued that caste feeling should be increased to prevent a coordinated attack against the British Raj, but not all missionaries were wedded to the Raj, and they felt that undermining caste would help to spread Christianity.

3. This law was to ensure that Christian converts get a share of ancestral property.

4. Ambedkar was rightfully critical of Gandhi's limited commitment towards the Dalits, on which he wrote trenchant critiques (B. R. Ambedkar and Rodrigues 2002).

5. Karna (1998) provides a useful overview of prominent movements in this region.

6. Josh (1979) and Sharma (2010) offer some perspective of the context.

7. One example is the failure of Ashok Ghelot to get re-elected despite introducing school feeding and providing massive drought relief during the drought of 2002–03. While there is no doubt that the relief work of 2003 was massive, it came after several years of struggles around persistent drought in the state.

8. For more details about the scheme see Echeverri-Gent (1988, 1993), Mahendra Dev and Ranade (2001) and Ravallion (1991).

9. For a review of education guarantee scheme see Leclercq (2003).

10. See Supreme Court of India (1993).

11. Some of these are covered in Drèze (2004) and Khera (2011c).

12. This argument has been powerfully made by Drèze and by Sinha (Drèze and Sen 2002; Sinha 2014).

13. Right to education activists have challenged this approach by asking if a society should not expand education if it does not lead to higher economic growth. Education has a social significance that goes well beyond economic growth.

14. The following works shaped my understanding of the movement: (Athreya and Chunkath 1996; Athreya, Djurfeldt, and Lindberg 1990; Chandra 1983; Dasgupta 1973; Ganeshan 2003; Heller 1999; Josh 1979; Kohli 1983; Mallick 1994; Menon 1994; Sharma 2010; Sundarayya 1973). More importantly, I have had extended interactions with people engaged with different communist movements in CPM, CPI, various trade unions, women's organizations affiliated with left parties, former Naxals and one of the mediators between the state government and the Naxals in Andhra Pradesh.

15. The complete lack of appointments was due to a case in the High Court that had led to a stay on appointments. While this was a genuine problem for the government, it is important to remember that courts respond to governmental priorities. The fact that the case lingered for nearly seven years illustrated the low priority of education in the state, and the complete lack of pressure from the government on the court.

6

The Voice of the Common Person: India

I started this work by asking why there is a high level of public action in Tamil Nadu and went on to identify a set of conditions that enabled such action in this region. In this chapter, I will look at whether similar conditions could have shaped public action in other parts of India. Specifically, I propose to ask if there were systematic differences that could have enabled more widespread and effective public action in the good performers while the opposite held in states that have been traditionally poor performers in delivering services.

It is now well agreed that common people have a much greater voice in shaping politics and society than they did decades ago in most parts of the country. Scholars have discussed this phenomenon as a deepening of democracy, a transformation of rural authority, and even as a silent revolution that has profoundly changed social and political structures in India (Jaffrelot 2003; Mendelsohn 1993; Varshney 2000; Yadav 1999). It is also agreed that this transformation took place much earlier in states that were good performers in delivering services while the states with the poorest record in services were also the ones that were the slowest in achieving social transformation. In this chapter, I will review some of the dynamics that have influenced this change.

Profound social and political transformations need concerted efforts that last for decades. In this book, I have referred to such efforts as public action, which ranges from organized social movements and political parties to simple acts of resistance or disobedience. It is not uncommon for even the most oppressed groups to engage in some acts of resistance, but this comes at a great cost and with little chances of success. The essence of democratization lies in the increasing ability of such groups to engage in public action that enables them to shape political agenda and social arrangements. In other words, the deepening of India's democracy can be seen in terms of the changing conditions of public action for the common person.

The story of that change took a particular shape in Tamil Nadu. Engaging in public action was a dangerous act for most common people given the dominance of the elite over their lives. The elite controlled political offices, administration, land and other avenues of influence. Even though the lower class/caste population was numerically dominant, this could not translate into political power in the colonial context because only a few were permitted to vote and in any case, elected governments had little power under the colonial administration. This landscape changed in part due to mobilization by the great social movements which organized people, formed viable political parties and provided the support structure for public action. When adult franchise was introduced, prior mobilization enabled people to exercise their voice and this created the basis for sustained political competition. Competition in-turn made it imperative for serious aspirants to pay attention to people's demands. Prior organization, political competition, and other supportive conditions unleashed the decentralized public action that lies at the heart of Tamil Nadu's commitment to services. This mutually reinforcing feature of mobilization fostering political change and political conditions fostering public action could be found in other parts of India as well, often with similar results. But these changes have not taken place at the same rate, with the Hindi heartland in particular lagging behind by decades due to certain adverse conditions. Let me start a discussion of that in regards to local domination.

Social change: reducing dominance

The increasing availability of people with the education, skills, resources and networks was integral to how the oppressed communities of Tamil Nadu developed the ability to challenge dominance. Such an impact of resources on action has been documented elsewhere in India and also internationally. From this perspective, one could ask if there were systematic differences in the availability of resources among oppressed communities between the good and poor performers which could explain the greater prevalence of public action in the former states. There is evidence that public action increased as the resource position of the oppressed communities improved in India, and that there were some important differences between states that could explain the differences in the level of public action.

The dominance of the elite communities owed to the fact that they were the primary employers and that they controlled the administration, policing functions, conflict resolution, and religious and cultural institutions. In a society that was predominantly agrarian and rural, most people had to depend on a small set of elite in their villages for their livelihood and even for the most basic amenities, giving the elite tremendous power over others. Oppressed communities also tended to be abjectly poor, which made their dependence on their employers acute. In addition to poverty and the consequent lack of education and other resources made mobilization challenging since sustained mobilization requires resources. Changing structure of livelihood opportunities was one of the key factors that led to the breakdown of dependence and an improvement in the resource base of oppressed communities–both of which increased their ability to engage in public action. These changes were not always emancipatory. Some changes in the economic organization have led to more repressive conditions, and in the colonial era the most egregious of these related to disenfranchizing people of land and providing the land to already dominant groups. The resulting disempowerment is not surprising since land was the main source of power. People living in Zamindari and tribal areas were the worst affected in this respect.

The East India Company developed a model of collecting land revenue as a way of sustaining their costly operations in India, and it developed three distinct models for doing so, viz. Zamindari, Ryotwari and Mahalwari. The Zamindari system involved the use of revenue farmers who paid a fixed amount each year to the colonial administration for which they were given the rights to collect any amount of revenue in their regions. Zamindars had to have large estates to be able to afford to pay such large sums, especially in lean years. This model, which was preferred by the powerful governors of the Bengal presidency, was implemented mainly in the eastern states of Bengal, Orissa and Bihar.[1] Zamindars were also prominent in Uttar Pradesh, and their holdings were especially large in the Oudh region, which was the last to be occupied by the British in Uttar Pradesh (Metcalf 1967). Overall, the system of revenue farming was concentrated heavily in the North and East of India and it produced powerful families that had vast stretches of land and other riches gained through rent collections. They also derived power through their administrative functions.

As Thomas Munro, an early colonial administrator, astutely observed (Mukherjee 1962), the Zamindari system would work only in areas where there were families with very large initial holdings. The Mughal system of revenue farming had created the basis for the Zamindari system in the North, but the company found it difficult to extend it to the South despite several decades of effort. There were strong inequalities in the first place between these regions, and the inequalities were exacerbated by the colonial policy of permanent settlement.[2] Faulty interpretations of local customs also led to a situation in which the zamindars were practically given ownership of the land, thus enabling their dominance for a long time. While the system started breaking down in Bengal during the last decades of the colonial administration, zamindars continued to be powerful even after the formal abolition of the system which happened after India's independence thanks to their accumulated wealth and power.

Similarly, legal fictions enabled the colonial government to appropriate large swatches of land in the tribal areas that were then used to alienate the land from the tribal people. This era increased the presence of outsiders in these areas, many of whom appropriated land from the tribal people through the lending of money at atrocious rates and other practices. Thus, colonial practices led to a major alienation of property from the tribal people and established a system of domination by outsiders that continues to affect these areas even today.

Land revenue and the regime of property rights introduced by the colonial power thus led to a worsening of inequalities and the creation of very powerful players who dominated social life in rural India. While some such effects were felt in most parts of colonial India, the worst affected were the Zamindari areas and the tribal belt covering states such as Bengal, Orissa, Bihar, Uttar Pradesh, Jharkhand, and Chhattisgarh. In contrast to these, the introduction of Ryotwari in most parts of South India led to a decrease in the influence of contemporary village power holders as the entrenched administration took over their functions. Even though there were complaints of excessive rents in the Ryotwari system, the rent was not collected by certain families that came to dominate the region. In other words, people in both regions were exploited through the imposition of high taxes. In the Zamindari areas, a part of the proceeds went to influential families who became even more dominant in those regions. In the Roytwari regions, taxes were collected directly by the administration and thus it did not lead to a few powerful families who could dominate the region. The South suffered the least in the process, while the Hindi heartland, Orissa, Bengal, and the tribal states suffered the worst.

Apart from revenue administration, there were also other practices that entrenched the domination of the elite in the poor performers while creating new opportunities for oppressed communities in the South and the West. As I argued before, public employment has been one of the most important sources of empowerment to oppressed communities, and an early form of it was employment with the colonial armies. In its initial years, the English East India Company created a system of temporarily recruiting agricultural workers during conflicts. Once the company was settled, it started recruiting sepoys (soldiers) on a regular basis offering new conditions of work for agricultural labourer communities (Cohen 1969; Riser-Kositsky 2009). This unprecedented opportunity led to a new generation of leaders whose parents had worked with the British, in the army or in a civilian capacity. Most major Dalit leaders in the South and West India, including the legendary Ambedkar, had fathers who worked in this capacity. The community that gained the most from such employment were the Mahars of Maharashtra, who had previous experience working in the army of the legendary Shivaji. The significance of this can be seen by the fact that almost one-third of the Bombay presidency army was comprised of Mahars by 1856 (Riser-Kositsky 2009). While other Dalit communities did not have such a strong presence in the army, there was a substantial presence of Parayars of Tamil Nadu in the army at that time. Unlike the Madras and Bombay presidency armies, the Bengal presidency had a policy of not recruiting Dalits even before the great Mutiny of 1857. In this region, employment in the army went to Bhumihar Brahmins, and this considerably strengthened their position in Bihar. Thus, an important avenue of empowerment for Dalits and other agricultural labourer communities that was available in the South and in parts of the West was never available in North and East India. It should be remembered that Bengal, Bihar, and Orissa were administered by the Colonial administration from the early years of colonialism whereas parts of Uttar Pradesh, Punjab, and other territories in the North were annexed just before the Mutiny of 1857.

Following the Mutiny, the British administration appointed the Peel commission to undertake an inquiry. The report of the commission was unclear and there were many different interpretations within the army, but one version of it came to dominate. This version argued that in order to prevent mutinies and to have a strong sense of discipline in the army, only 'Martial races' should be recruited to the army. With Dalits and many BC communities being considered non-martial, the Peel commission closed a major avenue of employment for these communities in colonial India.[3] Employment in the army and in other capacities with the Company or with Company officials gave Dalit families the income to educate their children and also the resources to support their public action. As a result, the late 1800s saw a number of educated, articulate leaders who helped to frame an agenda for their community. M C Rajah, Rettamalai Srinivasan, Ambedkar, among others, found a place in the legislative councils from the 1920s through which they were able to articulate policy demands. By independence, they had created substantial support for their agenda among Dalits and other communities. The colonial era also saw the rise of new trade and industrial opportunities that led to the empowerment of a few of the marginalized communities in some cases. A notable case being the Chamar Dalits of Uttar Pradesh (Pai 2001; Zelliot 1970). To take another case, Dalits of the Namasudra caste were able to become zamindars in the East and West Bengal, and this provided a support network for the Namasudra movement (Bandyopadhyaya 1997).

While exceptions can be found to the story, it is clear that the Southern states of India started at a more favourable position at India's independence. These conditions were compounded in the post-independence period by the creation of new livelihood opportunities that further weakened elite dominance. Movement leaders from Ambedkar to my discussants engaged in decentralized public action in Tamil Nadu and recognized that the traditional relationship of dependence was one of the most important stumbling blocks to their ability to mobilize. In order to overcome this they encouraged youngsters in their area to migrate in search of alternate job opportunities. This knowledge that there are alternate places where they can find work has emboldened oppressed communities to assert themselves in public affairs. Jobs in industries, services, and the public sector have been key sources of sustained alternative livelihood, and not surprisingly social transformation has happened at a faster pace where such alternatives were available. For example the states with the highest proportion of the population in 'regular jobs' as categorized by the NSS are Tamil Nadu, Punjab, Kerala, Maharashtra, and Haryana while the bottom five are Uttar Pradesh, Orissa, Jharkhand, Chhattisgarh, and Bihar (B. Paul et al. 2009).[4] In states with a narrow base of regular jobs, many of these are cornered by the dominant communities, and thus, the avenue for advancement is narrower for others.

While Southern and Western states of India are the leaders in creating such opportunities, there has also been a major change in the livelihood patterns in the Hindi belt where feudal conditions persisted for a longer period of time. As John Harriss argues (Harriss 2013), the phenomenon of landlords having a dominant say over the people of their village has significantly diminished in most parts of India. While stable and salaried jobs provide the greatest security, even agricultural work outside the village and other non-regular employment in brick kilns or construction have been important sources of non-traditional employment and a way to escape from the traditional relationships of dominance. Such opportunities are now availed by communities that traditionally been agricultural labourers. They now migrate within and outside their states for non-agricultural employment, which has resulted in a social ferment and the creation of a new cadre of leadership among oppressed communities in these regions (C. Jeffrey, Jeffery, and Jeffery 2008; Frankel and Rao 1990; Kapur et al. 2010; Lerche 1999). This phenomenon has provided the social basis for political change and democratization in much of North India.

The impact of industrialization and migration on social relations should be evaluated carefully, since these have not fundamentally challenged the social hierarchy. Dalits tend to work in lower end jobs and face discrimination in their places of work even in the urban areas (Patankar and Omvedt 1979). Despite this hierarchy, alternate job opportunities in industry, agriculture, or service industries offer alternatives, and can have an impact in reducing the dominance of the traditional elite. Similarly, the empowerment of BCs with the green revolution and other avenues of prosperity have led to the increased repression of Dalits in many parts of India. Increasing wealth has also had adverse consequences for women's freedoms. One cannot thus make direct associations between incomes of regions and the mobilization capacity of people. That said, in the context of social ferment, such opportunities can add to the strength of mobilization, and the change in material conditions have interacted with broader political changes such as the introduction of adult franchise in fostering an atmosphere of challenges and social change.

Identity, assertion, coalition

The material conditions of dominance discussed above give us some clue as to why public action was more challenging in the North than in the South or West of India. While they have an important impact on people's voice, economic opportunities are not the sole determinants of action. The ability of movements to encourage people to assert themselves, form coalitions, create organizations, and other factors had an impact on public action. In other words, no matter what the material conditions are, capable leaders have the opportunity to increase the level of public action if they are able to motivate their members and create support systems for activism. In addition, some movements were successful in developing large coalitions of the underprivileged, which can be a tremendous source of power. The strategy of using numbers to demand a greater share of public resources started at least in the colonial era, as illustrated in the Non-Brahmin manifesto. Such coalitions are all the more powerful in a democratic context, especially if they are large enough to influence elections. While there is a long history of such attempts, politically potent coalitions were formed much earlier in Tamil Nadu and Kerala whereas it took several more decades for such coalitions to succeed in the North.

One of the early attempts at creating a coalition of oppressed communities was taken up by Jyotirao Phule who sought to create the 'Bahujan Samaj' comprised of BC and Dalit communities that had common grievances against the caste elite. The importance of strength in numbers is represented by the very name, 'Bahujan Samaj', which can be translated as 'majority community'. But the majority community was fractured into many small caste groups, making it difficult to create a powerful coalition. Phule, like many others, did not succeed. By the late nineteenth century, movements had also started making claims for a greater share of political representation and other public resources by citing their numbers, which made it all the more important for competing groups to demonstrate a large social base. An opportunity to demonstrate arose with the censuses of 1901–31, which included a detailed account of a person's caste and Varna categories. This presented an opportunity to engineer new coalitions and establish a show of strength for many caste groups. A highly successful case was the fusing of three castes in Tamil Nadu to form a new caste called the *Mukkulathor*, literally meaning 'people of three castes'. A similar fusion was attempted by the Triveni Sang in Bihar to bring a coalition between major BC groups in the state – but without success (Jaffrelot 2003). Similarly, the Dalit leader of Punjab, Mangoo Ram, used the 1931 census to create a new caste identity and demonstrate a show of strength, and he was successful in enlisting hundreds of thousands of followers.

The most remarkable effort at creating a pan-India coalition of oppressed communities was led by Ambedkar who sought to create a coalition among 'untouchables' under the identity that he coined—'Dalit' or broken people. Prior to Ambedkar, there was some notion of people below the pollution line suffering from drastic unfreedoms across India, but for the most part, the dominant identity was that of the individual caste. Following Phule, Ambedkar tried to create a broad-based coalition of working classes but this did not succeed. He then played an instrumental role in creating a coalition among the untouchable castes throughout India.

Ambedkar too used the strategy of demonstrating the numerical strength of untouchable castes as a part of his political strategy. A show of numbers by the Dalits is a challenge to the caste Hindu elite in any context, and this was particularly sensitive during the caste censuses of 1901–31. In the context of the demand for proportional representation by Muslim leaders, caste Hindu leaders (often affiliated with the Congress) wanted to enlist Dalits in the larger category of 'Hindus' and thus resisted attempts by Dalits to form a distinct community. In his essay, *From millions to fractions* (Bhimrao Ramji Ambedkar and Moon 1979), Ambedkar presents a fascinating account of caste Hindu attempts at subverting this show of numbers essentially by arguing against enlisting various castes as untouchables with the census commission.

While there were many attempts to form politically formidable coalitions, only a few were successful in the early years of independence. The Dravidian movement was a notable success, and the Communist Party of India created a formidable class-coalition in Kerala and the Nationalist movement was able to form a coalition of other strong identity networks, thus creating two strong parties in the state. The policy history of these states would be inconceivable without this success. Another coalition that was briefly successful was the National Conference or NC (which was originally called the Muslim Conference). The NC was able to create a powerful coalition of the Muslim population of Kashmir, which was predominantly poor, to dislodge the powerful Dogra landlords with their ties to the king. The Indo-Pak conflict on Kashmir, violence against minorities and other factors quickly dislodged this victory, thus ensuring that the new coalition did not have a chance to rebuild the state on the basis of sustained political power.

South-western India had a relatively early success in building lower class or caste coalitions compared to North. In North India, backward castes were finally able to secure power only starting in the 1990s even though these areas have had powerful lower class and caste mobilization for more than a century. Remarkably, a Dalit-led party was able to occupy political centre stage by creating a strong Dalit coalition, thus achieving something that has not been done in any other part of India. This was enabled by the fact that Uttar Pradesh has a very high proportion of Dalit population and also by the fact that the other castes and communities were fractured.[5] Demographic factors did play a role in the coalition experiments elsewhere. As the Dravidian movement pointed out in the non-Brahmin manifesto, the Brahmins consisted of just 3 per cent of the Madras presidency's population, which did not constitute a viable political force in a democracy. Compared to this, Brahmins represented a much larger proportion of the population in the North–making it additionally difficult to challenge them electorally (Jaffrelot 2003). But in no case have they had numbers strong enough to be invincible if alternate groups were able to form a powerful coalition. Considering the oppressive conditions of action, it is not surprising that the consolidation of lower caste votes took much longer to materialize in the North–but credit should also go to the leaders of the southern movements that were able to accomplish the difficult task of forming supra-jati coalitions. As I mentioned in the previous chapter, the task of foregrounding caste or class identities was also disrupted in the Hindi heartland due to the dominance of Hindu-Muslim politics for decades in this region. Despite the hiccups, lower caste coalitions are now a powerful force and are shaping the political and social relations of the region.

Democratization of political institutions

The most important change in the external condition was in the domain of formal political institutions which underwent a dramatic change in 1951. India's new Constitution adopted that year initiated a remarkable experiment of transforming India into a democracy with adult franchise, a novel phenomenon for a low-income country at that time. This moment represented a major shift in the political arrangements in India. Even though there were elections in the colonial era, the elected bodies had only limited power. Even more importantly, only a small proportion of the population was allowed to vote since voters had to have property or education to vote, and in most cases, women were not allowed to vote even if they were highly educated or owned property. Thus, freedom from colonial bureaucracy and the dramatic expansion of the number of people who were allowed to vote through the introduction of adult franchise represented a paradigm shift in the voice of the common person in politics.

It is of course pedantic to say that the introduction of elections and adult franchise do not lead to a democracy. In a highly unequal society, material wealth, control of violence, and other factors can lead to a situation in which small elite communities are able to occupy political power even in the context of free elections and adult franchise.[6] Despite inequalities, the democratic turn in 1951 represented a considerable increase in power for the common person, but the degree of influence depended on people's ability to vote in practice, to be able to do so independently, to form associations, to form political parties and to contest for different positions in government. While the formal political structure opened up in 1951, the social structure did not permit many of the fundamental things that people do as democratic practice.

One indication of the adverse conditions prevalent in the Hindi heartland was the degree to which people were able to vote in elections under adult franchise. Where the conditions of social domination were severe, oppressed communities were routinely prevented from voting through intimidation and violence, and candidates had little engagement with the common person to secure their votes. One thus finds that states that had undergone early social transformation like Kerala, Punjab, and Tamil Nadu had the highest levels of voter turnout in the early years after India's independence while Uttar Pradesh,[7] Madhya Pradesh, Bihar, Rajasthan, and Orissa represent the states with the lowest turnouts. Southern states including Kerala and Tamil Nadu started with a very high proportion of people voting in elections immediately after independence. Kerala had a turnout of 78.4 per cent in 1957 and a whopping 84.4 per cent in 1960 which are enviable by any standards internationally. At the same time, many of the northern states had a turnout of less than 40 per cent. There was thus a remarkable correlation between voter participation a few decades ago and the levels of human development achieved by these states today.[8] This cannot be a coincidence given the fact that higher voter turnouts put pressure on governments to perform for a broader section of the population (Besley and Burgess 2002).

Systematic discrimination and intimidation of voters from oppressed communities enabled the upper castes to dominate politics. This enabled them to institute a partisan system of governance, including the creation of public services for the few. Social transformation and the resultant decline of domination have enabled more and more communities to participate in the electoral process starting with the first step of voting. If we look at the highest turnout in Lok Sabha elections between the Nehru era (1952–64) and the Post-Mandal era (1990 onwards), there has been an average increase of 14.7 percentage points in participation in the states of Bihar, Madhya Pradesh, Rajasthan, Orissa and Uttar Pradesh.[9] The increased participation was enabled by grassroots assertiveness which led to political changes similar to those in Tamil Nadu.

One change was in the social composition of governance both among elite-led parties and among new challengers to power with a strong root among the lower castes. In the first few decades after independence, Congress systematically accommodated new challengers to power. It was such an entrenched phenomenon, that it was labelled as the 'Congress system' by Rajni Kothari (Kothari 1964). Whenever some community started becoming vocal about their lack of representation, Congress managed to create some political space for them in order to sustain its electoral chances. Many scholars have argued that the Congress system enabled the sustenance of the party. Such an accommodation has also taken place in recent years in the other major national party–the BJP.

The emergence of these parties would not have been possible without people's assertion from the grassroots initially.

Numerically strong and mobilized groups offered a readymade constituency for ambitious leaders outside the dominant parties. Thanks to early mobilization in the South, communists were able to displace the Congress as early as 1957 in Kerala while the DMK succeeded in 1967 in Tamil Nadu on the strength of lower class/caste mobilization. In contrast, socialist parties and some BC groups had an early presence in the poor performers, but it was only in the 1990s that these parties were able to dislodge the established parties and establish their own formidable presence.

In this competitive environment politically marginalized groups have offered tremendous opportunities for aspirants to political office. Communities that had gained little from the ruling dispensations were often willing to offer support for even the most minimal promises. This opportunity led to the formation of many new parties, and changes in political strategies for others. In regions where there were multiple mobilized groups, parties were forced to form social coalitions consisting of multiple groups, in which each group is offered some benefits of power. This strategy is a far cry from the times when a very small number of elite groups were able to appropriate power through their social control over others. Electoral competition, in general, forces parties to create a 'formula' of securing the support of communities which can give them a chance of electoral success. What is significant from the perspective of this work is that the formulae have undergone changes with more and more communities finding a prominent place in the electoral equations. A related political activity has been to create new social categories based on the perceived grievances of groups who have been ignored by ruling coalitions. Nowhere is the broadening composition of the electoral formulae more apparent than in Bihar.

Immediately after India's independence, the dominant Bhumihar community of Bihar firmly established control not only in the higher levels of politics, but at every level of politics and administration. The main competition that this group faced until the 1970s was the Rajput community. The confusion of the 1970s and the intense competition between elite politicians in Bihar created a space for the first BC Chief Minister in the state viz. Karpuri Thakur, but his tenure did not last long. The social changes taking place in Bihar created a newly assertive constituency of selected BC communities, notably the Yadavs and the Kurmis. In the wake of the Mandal commission agitations, the Yadav community was able to wrest political power from the Congress, and in essence, also from the dominant Bhumihar and Rajput communities. Given the fact that the Yadav community by itself could not garner the required votes, a political coalition was created with the Muslim community, in what was called the M-Y formula. In addition, minor concessions were made to the Dalits and a broad appeal was made to the BC communities at large, even while power was concentrated within the Yadav community through the 1980s and 1990s.

This in turn enabled the creation of new social categories under the leadership of Nitish Kumar. These were based on groups that did not have a share of power in the previous dispensation. Recognizing that the assertive among the BCs and the Dalits had gained political favours in the previous dispensation, he created social categories of Most Backward and Maha Dalits. This social engineering created a new constituency, and with the support of a few assertive BC groups such as the Kurmis, he was able to form a formidable political combination. But in order for this political group to become viable, he had to secure further support from the upper caste groups; this was achieved by a coalition with the BJP. The new combination, which was broader and more inclusive of marginalized groups, was able to secure political power in Bihar. His attempts to secure the support of these communities would have been futile without their assertion, but at the same time the impetus to secure their support and create enabling conditions for their public action would not have happened without the introduction of adult franchise–indicating the two-way relationship between mobilization and political opportunities.

The two major regime changes in Bihar have both been politically impressive. The ascendance of Lalu Prasad Yadav created the first serious challenge to the elite, and through the process, it created serious political competition for the first time. This competitiveness increased in the two decades of government led by Lalu Prasad Yadav, which was a period of major social change. The initial victory of Nitish Kumar in 2004 happened with a thin margin, and his victory in the assembly elections was immediately followed by a defeat in the Parliament election. The fine balance of social combinations led to intense political competition and insecurity of tenure. This forced Nitish Kumar to adopt a strategy of delivering broad-based benefits, especially by delivering basic public services. This enabled him to return to power with a more significant majority in the assembly election of 2009, encroaching in the process on some of the core support groups of Lalu Prasad Yadav.

The political competition initially took the shape of appropriating newly assertive communities that did not have a share in power. Even minor contributions, sometimes merely symbolic, secured the support of these groups. But this strategy was successful only while there were large numbers of un-mobilized communities. Once that political opportunity was exhausted, new approaches had to be undertaken in order to secure support, and this required serious aspirants to offer benefits beyond political participation. Political competition thus ensured that the benefits of power were not restricted to very narrow social groups as in the past and forced the government to be more responsive to the concerns of common people at large.

I argued that sustained competition in Tamil Nadu led to a situation where organized local groups were able to bargain with competing parties and this process helped them to secure public services and resources that were previously unavailable to them. This would not have been possible without the democratization of political institutions accompanied by some degree of social transformation. The process of social and political transformation leading to a prioritization of public services that one saw in Tamil Nadu resonates with the history in other parts of India. In states that are good performers today, that transformation started earlier and it was sustained for decades. The favourable conditions for public action enabled people to bargain for services over decades and these little victories have accumulated into a broad set of well-functioning public services in their neighbourhoods. In the Hindi heartland and other poor performers, these transformations have happened only recently–and so we find only a few benefits that are being offered to large sections of the population. In the context of increasing democratic assertion, it is likely that each new government will have to offer tangible benefits to a broad section of the population in the years to come.

In summary, my argument is that the voice of the common person has been increasing in India, and that India is much more democratic today than it was six decades ago at independence. But this has happened at a varied pace across India's states. I do not make the claim that this was inevitable or irreversible, but I make a limited claim that this has been the case over the last six decades. In the highly imperfect democracy that India has been, a small elite has been successful in cornering the benefits of power in a highly parochial manner. This ability has been challenged by the increasing power of the common person driven by socio-economic, cultural, and political changes. In places where these challenges succeeded early, people have been able to put pressure on governments to deliver–and public services have been one of the routes for doing so. Thanks to consistent pressure lasting decades in the early reformers, we find a broad array of well-functioning services in operation. The beginnings of this pressure are now found in other states, and services will inevitably become a major political priority in the years to come.

Notes

1. There were some Zamindari districts in most states ruled by the Company, but there were only a few districts with the Zamindari system outside the Bengal presidency.

2. The Permanent Settlement is one of the forms of Zamindari system wherein the revenue farmers had to pay a fixed sum annually to the colonial administration and was in turn allowed to collect any amount of revenue from people in these regions.

3. For a discussion on the evolution of these policies see Alavi (1995), Cohen (1969, 2001), Constable (2001), Rand (2006) and Saha (2004).

4. The report has the number of people in the labour market, the proportion of which are employed and the proportion of employed who have regular jobs as separate tables. The assessment here is calculated from the three tables.

5. This demographic feature compares favourably with Punjab which has the highest proportion of Dalit population in India, but is confronted by a relatively homogenous Jat–Sikh population majority.

6. The most forceful arguments on this subject were made by Ambedkar in his essays on social democracy and also on the question of 'whose freedom' the Indian National Congress was championing (B. R. Ambedkar and Rodrigues 2002).

7. Uttar Pradesh had a relatively high turnout in 1952, which then went down remarkably through the 1960s.

8. Himachal Pradesh was a part of Punjab until 1972 and is not represented in this list.

9. Uttar Pradesh is an outlier in this with a slight decline in this period thanks to very high participation in the first election in 1952.

Conclusion

In the preface of this book, I asked if the recent trend of criticizing public services would lead to the dismantling of India's bare minimum welfare-programmes. In a bid to answer that, this book has looked at the politics of public services in India's past. I argued that India has a long history of discrimination and that the fight against it has been the defining feature of politics in India over the last few decades. Political parties were able to ignore the aspirations of the majority in the past when common people had no leverage over the government. This has changed decisively in India.

Now that common people have the ability to affect electoral chances, political parties increasingly find that there is no alternative but to offer concrete promises to the common people. The very indirect path to well-being advocated by neo-liberal ideologues does not have much resonance among the newly assertive. We also live in an era in which the radical reform of property and labour relations does not have the appeal they had during India's independence. In other words, the classic Left and Right policy agendas are unlikely to have much appeal among the vast majority of India's electorate, at least in the near future.

While the Left and the Right fail to appeal to the majority today, two factors have gained popular appeal. These are the quest for dignity and the delivery of basic public services. As the story from

Erani illustrated, these demands are closely related for historically marginalized groups. Good schools, clean drinking water, functional public health systems, nutrition support, child care and other basic services have a tremendous impact on people's lives, leading to their widespread support. Even those of us who do not have to walk miles to get clean water or suffer from lack of health care should not find it difficult to understand why these services are valued.

Accepting this fact and making it a political priority can bring important social dividends. One of the earliest people to recognize this was Kamarajar, who understood that ignoring the aspirations of the majority will lead to political instability and class warfare. Based on this recognition, he laid the foundation of Tamil Nadu's welfare system, which ensured that rapid social change happened in Tamil Nadu without violent conflicts. Chief Ministers like YSR, Raman Singh, and others have also used the promise of services to gain political stability and some semblance of trust in government. Such political stability based on the recognition of the aspirations of the majority can go a long way in helping us as a nation to escape poverty and embark on a path towards development.

As I have consistently argued in this book, it is conceivable that an agenda could evolve in the future which has popular appeal. While that is a possibility, the only concrete policy with mass appeal currently is the widespread provision of basic public services. Making that promise can lay the foundation of political stability. What remains to be seen is whether the elite will recognize this demand and accommodate it or if they will continue to demand discrimination, and accommodate the inevitable the hard way.

Glossary

AIADMK	All India Anna Dravida Munnetra Kazhagam, one of the two main Dravidian parties in Tamil Nadu
Backward Castes	Backward Castes or Classes refers to caste groups and certain other groups that cannot be neatly classified as castes. These groups are above the pollution line and thus are not untouchable, but are deprived socially and economically in many ways. They are not clearly defined.
Backward Classes	See 'Backward Castes'.
BC or BCs	See 'Backward castes'.
Caste Hindus	Hindu castes that are above the pollution line and so are not untouchable.
Cheri	Habitation of Dalits, also called colony' in some regions.
Collector	The administrative head of a District
Colony	See note on 'Cheri'.
Congress, Congress (I)	Congress is one of the main national parties in India. After a major split in 1969 the faction led by Indira Gandhi became dominant and it is called Congress (I).

Dalits	Refers to castes that are considered Untouchable.
Depressed classes	See note on 'Dalits'
DMK	Dravida Munnetra Kazhagam, one of the two main Dravidian parties in Tamil Nadu formed in 1949 after it split from DK.
Jati	Refers to caste, and should be distinguished from Varna that stands for a major categorization of castes by their order in the hierarchy.
Kumbabishegam	A major temple festival celebrated periodically in each temple.
Legislative Assembly	The apex political body at the state level comprising of elected members, headed by the Chief Minister.
Legislative Council	Apex political body at the state level comprising of nominated members. Legislative councils were started in 1861 and most states today do not have legislative councils.
Madras Presidency & Tamil Nadu	One of the major provinces during British era that was split after independence along linguistic lines. Tamil Nadu was formed out of the Tamil speaking areas of the province.
MGR	M G Ramachandran, an actor turned politician who split from the DMK to form AIADMK. He was the Chief Minister of Tamil Nadu from 1977–89.
MLA	Member of Legislative Assembly
Most Backward Classes	Sub classification of most backward among Backward Classes
MP	Member of Parliament
OHT	Overhead tank for water
Other Backward Classes	Sub classification of backward among Backward Classes

Panchayat	Village level government comprising of elected members. It can also refer to the informal judicial body of the village or of a caste.
Reservation	Refers to reservation of certain proportion of jobs, seats, etc. for a certain categories of people. There is mandatory reservation for SCs and STs in all government jobs and educational institutions apart from reservations for Backward Classes, for women in some cases, etc.
Ryotwari system	System of tax collection during British era that involved direct collection of taxes from farmers by the administration. To be distinguished from the Zamindari system
SC	Scheduled Castes
Scheduled Castes	Official classification of castes that could be considered untouchables. Synonymous to Dalits.
Scheduled Tribes	Official classification of Tribal groups
ST	Scheduled Tribes
Untouchables	See note on 'Dalits'.
Varna system	Broad categorization of castes into Brahmin (Priests), Kshatriya (warriors), Vaishya (Traders) and Shudras (Workers). Untouchables and tribals are outside the caste system.
Village level workers (VLW)	Government workers at the village level who are in charge of implementing programmes at the grassroots.
Zamindari system	System of tax collection through intermediaries called Zamindars.

Bibliography

Agarwal, Bina, Jane Humphries, and Ingrid Robeyns. 2005. *Amartya Sen's Work and Ideas: A Gender Perspective*. London: Routledge.

Aiyappan, A. 1965. *Social Revolution in a Kerala Village: A Study in Culture Change*. London: Asia Pub. House.

Alavi, Seema. 1995. *The Sepoys and the Company: Tradition and Transition in Northern India, 1770–1830*. Delhi; New York: Oxford University Press.

Ambedkar, B. R. and Valerian Rodrigues. 2002. *The Essential Writings of B.R. Ambedkar*. New Delhi.; Oxford: Oxford University Press.

Ambedkar, Bhimrao Ramji and Vasant Moon. 1979. 'From Millions to Fractions', In *Dr. Babasaheb Ambedkar, Writings and Speeches*. Education Department, Government of Maharashtra.

Anand, S. 2013. 'No Pink Chaddis for PMK', *The Hindu*, July 13. Retrieved from http://www.thehindu.com/todays-paper/tp-opinion/no-pink-chaddis-for-pmk/article4910536.ece.

Athreya, Venkatesh B. and Sheela Rani Chunkath. 1996. *Literacy and Empowerment*. New Delhi; Thousand Oaks, CA.: Sage Publications.

Athreya, Venkatesh B., Göran Djurfeldt, and Staffan Lindberg. 1990. *Barriers Broken: Agrarian Change in Tamil Nadu*. New Delhi; Newbury Park, CA.: Sage Publications.

Balasundaram, F. J. 1997. *Dalits and Christian Mission in the Tamil Country: The Dalit Movement and Protestant Christians in the Tamil Speaking Districts of Madras Presidency 1919–1939 with Special Reference to London Mission Society Area in Salem, Attur, Coimbatore, and Erode*. Bangalore: Asian Trading Corp.

Baliga, B. S. 1962. *South Arcot District Gazetteer*. Madras: India: Printed by the Supt., Govt. Press.

Bandyopadhyaya, Sekhara. 1997. *Caste, Protest and Identity in Colonial India: The Namasudras of Bengal, 1872–1947*. Richmond, Surrey: Curzon.

Banerjee, Abhijit, Rukmini Banerji, and Esther Duflo. 2007. 'Can Information Campaigns Raise Awareness and Local Participation in Primary Education? *Economic and Political Weekly* (April 14): 1365.

Banerjee, Abhijit and Lakshmi Iyer. 2005. 'History, Institutions, and Economic Performance: The Legacy of Colonial Land Tenure Systems in India', *The American Economic Review* 95 (September): 1190–1213. doi:10.1257/0002828054825574.

Banerjee, Abhijit, Lakshmi Iyer, and Rohini Somanathan. 2005. 'History, Social Divisions, and Public Goods in Rural India', *Journal of the European Economic Association*, 3 (2–3) (May): 639–647.

Basu, Aparna and Bharati Ray. 2003. *Women's Struggle: A History of the All India Women's Conference, 1927–2002*. Vol. 2nd. New Delhi: Manohar.

Besley, Timothy and Robin Burgess. 2002. 'The Political Economy of Government Responsiveness: Theory and Evidence from India', *Quarterly Journal of Economics*, 117 (4): 1415–1451.

Béteille, André. 1996. *Caste, Class, and Power: Changing Patterns of Stratification in a Tanjore Village*. Delhi; New York: Oxford University Press.

Bharathiyar. 2000. *Bharathiyar Kavithaigal*. Chennai: Giri Trading Agency.

Brulé, Rachel. 2013. 'Gender Equity, Legal Reform and Local Institutions: The Political Economy of Gender-Equalizing Land Inheritance Reform in Rural India'. Ph.D. Dissertation, Palo Alto: Stanford.

Caplan, Lionel. 1980. 'Caste and Castelessness among South Indian Christians', *Contributions to Indian Sociology*, 14 (2) (July 1): 213–238.

Casinader, Rex. 1995. 'Making Kerala Model More Intelligible: Comparisons with Sri Lankan Experience', *Economic and Political Weekly*, 30 (48) (December 2): 3085–3092. doi:10.2307/4403512.

Chand, Attar. 1988. *M.G. Ramachandran, My Blood Brother*. New Delhi: Gyan Publishing House.

Chandra, Bipan. 1983. *The Indian Left: Critical Appraisals*. New Delhi: Vikas.

Chattopadhyay, Raghabendra and Esther Duflo. 2004. 'Women as Policy Makers: Evidence from a Randomized Policy Experiment in India', *Econometrica*, 72 (5) (September): 1409–1443.

Chokalingam, T.S. *Mudhukulathoor Baiangaram* [Terror in Mudhukulatoor].

Citizens' Initiative for the Rights of Children Under Six. 2006. 'Focus on Children under Six.' Delhi: Circus. Retrieved from http://www. righttofoodindia.org/icds/icds_index.html.

Cohen, Stephen P. 1969. 'The Untouchable Soldier: Caste, Politics, and the Indian Army', *The Journal of Asian Studies*, 28 (3) (May): 453–468. doi:10.2307/2943173.

————. 2001. *The Indian Army: Its Contribution to the Development of a Nation*. Berkeley: University of California Press.

Constable, Philip. 2001. 'The Marginalization of a Dalit Martial Race in Late Nineteenth and Early Twentieth-Century Western India', *The Journal of Asian Studies*, 60 (2) (May 1): 439–478. doi:10.2307/2659700.

Das Gupta, Monica, B.R. Desikachari, T.V. Somanathan, and P. Padmanaban. 2009. 'How to Improve Public Health Systems: Lessons from Tamil Nadu', The World Bank. Retrieved from http:// ideas.repec.org/p/wbk/wbrwps/5073.html.

Dasgupta, Biplab. 1973. 'Naxalite Armed Struggles and the Annihilation Campaign in Rural Areas', *Economic and Political Weekly*, 8 (4/6) (February): 173–188.

Desai, Manali. 2005. 'Indirect British Rule, State Formation, and Welfarism in Kerala, India,1860–1957', *Social Science History*, 29 (3): 457–488.

Devarajan, G. 1990. *Social Reform Movements in Kerala: An Annotated Bibliography of Source Materials*. Vol. 14. Gurgaon, Haryana: Indian Documentation Service.

Diani, Mario and Doug McAdam. 2003. *Social Movements and Networks: Relational Approaches to Collective Action*. Oxford; New York: Oxford University Press.

Dickey, Sara. 2005. 'Still One Man in a Thousand', In David Blamey and Robert D'Souza (eds), *Living Pictures*, pp. 69–79. London: Open Editions.

Dietrich, Gabriele. 1992. *Reflections on the Women's Movement in India: Religion, Ecology, Development*. New Delhi: Horizon India Books.

Divekar, V. D., G. T. Kulkarni, and M. R. Kantak. 1991. *Social Reform Movements in India: A Historical Perspective*. Pune; Bombay: Bharat Itihas Samshodhak Mandal; Popular Prakashan.

Drèze, Jean. 2004. 'Democracy and Right to Food', *Economic and Political Weekly*, 39 (17): 1723–1731.

Drèze, Jean, Nikhil Dey, and Reetika Khera. 2006. *NREGA: A Primer*. Delhi, India: National Book Trust. Retrieved from www.righttofood-india.org.

Drèze, Jean and Aparajita Goyal. 2003.'The Future of Mid-Day Meals', *Economic and Political Weekly* (1 Nov): 4673.

Drèze, Jean and Yamini Jaishankar. 2005. 'Supreme Court Orders on the Right to Food: A Tool for Action', Retrieved from Right to Food Campaign. www.righttofoodindia.org.

Drèze, Jean and Reetika Khera. 2011. 'PDS Leakages: The Plot Thickens', *The Hindu*, August 12, sec. Opinion. Retrieved from http://www. thehindu.com/opinion/lead/pds-leakages-the-plot-thickens/ article2351414.ece.

———. 2012. 'Regional Pattern of Human and Child Deprivation in India', *Economic & Political Weekly*, XLVII (39) (September 29): 42–49.

Drèze, Jean, Vandana Prasad, and Vandana Bhatia. 2005. 'Mid-Day Meals: A Primer', Right to Food Campaign. Retrieved from www.righttofoodindia.org.

Drèze, Jean and Amartya Sen. 1995. *India: Economic Development and Social Opportunity*. Delhi: Oxford University Press.

———. 2002. *India: Development and Participation*. New Delhi: Oxford University Press.

———. 2013. *An Uncertain Glory: India and Its Contradictions*. Princeton University Press.

Echeverri-Gent, John. 1988. 'Guaranteed Employment in an Indian State: The Maharashtra Experience', *Asian Survey*, 28, (December, 12): 1294–1310.

———. 1993. *The State and the Poor: Public Policy and Political Development in India and the United States*. Berkeley and Oxford: University of California Press.

Franke, Richard W. and Barbara H. Chasin. 1989. *Kerala: Radical Reform as Development in an Indian State*. Vol. 6. San Francisco, CA: Institute for Food and Development Policy.

Frankel, Francine R. and M. S. A. Rao. 1990. *Dominance and State Power in Modern India: Decline of a Social Order Volume 1 (Dominance & State Power in India)*. Oxford University Press.

Ganeshan, P C. 2003. *Communisa Iyakkamum Tamizhaga Arasialum* [Communist Movement and Tamil Politics]. 1st ed. Chennai: Arunthathi Nilayam.

Geetha, V., and S. V. Rajadurai. 1993. 'Dalits and Non-Brahmin Consciousness in Colonial Tamil Nadu', *Economic and Political Weekly*, 28 (39) (September 25): 2091–2098.

Giugni, Marco, Doug McAdam, and Charles Tilly. 1999. *How Social Movements Matter*. Vol. 10. Minneapolis, MN: University of Minnesota Press.

Goodwin, Jeff and James M. Jasper. 1999. 'Caught in a Winding, Snarling Vine: The Structural Bias of Political Process Theory', *Sociological Forum*, 14 (1): 27–54.

Gorringe, Hugo. 2005. *Untouchable Citizens: Dalit Movements and Democratisation in Tamil Nadu*. New Delhi; Thousand Oaks, Calif.: Sage Publications.

Goyal, Sangeeta. 2006. 'Human Development in Tamil Nadu and Karnataka', In Vikram K. Chand (ed), *Reinventing Public Service Delivery in India: Selected Case Studies*, pp. 294–332. Washington, DC: World Bank.

Guha, Ramachandra. 2008. 'The Biggest Gamble in History', In *India After Gandhi*. New York, NY: Harper Perennial.

Gupta, Dipankar. 2000. *Interrogating Caste: Understanding Hierarchy and Difference in Indian Society*. Penguin Books.

Hardgrave, Robert L. 1964. 'The DMK and the Politics of Tamil Nationalism', *Pacific Affairs*, 37 (4): 396–411.

Harriss, John. 2001. 'Populism, Tamil Style. Is It Really a Success? *LSE Development Studies Institute DESTIN Working Paper Series* 15.

———. 2013. 'Does "Landlordism" Still Matter? Reflections on Agrarian Change in India', *Journal of Agrarian Change*, 13 (3): 351–364. doi:10.1111/joac.12024.

Heller, Patrick. 1999. *The Labor of Development: Workers and the Transformation of Capitalism in Kerala, India*. Cornell University Press.

———. 2000. 'Degrees of Democracy: Some Comparative Lessons from India', *World Politics*, 52 (04): 484–519. doi:10.1017/S0043887100020086.

International Institute for Population Studies, and Macro International. 2008. 'National Family Health Survey India 2005–06: Tamil Nadu', Mumbai: IIPS. http://www.nfhsindia.org/NFHS-3%20Data/TamilNadu_report.pdf.

Jadhav, Vishal. 2006. 'Elite Politics and Maharashtra's Employment Guarantee Scheme.', *Economic and Political Weekly*, 41 (50) (December 16): 5157–5162.

Jaffrelot, Christophe. 2003. *India's Silent Revolution: The Rise of the Lower Castes in North India*. New York: Columbia University Press.

Jaywardena, Lal. 2004. 'Understanding Reforms: 1960–2000', In Saman Kelegama (ed.) *Economic Policy in Sri Lanka: Issues and Debates: A Festschrift in Honour of Gamani Corea*, pp. 96–108. Economic Policy in Sri Lanka. New Delhi: Sage Publications.

Jeffrey, Craig, Patricia Jeffery, and Roger Jeffery. 2008. 'Dalit Revolution? New Politicians in Uttar Pradesh, India', *The Journal of Asian Studies*, 67 (04): 1365–1396. doi:10.1017/S0021911808001812.

Jeffrey, Robin. 1976. *The Decline of Nayar Dominance: Society and Politics in Travancore, 1847–1908*. New York: Holmes & Meier Publishers.

———. 1994. 'Kerala's Story', *Economic and Political Weekly*, 29 (10) (March 5): 549. doi:10.2307/4400896.

———. 2001. *Politics, Women and Well Being: How Kerala Became 'a Model'*. New Delhi: Oxford University Press.

Josh, Bhagwan. 1979. *Communist Movement in Punjab, 1926–47*. Delhi: Anupama Publications.

Juergensmeyer, Mark. 1982. *Religion as Social Vision: The Movement against Untouchability in 20th Century Punjab*. Berkeley, CA: University of California Press.

K. Veeramani, 1998. *The History of the Struggle for Social Justice in Tamil Nadu*. 3rd ed. Chennai: India: Dravidar Kazhagam.

———. 2002. *Cheranmadevi Gurukkula Porattam: Varalatru Chuvadugal*. 1st ed. Chennai: India: Dravidar Kazhagam.

Kamarajar. 2003. *Makkalathchi*. Edited by M. Namachivayam. 2nd ed. Chennai: India: Palaniappa Brothers.

Kapur, Devesh, Chandra Bhan Prasad, Lant Prichett, and Shyam Babu. 2010. 'Rethinking Inequality: Dalits in Uttar Pradesh in the Market Reform Era', *Economic & Political Weekly*, XLV (35) (August 28): 39–49.

Karna, Mahendra Narain. 1998. *Social Movements in North-East India*. New Delhi: Indus Publishing.

Khera, Reetika. 2006. 'Political Economy of State Response to Drought in Rajasthan, 2000–03', *Economic and Political Weekly* (December 16): 5163.

———. 2011a. 'Revival of the Public Distribution System: Evidence and Explanations', *Economic & Political Weekly*, 46 (44): 36–50.

———. 2011b. 'Trends in Diversion of PDS Grain', Centre for Development Economics, Delhi School of Economics. http://ideas.repec.org/p/cde/cdewps/198.html.

———. 2011c. *The Battle for Employment Guarantee*. Oxford University Press, USA.

Kohli, Atul. 1983. 'Regime Types and Poverty Reform in India', *Pacific Affairs*, 56 (4): 649–672.

———. 2012. *Poverty Amid Plenty in the New India*. Cambridge, MA: Cambridge University Press.

Koopmans, Ruud. 1999. 'Political. Opportunity. Structure. Some Splitting to Balance the Lumping', *Sociological Forum*, 14 (1): 93–105.

Kothari, Rajni. 1964. 'The Congress "System" in India', *Asian Survey*, 4 (12) (December 1): 1161–1173. doi:10.2307/2642550.

Kreisi, Hans Peter and Dominique Weisler. 1999. 'Impact of Social Movements on Political Institutions: A Comparison of the Introduction of Direct Legislation in Switzerland and the United States.' In Marco Giugni, Doug Mcadam, and Charles Tilly eds, *How Social Movements Matter*, pp. 42–65. Minneapolis, MN: University of Minnesota Press.

Kshīrsāgara, Rāmacandra. 1994. *Dalit Movement in India and Its Leaders, 1857–1956*. M.D. Publications Pvt. Ltd.

Lerche, Jens. 1999. 'Politics of the Poor: Agricultural Labourers and Political Transformations in Uttar Pradesh', *The Journal of Peasant Studies*, 26 (2–3): 182–241.

Lieten, G. K. 2002. 'Human Development in Kerala: Structure and Agency in History', *Economic and Political Weekly*, 37 (16) (April 20): 1539–1544. doi:10.2307/4412015.

Ma.Pa. Gurusamy. 2006. *Vazhvikka Vantha Vallalar*. Chennai: India: New century book house.

Mahendra Dev, S. 2001. *Social and Economic Security in India*. New Delhi: Institute for Human Development: Distributed by Manohar Publishers.

Mallick, Ross. 1994. *Indian Communism: Opposition, Collaboration, and Institutionalization*. New Delhi: Oxford University Press.

Markandan, K. C. 1964. *Madras Legislative Council: Its Constitution and Working between 1861 and 1909; Being a Report, Submitted to the Madras University, as a Fellow in the Politics Department between October 1952 and October 1953*. Delhi: S. Chand.

Mathew, E. T. 1999. 'Growth of Literacy in Kerala: State Intervention, Missionary Initiatives and Social Movements', *Economic and Political Weekly*, 34 (39) (September 25): 2811–2820.

McAdam, Doug, John D. McCarthy, and Mayer Zald. 1996. *Comparative Perspectives on Social Movements: Political Opportunities, Mobilizing Structures, and Cultural Framings*. Cambridge England; New York: Cambridge University Press.

McAdam, Doug, Sidney G. Tarrow, and Charles Tilly. 2001. *Dynamics of Contention*. New York: Cambridge University Press.

Mendelsohn, Oliver. 1993. 'The Transformation of Authority in Rural India', *Modern Asian Studies*, 27 (4): 805–842.

Menon, Dilip M. 1994. *Caste, Nationalism, and Communism in South India: Malabar, 1900–1948.* New York, NY, USA: Cambridge University Press.

Metcalf, Thomas R. 1967. 'Landlords Without Land: The U. P. Zamindars Today', *Pacific Affairs*, 40 (1/2) (April): 5–18. doi:10.2307/2754619.

Miran, Paimpozhil. 2007. *Talai Nimirntha Tamizhachigal.* Chennai: India: Tozhmai Veliyeedu.

Mohan, P. E. 1993. *Scheduled Castes, History of Elevation, Tamil Nadu, 1900–1955.* Madras: New Era Publications.

Mooij, Jos. 2005. *The Politics of Economic Reforms in India.* New Delhi and Thousand Oaks, CA.: Sage Publications.

Mooij, Jos, and S. Mahendra Dev. 2004. 'Social Sector Priorities: An Analysis of Budgets and Expenditures in India in the 1990s', *Development Policy Review*, 22 (1) (January): 97–120.

Mukherjee, Nilmani. 1962. *The Ryotwari System in Madras, 1792–1827.* Firma K. L. Mukhopadhyay.

Muthulakshmi Reddi, S. 1964. *Autobiography'of Mrs. S. Muthulakshmi Reddy.* Madras: M.L.J. Press.

Narula, Smita and Human Rights Watch. 1999. 'Broken People: Caste Violence against India's 'Untouchables', New York: Human Rights Watch. Retrieved from http://www.hrw.org/en/node/24486/section/1.

Natarajan, Swaminath. 1959. *A Century of Social Reform in India,* Bombay: Asia Publishing House.

National Seminar on the Role of Women in Education in India. 1975. *Women Pioneers in Education, Tamil Nadu.* Madras: Society for the Promotion of Education in India.

Negi, Jaideep. 1995. *The Beg–ar & Beth System in Himachal Pradesh: A Study of Erstwhile Shimla Hill States.* New Delhi: Reliance Pub. House.

Oddie, G. A. 1969. 'Protestant Missions, Caste and Social Change in India, 1850–1914', *Indian Economic & Social History Review*, 6 (3) (September 1): 259–291. doi:10.1177/001946466900600302.

———. 1975. 'Christian Conversion in the Telugu Country, 1860–1900: A Case Study of One Protestant Movement in the Godavery-Krishna Delta.' *Indian Economic & Social History Review*, 12 (1) (January 1): 61–79. doi:10.1177/001946467501200103.

Offe, Claus. 1987. 'Democracy against the Welfare State?: Structural Foundations of Neoconservative Political Opportunities', *Political Theory*, 15 (4) (November): 501–537.

Olson, Mancur. 2012. 'The Logic of Collective Action', In Craig Calhoun, Joseph Gerteis, James Moody, Steven Pfaff, and Indermohan Virk (eds), *Contemporary Sociological Theory*, pp. 124–141. Oxford: John Wiley & Sons.

Omvedt, Gail. 2008. *Seeking Begumpura*. New Delhi: Navayana.

Pai, Sudha. 2001. 'Social Capital, Panchayats and Grass Roots Democracy: Politics of Dalit Assertion in Uttar Pradesh', *Economic and Political Weekly*, 36 (8) (February 24): 645–654. doi:10.2307/4410321.

Pandian, M. S. S. 1992. *The Image Trap: M.G. Ramachandran in Film and Politics*. New Delhi: Sage.

Pandian, M. S. S. 1989. 'Culture and Subaltern Consciousness: An Aspect of MGR Phenomenon', *Economic and Political Weekly*, 24 (30) (July 29): PE62–PE68. doi:10.2307/4395134.

———. 1990. 'From Exclusion to Inclusion: Brahminism's New Face in Tamil Nadu', *Economic and Political Weekly*, 25 (35/36) (September 1): 1938–1939.

———. 1994. 'Notes on the Transformation of 'Dravidian' Ideology: Tamilnadu, C. 1900–1940', *Social Scientist*, 22 (5/6) (June): 84–104.

Pandit, Nalini. 1979. 'Caste and Class in Maharashtra', *Economic and Political Weekly*, 14 (7/8) (February 1): 425–436.

Patankar, Bharat and Gail Omvedt. 1979. 'The Dalit Liberation Movement in Colonial Period', *Economic and Political Weekly*, 14 (7/8) (February 1): 409–424.

Paul, Binu, Kishore Bhirdikar, Shabnam Shaoni, Piu Mukherjee, M Krishna, Radhika Bhardwaj, K Purandaran, and R. Venkatesha Murthi. 2009. 'India Labour Market Report 2008', Adecco-TISS Labour Market Research Initiatives (ATLMRI). Bombay: TISS.

Paul, Samuel, Suresh Balakrishnan, and Public Affairs Centre. 2006. *Who Benefits from India's Public Services?* Bangalore: India: Academic Foundation.

Pe. Maniyarasan and A. Marx. 2007. *Bharathi: Oru samugaviyal paarvai* [A sociological reading of Bharathi]. Chennai: India: Thozhamai Veliyeedu.

Planning Commission. 2001. *National Human Development Report 2001*. Human Development Reports of India. New Delhi: Planning Commission, Government of India.

Radhakrishnan, P. 1990. 'Backward Classes in Tamil Nadu: 1872–1988', *Economic and Political Weekly*, 25 (10) (March 10): 509–520.

———. 1998. 'A Costly Digression', *Frontline*, September 12. http://www.hinduonnet.com/fline/fl1519/15191010.htm.

Raj Gauthaman. 2005. *Dalitiya Vimarsana Katturaikal*. 2nd ed. Chennai: India: Kalachuvadu Publishers.

Raj Ratnam. 2003. 'Discussion on Tamil Nadu PDS with Adl. Secretary, Food & Civil Supplies, Government of Tamil Nadu' Informal discussion.

Raman, Sita Anantha. 2004. 'Prescriptions for Gender Equality in South India: The Work of Dr. Muthulakshmi Reddi', In *Charisma and Commitment in South Asian History: Essays Presented to Stanley Wolpert*, 331–366. Orient Longman.

Ramasamy, E.V (Periyar). 2005. *Jaati-Teendamai (2) [Caste-Untouchability]*. In K. Veeramani (ed.), Vol. 8. *Periyar Kalanjiyam* [Collected works of Periyar]. Chennai: India: The Periyar Self-respect Propaganda Institution.

Ramusack, Barbara N. 2003. *The Indian Princes and Their States.* Cambridge University Press.

Rand, Gavin. 2006. '"Martial Races" and "Imperial Subjects": Violence and Governance in Colonial India, 1857–1914', *European Review of History: Revue Europeenne d'Histoire*, 13 (1): 1.

Ravallion, Martin. 1991. 'Employment Guarantee Schemes: Are They a Good Idea?', *Indian Economic Journal*, 39 (2, December): 50–65.

Ravikumar. 2008. 'Re-Reading Periyar', *Seminar* 558 (Feb). A Symposium on the Changing Contours of Dalit Politics (February). Retrieved from http://india-seminar.com/2006/558/558%20ravikumar.htm.

Right to Food Campaign. 2001. *PUCL Vs UoI and Others 196 of 2001.* Supreme Court of India.

Riser-Kositsky, Sasha. 2009. 'The Political Intensification of Caste: India Under the Raj', *Penn History Review*, 17 (1): 3.

Robinson, Rowena. 2010. 'Christian Communities of India: A Social and Historical Overview', In *Religions and Development Research Program. Working Paper Series*, Volume 1, Number 1:41. New Delhi: Indian Institute of Dalit Studies.

Roy, Jagat Jyoti. 1998. 'Youth Movement for Social Reformation in Tripura', In Mahendra Narain Karna (ed.), *Social Movements in North-East India*, pp. 133–39. New Delhi: Indus Publishing.

Rukmani, R. 1994. 'Urbanisation and Socio-Economic Change in Tamil Nadu, 1901–91', *Economic and Political Weekly*, 29 (51/52) (December 17): 3263–3272.

Rural Development and Panchayati Raj Department, Government of Tamil Nadu. 2006. *Rural Schedule of Rates Order. G.O. Ms. No. 77.*
———. 2007. *Revised Rural Schedule of Rates for the Year 2007–08 Order. G.O. Ms. No. 101.*

Sadasivan, D. 1974. *The Growth of Public Opinion in the Madras Presidency, 1858–1909.* Madras: University of Madras.

Saha, Sheela. 2004. *The Company Rule in India: Some Regional Aspects*. Delhi: Kalpaz Publications.

Sarkar, Sumit and Tanika Sarkar. 2008. *Women and Social Reform in Modern India: A Reader*. Indiana: Indiana University Press.

Seeta Prabhu, K. 2001. *Economic Reform and Social Sector Development: A Study of Two Indian States*. Vol. 3. Thousand Oaks, CA: Sage Publications.

Seeta Prabhu, K. and R. Sudarshan. 2002. *Reforming India's Social Sector: Poverty, Nutrition, Health and Gender*. New Delhi: Social Science Press: Distributed by D.K. Publishers and Distributers.

Sen, Amiya P. 2005. *Social and Religious Reform: The Hindus of British India*. Oxford University Press.

Shah, Mihir. 2009. 'Taking Goals of NREGA-I Forward', *The Hindu*, August 14, Online edition.

Sharma, Shalini. 2010. *Radical Politics in Colonial Punjab: Governance and Sedition*. London: Routledge.

Sinha, Dipa. 2014. 'Health and Human Development: Comparative Experiences of Tamil Nadu and Uttar Pradesh'. Ph.D. Dissertation, New Delhi: Jawarharlal Nehru University.

Sivasubramanian A. 2001. *Kiruthuvamum Chatium* [Christianity and Caste]. Nagarcoil: India: Kalachuvadu Publishers.

Srinivas, Mysore Narasimhachar. 1987. *The Dominant Caste and Other Essays*. Delhi; New York: Oxford University Press.

Subramanian, Narendra. 1999. *Ethnicity and Populist Mobilization: Political Parties, Citizens, and Democracy in South India*. Delhi; New York: Oxford University Press.

Sundarayya, P. 1973. 'Telangana People's Armed Struggle, 1946–51. Part Three: Pitted against the Indian Army', *Social Scientist* 1 (9) (April): 23–46.

Supreme Court of India. 1993. *Unni Krishnan v. State of Andhra Pradesh*. Supreme Court of India.

Suri, K. C. 2005. *Parties Under Pressure: Political Parties in India Since Independence*. State of Democracy in South Asia. New Delhi: Centre for the Study of Developing Societies. Retrieved from http://democracy-asia.org/workingpapers/scsuri.pdf.

Swaminathan, Padmini. 1999. ''Women's Education in Colonial Tamil Nadu, 1900–1930: The Coalescence of Patriarchy and Colonialism.' *Indian Journal of Gender Studies*, 6 (1): 21–42.

Tamizhvanan. 1985. *A.THI.MU.KA Vin Thotramum Valarchium* [Birth and Growth of AIADMK]. Chennai: India: Manimegalai prasuram.

Tarrow, Sidney G. 1996. 'States and Opportunities: The Political Structuring of Social Movements.' In *Comparative Perspectives on*

Social Movements: Political Opportunities, Mobilizing Structures, and Cultural Framings, 41–61. Cambridge Studies in Comparative Politics. Cambridge England; New York: Cambridge University Press.

The Probe Team, Jean Drèze, and Anuradha De. 1999. Public Report on Basic Education in India. New Delhi: Oxford University Press.

Tilakam, P. V. 1989. "Women's Franchise in Tamil Nadu 1900–1950". M.Phil Thesis, Chennai: India: Ethiraj College.

Tiruchy Selventhan. 2007. Jathiyai Ozhikka Satta Erippu Porattam [Constitution Burning Protest to Destroy Caste]. Pollachi: India: Periyar dravidar kazhagam, Coimbatore District.

UNDP and Richard Jolly. 2000. 'Human Development Report 2000'. New York: OUP.

Vaitheespara, Ravi. 2009. 'Maraimalai Atigal and the Genealogy of Tamilian Creed', Economic and Political Weekly, XLIV (14) (April 4): 45–51.

Valarmathi, Munaivar M. 2008. Suyamariyathai Veeranganaigal. 2nd ed. Chennai: India: Karuppu Prathigal.

Varshney, Ashutosh. 2000. "Is India Becoming More Democratic?" The Journal of Asian Studies, 59 (1) (February): 3–25.

Vijay Shankar, P. S., Rangu Rao, Nivedita Banerji, and Mihir Shah. 2006. 'Revising the Schedule of Rates: An Imperative for NREGA', Economic & Political Weekly, (April 29).

Vikalp. 2005. Contextualising Dalit Movement in South India: Selfhood, Culture and Economy. Chennai: India: Vikalp. http://vakindia.org/archives/Vikalp-Aug2005.pdf.

Visaria, Leela. 2000. "Innovations in Tamil Nadu." Seminar 489.

Vivek, S. and Basudeb Guha-Khasnobis. 2007. 'Rights Based Approach To Development: Lessons From The Right To Food Movement', In Food Insecurity, Vulnerability and Human Rights Failure. Studies in Development Economics and Policy, pp. 308–28. Basingstoke: UK: Palgrave-Macmillan.

Vivek, S. and Sudha Narayanan. 2007. "Food Policy and Social Movements: Reflections on the Right to Food Campaign in India." In Food Policy for Developing Countries: The Role of Government in the Global Food System. Ithaca: New York: Cornell University. http://cip.cornell.edu/DPubS?service=UI&version=1.0&verb=Display&page=current&handle=dns.gfs&collection=.

Washbrook, D. A. 1976. The Emergence of Provincial Politics: The Madras Presidency, 1870–1920. Vol. 18. Cambridge Eng.; New York: Cambridge University Press.

Washbrook, David. 1989. 'Caste, Class and Dominance in Modern Tamil Nadu: Non-Brahmanism, Dravidianism and Tamil Nationalism',

In *Dominance and State Power in Modern India: Decline of a Social Order,*.Vole 1, pp. 117–37.New Delhi: Oxford University Press.

Weiner, Myron. 1991. *The Child and the State in India: Child Labor and Education Policy in Comparative Perspective.* Princeton, N.J.: Princeton University Press.

Myron Weiner. 1996. 'Child Labour in India: Putting Compulsory Primary Education on the Political Agenda', *Economic and Political Weekly,* 31 (45/46) (November 9): 3007–3014.

Yadav, Yogendra. 1999. 'Electoral Politics in the Time of Change: India's Third Electoral System, 1989–99', *Economic and Political Weekly,* 34 (34/35) (September 21): 2393–2399.

Zelliot, Elenor. 1970. 'Learning the Use of Political Means: The Mahars of Maharashtra', In *Caste in Indian Politics.* New Delhi: Orient Longman.

Index

access 4–6, 9–10, 14, 41, 45–6, 54,
68, 82, 93, 126, 129, 159,
163, 173, 185, 187;
to available services 162;
to education 130; to funeral
facilities 56–7, 60, 68;
to information 157; to jobs
127; of health to women
105; to pensions 161; to
prohibited services 113;
to public amenities 57, 127,
138–9; to public services
41, 65, 71, 76, 84, 105, 107,
119, 126, 169, 171, 179,
185; to road 60; to school
5, 82, 89, 172; to social
networks 136; to water 139,
169
Adigalar, Ramalinga 94, 120, 128,
129
Adivasis/Scheduled Tribes 106,
114, 146–7, 163, 184, 196,
201–3; land alienation of
202;

adult franchise 71–2, 97, 99–101,
106, 200, 206, 210, 213,
see also election;
agricultural labourers 39–40, 66,
92, 101, 107, 130, 133, 162,
203–4, 206;
agricultural work 39, 47, 66, 84,
205; wages scales of 66
All India Anna Dravida Munnetra
Kazhagam (AIADMK) 64,
103, 105, 143, 146; to power
in 1977 54, 144–5
All India Trade Union Congress
(AITUC) 110
All India Women's Democratic
Association (AIDWA) 64, 92
allies 71–2, 81–2, 89, 93, 96, 110,
112, 132, 145
Ambedkar *Mandram* (Ambedkar
Society) 50–1, 66, 69–70, 76,
139
Ambedkar, B.R. 52, 137–8, 170,
175, 195, 203–5, 208;
Dalit movement by 173;

amenities 74–5, 128, 136, 139, 168–9, 172; demand for 58

Andhra Pradesh 6, 14, 102, 134, 158, 160, 178, 180, 183, 188, 194–5; Self Help Groups in 160

Anganwadis 6–7, 160; workers of 147

Annadurai, C. N. 132

ante-natal care (ANC) 5

anti-caste movements 50, 94

army 48, 203–4; to Bhumihar Brahmin 204; and Dalits 204; employment in 204; and suppression of rebellion 101

Arunthathiyar community 95

Arya Samaj 94, 119, 168, 170–1, 173–4

Aryan invaders 100;

associations 92, 95, 111, 118; caste based 90, 94–5, 103, 135–7; of Vanniyars 94

Backward Caste (BC) 21, 41, 46, 63, 67, 69, 71, 82, 84, 91, 95, 99, 103, 106, 108, 121–2; communities 95, 103, 213; and Dalits 99; groups of 94–5, 141, 207, 212; leaders of 91, 98, 103

Bahujan Samaj 207;

ban 113; on bicycles 49; on Communism 110; protest against 109; on raising goats 66; on using public services 113

below the poverty line 6, 162, 188

Bengal 174–5, 190, 195, 202–4

Bharathidasan 89, 120

Bharathiyar 89, 120–1

Bihar 107, 155–6, 158, 163–4, 178, 180, 196, 202–5, 210–13

Bhumihar community of 212; Triveni Sang in 175, 207;

bonded labour, elimination of 67

Brahmins 90, 98–100, 123–4, 143, 209

Brahmo Samaj 94, 168, 170, 174

bureaucracy/bureaucrats 38, 147–9, 35, 38–9, 145, 147–8, 179

burning puppets, as collective action 74

caste: based education scheme 103, 126, 140. (see also Rajaji) discrimination 57, 129; elites 14, 108, 207; groups 44, 46, 94–5, 167, 185, 207; Hindus 46–7, 49, 62, 66–9, 95, 109, 208; mobilization 113, 137; movements 90, 175, 196; organizations 136; system of 14, 57, 169–70; tensions 58; violating bans on 68;

Chettiyar, Thyagaraja 98

Chhattisgarh 8, 14, 107, 163–4, 178, 180, 184, 188, 203, 205

child care 3–4, 6, 10, 158, 182, 218

Christianity 56, 129, 169

civic unfreedoms 69, 86, 169, 193–4, see also social unfreedom

class agenda 18, 104, 131, 134, 141, 174, 189, 191–2, 195

class mobilization (analysing) 16–18, see also communism/communists

coalition 99, 206–9; with BJP in Bihar 213; of Congress 103, 192; of National Conference 208; of supra-jati 209; with Vanniyar castes 101

collective: action 20–2, 24, 30, 39, 43–5, 51, 54, 72–3, 75,

Dravidian parties 13, 91, 120, 124, 132, 134, *see also under separate names*
dress restrictions 68, *see also* social unfreedom
drought 1–2

East India Company 97, 168, 201
education xv, 12–16, 138–65, 181 campaigns for right to 181; mass education 126, 128, 141; World Bank support to 187; policy in Tamil Nadu 4–10, 18, 72, 76, 82, 102–5, 126–150
election: legislative assembly 62; of Panchayats 37, 53, 63, 72;
electoral: politics 71, 102, 196; pressures 14, 19, 148
electrification of villages 143, *see also under* Karnataka
English East India Company 97, 168, 201–4
entitlements 4, 10–11, 32, 140, 162, 183
ethnic identity 21
Ezhava community 127

fasting 74
feeder roads 143
First communal G.O. in 1923 123
funeral processions 56–7, 75

Gandhi, M.K. 90, 108, 170, 174
Goa 159
goats rearing 66–7
Government of India Act (1919) 98, 122
government offices, locking of 75
grazing, as demeaning 67–8

Gujarat 9, 159, 161, 195; public transport in 160

Harriss, John 176, 205
health system 8–9
Heller 16, 19, 21
Himachal Pradesh 8, 11, 22, 159, 184, 188, 193–4; women's freedom in 194
Hindu-Muslim politics 193, 209
homestead lands 45, 52, 54, 60; for landless 133
housing programmes 161
human well-being 15, 19–20, 166–7
hunger 1–3, 105, 129, 131, 135, 139, 143–4, 182, 189
hunger strikes 72, *see also* fasting
Hut Service Scheme 53

identity movements 16–18, 130, 155, 167, 183, 185
identity politics 184, 186
immunization 159, 161–3
implementing agents 30–2, 40
India Human Development Survey (IHDS) 157–8, 159–60, 162–3
Indian National Congress 46, 90, 100–4, 110–11, 122–3, 126, 132, 140–1, 143, 178, 190–1, 208, 211–13
Indira Awas Yojana 36, 160
industrialists 102, 110–11, 141
inequalities 57, 84, 97, 114, 128–9, 162, 185–6, 202–3, 210
Integrated Child Development Services (ICDS) 6–7, 144, 160–1, 163

Jaffrelot, Christophe 173
Jharkhand 163, 184, 203, 205

Ramachandran, M.G. *See* MGR
Ramakrishna Mission 168, 171,
    173
Ramanathapuram 108–9
Ranade 175, 195
Rao, Subba 98
ration card 5, 10
Ravidasis, Uttar Pradesh 175
Reddiar, lands as 48, 51, 59
Reddy, Muthulakshmi 85
redistributive issues 109
reform marriages by Periyar 70
reform movements 130, 150, 168,
    170–5, 180, 183, 190, 195–6
regional identity 183
religious conversion 76, 137, 179–80
representations 40, 73–6, 81, 142,
    211
repression, violent 106–7, 113
Republican Party of India (RPI) 49,
    52–3, 61, 64, 66–7, 95–6, 138
reservation 63, 76, 82–3, 118, 123,
    139
retaliatory violence 96, 109, 111
Right to Food Campaign (RFC)
    3–4, 182
riots 56–7, 104, 111–12, 166
road blocking 54–5, 73–4
road connectivity 143, 160
rowdies 114
Roy, Raja Ram Mohun 170, 195
Ryotwari system 202–3

Sanskritization 136
Scheduled Caste and Scheduled
    Tribe (Prevention of
    Atrocities) Act, 1989 112–13
scholarships 18, 20, 22, 32, 119,
    138
school feeding 2–5, 14, 17, 119,
    138, 144, 146, 160, 163, 182

schooling/school system 17, 82,
    127, 141–2, 163, 182, 184,
    192; expansion of 142
self-help groups (SHGs) 92, 140,
    146, 160; networks of 105
self-respect: marriage 124, (*see also*
    reform marriages; self-respect
    marriage); movement 86–9,
    123, 126
self-respecters 88, 123, 125;
    fire-walking festival by 124
services, expansion of 19, 168, 171,
    176, 179–80
Shivaji 204
Silent Revolution 173, 199
Singh, Digvijay 14
Singh, Raman 14, 178, 218
sit-ins, as collective action 72
SNDP 173, *see also* Narayana Guru
Social Justice Liberation Front. *See*
    Justice Party
social reform 119, 155, 167–8,
    170, 172, 175, 189, 195;
    movements 128, 149, 167–8,
    172–3, 189, 194–5
Social Reform Congress 168, 171
social tensions 37, 57; creative use
    of 55–6
social unfreedoms 50, 82, 85,89,
    113, 121, 127–8, 136, 138,
    185, 208; Church criticizing
    129; removal of 136
social: change 40, 43, 69, 86, 88,
    119, 121, 123, 126–7, 129,
    137, 168, 173, 201, 206,
    212–13; movements 15, 24,
    30, 51, 62, 79, 86, 89–90,
    94, 105–7, 118–21, 131,
    140, 142, 190–1, 193, 200;
    priorities 122, 126, 128, 166,
    174, 190, 193; protection

About the Author

Vivek S. works with the Program on Liberation Technology at Stanford University, and has recently completed his PhD in social sciences at the Maxwell School of Syracuse University. His passion is to ensure that everyone in India has access to basic public services, which started during his days with the Right to Food Campaign. His current research looks at how citizens can use technology to fight corruption and make governments accountable in delivering services.